# Higher, Faster, and Farther

# HIGHER, FASTER, and FARTHER

by **Mark P. Friedlander, Jr.**
and **Gene Gurney**

**William Morrow & Company, Inc.**

**New York   1973**

# DEDICATION

Joe C. Sweet, a fellow pilot and close friend of the authors, was killed in an attempt to set a new record for a New York to London and return nonstop flight. It is to Joe and the other fourteen persons who perished in the crash of a jet tanker on takeoff on June 27, 1958, at Westover Air Force Base, Massachusetts, that we dedicate this book.

**CREW MEMBERS**
Brig. Gen. Donald W. Saunders
Lt. Col. George M. Broutsas
1st Lt. Joe C. Sweet
Capt. James E. Shipman
M/Sgt. Donald H. Gabbard
T/Sgt. Joseph B. Hutter
Capt. John B. Gordon

**OFFICIAL TIMERS OF THE NATIONAL AERONAUTIC ASSOCIATION**
William Cochran
William Enyart

**JOURNALISTS**
Robert A. Ginsburgh (*U. S. News and World Report*)
Glenn A. Williams (*U. S. News and World Report*)
Norman Montellier (United Press International)
Dan J. Coughlin (Associated Press)
James McConaughey (*Time* magazine)
Bob Sibley (Aviation Editor, Boston *Herald*)

Copyright© 1973 by Mark P. Friedlander, Jr. and Gene Gurney

Printed in the United States of America.

1 2 3 4 5 77 76 75 74 73

Library of Congress Cataloging in Publication Data

Friedlander, Mark P
    Higher, faster, and farther.

    Includes bibliographical references.
    1. Aeronautics—Flights.   2. Aeronautics—Competitions.   I. Gurney, Gene, joint author.
II. Title.
TL515.F755           629.13'09           73-9377
ISBN 0-688-00204-8

10.00

# TABLE OF CONTENTS

**Chapter 1**  *A Thousand Miles per Hour*  *11*

**Chapter 2**  *The Airplane Goes Faster*  29

**Chapter 3**  *The Rocket Airplane Carries Man to Record Speeds*  53

**Chapter 4**  *Balloons Study Space First*  69

**Chapter 5**  *The Airplane Reaches Outer Space*  88

**Chapter 6**  *The Balloon Answers the First Challenge of the Sky*  105

**Chapter 7**  *The Balloon Goes Farther*  119

**Chapter 8**  *The Dirigible Goes Around the World*  128

**Chapter 9**  *Aviators Reach for Distant Shores*  145

**Chapter 10**  *The Airplane Circles the World*  156

**Chapter 11**  *Over the North Pole by Air*  180

**Chapter 12**  *A Long Flight Across the Pacific*  210

**Chapter 13**  *Faster and Faster Around the World*  219

**Chapter 14**  *Man Goes to the Moon*  243

Acknowledgments, Permissions, and Credits  260

## Appendices

Record Flights

| | | | |
|---|---|---|---|
| **Appendix** | **1** | Official F.A.I. Records | 264 |
| **Appendix** | **2** | Official F.A.I. Absolute World Records (Maximum Performance in Any Class) | 268 |
| **Appendix** | **3** | Official F.A.I. World Class Balloon Records | 271 |
| **Appendix** | **4** | Official F.A.I. World Class Dirigible Records | 290 |
| **Appendix** | **5** | Official F.A.I. World Records for Altitude | 291 |
| **Appendix** | **6** | Official F.A.I. World Records for Maximum Speed | 298 |
| **Appendix** | **7** | Official F.A.I. World Records for Distance | 305 |
| **Appendix** | **8** | Selected Chronology of Round-the-World Flights | 313 |
| **Appendix** | **9** | Selected Chronology of Transcontinental Flights | 319 |
| **Appendix** | **10** | Selected Chronology of Transatlantic Flights | 326 |
| **Appendix** | **11** | Selected Chronology of Transpacific Flights | 332 |
| **Appendix** | **12** | Selected Chronology of Polar Flights | 336 |
| **Appendix** | **13** | Selected Chronology of X-Model Rocket Aircraft Flights | 337 |
| **Appendix** | **14** | Selected F.A.I. Manned Spacecraft Record Flights | 342 |

# INTRODUCTION

On June 10, 1905, only eighteen months after the invention of the airplane, the Olympic Congress in Brussels passed a resolution which recognized the special importance of aeronautics and expressed the desire that in each country there be created an association for regulating flying. From these national associations would be formed a Universal Aeronautical Federation to regulate the international aviation meetings and advance the science and sport of aeronautics.

This resolution was the result of the entreating of Count de La Faulx, vice-president of the Aero Club of France, Fernand Jacobs, president of the Aero Club of Belgium, and Major Moedebeck of the German Airship League, all of whom foresaw the need for worldwide coordination and standards in the development of aviation and aviation records.

By October of the same year, representatives of Belgium, France, Germany, Great Britain, Italy, Spain, Switzerland, and the United States assembled in Paris, where they formed the Fédération Aéronautique Internationale, the F.A.I. Today the F.A.I. includes the National Aero Clubs of some sixty-five member nations and continues as the governing body of the world for official aircraft and space records, and for sport aviation competitions.

In the United States, the National Aeronautic Association (N.A.A.), originally founded in 1905 as the Aero Club of America, is the sole representative of the United States in the F.A.I.

The rules for all official world aircraft and space record flights are proposed initially by the various member clubs, evaluated by an international commission of the F.A.I., and then submitted for final approval to the delegates in attendance at the Annual General Conference of the F.A.I. The present rules, developed and refined over more than half a century, are now extremely sophisticated and detailed, promising all aviators who attempt to establish an official aviation record flight that the standards applied will be identically administered and measured wherever the challenge is made.

In the United States, all F.A.I. activities fall under the administration and regulation of the N.A.A., which organization enforces the goals of these regulations—namely, (1) an equal opportunity to every competitor, (2) competent, unbiased judging, and (3) scientifically accurate records.

The N.A.A. often sponsors major aviation gatherings in the United States and regulates air-race events and other sport aviation competitions. The organization also sponsors many programs dealing with aviation education and better public understanding of aeronautics.

Both the F.A.I. and the N.A.A. have a very broad schedule of activities, giving recognition to the special contributions to aviation and aerospace progress by individuals and groups. Typical is the administration of the renowned Wright, Collier, and Brewer trophies. The annual winners of these prestigious awards are chosen by committees appointed by the N.A.A. The ceremonies associated with the presentation of the trophies are major events on the aviation calendar. Traditionally, the Collier Trophy has been given annually to the recipient by the President of the United States. For some years, the Wright Trophy has been awarded as the highlight of the annual Wright Day Dinner sponsored by the Aero Club of Washington, a chapter of the N.A.A. The Brewer Trophy ceremony takes place at the Annual Conference of Aerospace Education.

The record code has been designed so that all aircraft—balloons, airplanes, gliders, and spacecraft—are classified according to weight, type, engine specifications, and so forth, in order to insure that everyone attempting a record flight will be competing against airmen in comparable vehicles.

The N.A.A. also contains many divisions and affiliates, including a wide range of aeronautical organizations dealing with every facet of aviation—antique airplanes, model airplanes, soaring, balloons, air racing, aerobatics, home-builts, general aviation, rocketry, and parachuting, among many. There are more than a hundred thousand men and women in America whose aviation interests are served by the N.A.A. through the affiliated groups or through direct membership.

The headquarters of the N.A.A. are located in Washington, D.C., in the Shoreham Building, 806 15th Street, N.W. (zip code 20005; telephone 202-347-2808), where information may be obtained regarding membership or the numerous activities of the organization. This is also the first place to apply to for official sanction of an attempt at a record flight.

The great advances made in aviation are remarkable to contemplate, and are in large measure due to the contributions made by the aviators seeking to beat a record—a record of altitude, of distance, or of speed. Many of the flights were official—that is, F.A.I.-sanctioned—and officially measured against the same standards applied to the prior record holder. Others were unofficial. But all were part of the remarkable spirit of aviation that has been and continues to be a part of the thrilling times in which we live. The challenge of these record flights is captured in this publication, and a tabulation of the record flights is contained in the Appendices.

More detail about any of these record flights and recent information about current records can all be obtained from the offices of the N.A.A.

MAJOR GENERAL BROOKE E. ALLEN
*Executive Director,*
*National Aeronautic Association*

# CHAPTER 1

# *A Thousand Miles per Hour*

It took the combined ingenuity of one thousand generations to progress from the wheel to the airplane—from one mile per hour to fifty. It took only one generation to fly a thousand miles per hour. Without fanfare or much public acclaim, this mark was reached on March 10, 1956.

On that date, high above the English Channel in a sleek, dart-winged, Delta-2 jet, Lionel Peter Twiss, a thirty-five-year-old test pilot for the Fairey Aviation Company, Limited, knifed through the thin air to a record 1,132 m.p.h. The timed run required two flights in opposite directions on a preset course—an imaginary tube 38,000 feet above sea level, 328 feet in diameter, 9.4 miles long. Officials of the Fédération Aéronautique Internationale (F.A.I.), the internationally recognized umpires of all air records, were on hand for the event.

Inside the cockpit, Twiss checked and rechecked his instruments as the turbine buckets and compressors of the Rolls-Royce Avon turbojet engine poured an invisible stream of superheated power from the tail. The concrete runway, the nearby fields and little English villages dropped swiftly away as the jet climbed almost vertically to the preassigned altitude. The earth below became haze as the altimeter needle swept around like a hand on a runaway clock. Twiss held firmly on his course. Approaching 38,000 feet, he rolled his craft to the left and eased the Delta-2 into level flight.

Peter Twiss recalled that moment:

Far over to the left at thirty-eight thousand feet, I could

see the contrails produced over the measured course by R.A.F. Meteors and mentally ticked off another vital check. The Delta-2 has a wingspan of under twenty-seven feet and would have been almost invisible to the telescopes that form a part of the timing gear if contrails were not used to sight on. But even the fickle English weather was on our side. The contrails were there, with not a cloud between them and the camera sights.

In the buildings below, the green luminescence of the sweeping finger of the radar scopes cast its eerie glow upon the intent faces of the operators. Carefully and calmly they tracked the fast target, broadcasting course and altitude directions to bring the jet into the invisible hoop high above them. Only precise maneuvering could make optimum use of the thrust of the jet in order to push the jet over the 1,000-m.p.h. mark.

The radio crackled. "Timing check, timing check . . . three . . . two . . . one."

Peter Twiss's gloved hand snapped the toggle to mark the recording tape, and simultaneously an official F.A.I. observer from the Royal Aero Club at his ground post double-checked his synchronized watch.

The Delta-2, airborne four and a half minutes, had reached its altitude and had slid through the sound barrier with only a slight flicker on the instrument panel.

The voice from control crackled over the radio: "You are over Point Able."

From the cockpit Twiss glanced to the south. "I could see only the coast of France," he recalled, "but knew I was over the New Forest."

Following a carefully prepared flight plan, he fired the afterburner. Instantly the Delta-2 burst into life, the sudden acceleration slamming Twiss back into the seat. The limited fuel capacity of the swift jet prevented a buildup to top speed before entering the measured course. So the Delta-2 accelerated through the first hoop at one and one-half times the speed of sound, over the timing camera at Chichester, straight along the course and over the second camera at Ford Naval Air Station.

"Cancel, cancel." The voice of Gordon Slade, ground controller, signaled the end of the run. Twiss switched off the afterburner.

"There was a sudden deceleration like the shock of catching

the arrester wires of an aircraft carrier," he remembered. "The first part of the job was over. A wide sweep out to sea, with the Thames estuary away to one side and the French coast on the other. I noticed stubble fields being burned off in Normandy and how the smoke was blowing across the Channel toward the white cliffs of England. But this was no time to relax."

In a wide climbing turn Twiss swung the jet in a 180-degree arc to bring it back to the precise point he had passed in the opposite direction. The rules of the F.A.I. required that the airplane in the turn at the end of the run could not gain more than 2,460 feet. Any error would be disqualifying, and at supersonic speeds the slightest overcontrol of the jet could carry it up or down thousands of feet in a fraction of a minute.

Twiss did not move the control stick; instead, he reacted through the instincts acquired from years of flying, applying slight directional pressures to guide the jet more as a living part of himself than as a separate machine.

"This was the most critical moment of the whole show," he recalled. "There was no sensation of speed. Yet every second brought me a thousand feet nearer to the gate of the second test run. The outside temperature was sixty degrees below zero, but I was sweating partly from tense excitement, partly because air friction over the Delta-2's smooth skin had caused the inside temperature to rise to over a hundred degrees in a few seconds—a warning of the heat barrier that must be overcome before record speeds can be raised much higher."

Now the Delta-2 passed through the loop to begin the timing for the second run. The airplane again had to be held to a precise course and at a precise altitude.

"I tried to concentrate my whole attention on the instruments," he continued. "All the time, instructions from the ground were dinning in my ears. They ordered a slight correction of course. And then once again the sharp push in the back as the afterburner came on."

The delta-winged craft darted through the invisible hoop over the camera and right on the mark. The airplane continued to accelerate as Twiss held it precisely on its course. "Throughout it," reported Twiss, "my eyes switched continuously from altimeter to fuel gauge, because if the fuel level had dropped below a certain figure I knew that the afterburner would switch itself off as a safety measure, and all our efforts would have been wasted.

"But, after what seemed the longest half-minute in history, the signal 'Cancel, cancel' came over the radio. I felt a great surge of relief as I switched off the afterburner and banked round for the smooth, quiet, peaceful descent toward Boscombe, forty-five miles away."

The Delta-2, an airplane which had taken off from the ground under its own power, had at last carried an aviator across the 1,000 m.p.h. threshold. Within another decade man and machine would have flown four times this speed in a rocket plane air-launched from the underside of the wing of a jet bomber; Russian cosmonauts and American astronauts launched in capsules astride monstrous rockets would have hurled around the earth faster than 17,000 m.p.h. And before 1970 American space vehicles would have carried men to the moon and back, reaching speeds of more than 25,000 m.p.h. L. Peter Twiss, then, had lifted man up another rung on the ladder of record flights, a record that had begun forty-seven years earlier at Rheims, France, when Glenn H. Curtiss flew his *Golden Flyer,* a machine made of wood and linen, in the first Gordon Bennett Cup race, clocking a little faster than 43 m.p.h. to win the race and establish the first major official speed record for aerial flight.

One hundred years before that race, an English baronet, Sir George Cayley, had theorized how future flight would develop. In his essay, *On Aerial Navigation,* published in *Nicholson's Journal* in 1809, Cayley wrote: "The whole problem is confined within these limits, viz.—to make a surface support a given weight by the application of power to the resistance of air." His papers advocated the fixed-wing concept. The fixed wing was a radical and significant departure from the endless number of abortive flapping-wing devices created by the aeronautical neophytes who believed that only a strict translation of the movement of birds in flight could provide man with a heavier-than-air flying craft. Cayley's studies received close attention from serious aviation enthusiasts, and the nineteenth century was replete with daring young men who attempted the seemingly impossible goal of powered heavier-than-air flight.

In 1842, William Henson, an English manufacturer, constructed a monoplane to be propelled by twin pusher blades and powered by a steam engine. He was aided by John Stringfellow, also a manufacturer, who developed a lightweight steam engine to power the Henson monoplane. In order to perfect the machine, Henson organized the Aerial Transit Company and attempted to sell the necessary stock to finance the project. The company was widely advertised with fanciful artistic renderings of the vehicle in flight carrying passengers to the key cultural centers of the world. But, in fact, the steam engine was too heavy for the power it delivered; and neither the Aerial Transit Company nor the aircraft for which it was organized ever got off the ground.

Other attempts at powered flight were similarly without success. In 1890, Clément Ader unsuccessfully attempted to fly in a craft resembling a bat. Seven years later, with a grant from the French army, he completed a larger and more highly perfected machine. This bat-shaped, linen-and-metal-tube airplane he dubbed the *Avion III*. Those who saw it did not doubt for a moment that the great bat-bird would lift easily into the blue horizon. Not

The Henson airplane, 1842 ... the steam engine was too heavy.
**(U.S. Air Force)**

only did it look as if it would fly, but it sounded as if it should. It did not, but its name did, and *avion* was absorbed into the French language as the word for *airplane.*

An Austrian piano-maker, Wilhelm Kress, built an airplane that used, for the first time, a gasoline engine. This machine, majestic in creation, capsized during a water launching and it, too, joined the long parade of aviation failures.

Even before he became secretary of the Smithsonian Institution in Washington, D.C., in 1887, Samuel Pierpont Langley had taken a lively interest in aerodynamics. In 1889, he had had occasion to see the small aero steam engine designed twenty years before by John Stringfellow. Impressed by the engine, he began work on steam-powered model airplanes. The models flew, but he lacked funds to build a full-sized machine, although the powered flights of the unmanned models seemed to assure the success of his design.

Then came the Spanish-American War. The War Department, now vitally interested in work on heavier-than-air flight, recommended a Congressional grant of fifty thousand dollars to Lang-

Samuel Pierpont Langley with his assistant, Professor Charles M. Manly.

**(National Air and Space Museum, The Smithsonian Institution)**

ley so that he could build his machine. At the same time, Langley became convinced that gasoline was more practical than steam. His assistant, Professor Charles M. Manly, a small, light-framed man with a dark moustache and pince-nez glasses, modified a five-cylinder radial engine originally designed by Stephen Balzer of New York, to create a one-hundred-pound engine that produced fifty-three horsepower.

A full-sized "aerodrome" (the name given the machine by Langley) was completed and ready in October, 1903, for the first manned, powered flight of an airplane.

The launching device was a catapult mounted on a sturdy, square houseboat anchored on the Potomac River at Washington. At noon on October 17, all was in readiness. Newspaper reporters, who had been watching from a nearby encampment for three months, assembled in several rowboats a few dozen feet from the houseboat. The aerodrome had been pretested with models; it embraced every modern theory of flight and was supported by both the finances of the United States Treasury and the expertise of the Smithsonian Institution. Thus the stage was set for what was to be aviation's finest moment. Charles Manly was in the "aviator's car" with a firm grip upon the controls of the aerodrome. It started without flaw, purring with the hum of a well-oiled internal-combustion engine.

The *Washington Post* carried the story of that moment:

> The newspapermen waved their hands. Manly looked down and smiled. Then his face hardened as he braced himself for the flight, which might have in store for him fame or death. The propeller wheels, a foot from his head, whirred around him one thousand times to the minute. A man forward fired two skyrockets. There came an answering "toot, toot" from the tugs. A mechanic stooped, cut the cable holding the catapult; there was a roaring, grinding noise—and the Langley airship tumbled over the edge of the houseboat and disappeared in the river, sixteen feet below.
>
> It simply slid into the water like a handful of mortar.

Manly was plucked from the river and the wreckage of the aerodrome was returned to the shore, both to be refurbished for another attempt at heavier-than-air flight.

The Langley airplane perched on its catapult.

Less than two months later, Manly was in the "aviator's car" again. The weather was cold and raw, with the chilling dampness of approaching winter. Ice was floating on the Potomac, unusual for December 8, and an ominous sign. It was late in the afternoon before everything was ready. The newsmen shivered as the comfortless rowboats bobbed in the icy waters.

As before, the engine was started without difficulty. Upon order the catapult cable was cut and the roaring airplane began to move. The movement was followed by a grinding sound, then the rending and ripping of metal. The aerodrome lifted from the houseboat, and when it was but a few feet in the air the fuselage spar snapped and the rear wings fell, followed by the remainder of the airplane and Mr. Manly.

The next day, the *Evening Star* reported that "the test of the Langley Aerodrome at the confluence of the Potomac River with the Eastern Branch yesterday afternoon was a complete failure. The sixty-foot machine, a perfect bit of mechanism, was launched at exactly 4:45 o'clock. Within thirty seconds it had described a half somersault, doubled up like an athlete taking a hurdle, and had fallen into the river, broken and twisted into a mass of wood, steel and linen, with its nose in the mud on the river bottom. Professor Charles M. Manly, who attempted to fly the machine, was buried under the mass of debris, but was quickly rescued by Fred Hewitt, one of the workmen on the houseboat, and Private Adelson of the Signal Corps, U.S.A.''

The U. S. Army promptly announced it was no longer interested in having this work go forward and withdrew its support from Langley. Langley's success had seemed so certain; his failure convinced many that manned heavier-than-air flight was a fantasy never to be achieved.

Both Langley and Manly, convinced of the correctness of their theory of flight, were perplexed by the failure. Langley told reporters shortly after the crash, ''The accident was a most peculiar one, and I am at a complete loss to tell how it was brought about. I am positive that the trouble lay with the launching apparatus and not with the machine itself, but what caused it I have not been able to find out.''

A writer for the *Boston Globe* declared, ''Perhaps if Professor Langley had only thought to launch his airship bottom-side up, it would have gone into the air instead of down into the water.'' And another columnist suggested, ''If Professor Langley had only thought to hitch his airship to the price of beef!''

Ambrose Bierce, a writer notorious at the turn of the century for his merciless and brilliant wit, could not resist joining in the levity of the moment: ''I don't know how much larger Professor Langley's machine is than its flying model was—about large enough, I think, to require an atmosphere a little denser than the intelligence of one scientist and not quite so dense as that of two.''

The Langley disaster became the subject of cruel cartoons, vaudeville skits, and comic writers. The professor was ridiculed for being silly enough to believe that man could fly. Two years later, saddened by the catastrophe and crushed by the sensational rebukes and humiliation, Langley fell seriously ill and died on February 27, 1906.

Langley's supporters at the Smithsonian Institution stood by him in his adversity, maintaining that his machine, in spite of the failures, was still capable of aerial flight. In 1914, eight years after his death, the aerodrome, reconstructed and modified to operate as a seaplane, was successfully flown from Lake Keuka at Hammondsport, New York.

Only nine days after Langley's second failure, on December 17, 1903, two unknown bicycle manufacturers, Wilbur and Orville Wright, achieved success with powered heavier-than-air flight on the windswept dunes of Kitty Hawk, North Carolina. Almost no American papers carried the story, and, possibly because of stories about Langley, those who heard of the event did not believe it.

The accomplishment of the Wright brothers was not a casual accident, but the result of years of thought and imaginative engineering. Before undertaking their early experiments, they studied already existing works on aerodynamics, particularly the book of their mentor and friend, Octave Chanute, *Progress in Flying Machines* (published in 1894), and Langley's writings.

What the Wright brothers learned in the steady onshore breezes at Kitty Hawk was the significance and importance of what is now called aspect ratio—the ratio of the span of an airfoil to its mean chord. They found that the lift of a wing does not come from air striking the bottom and lifting the surface, but from air flowing around a cambered foil, separating, and racing to meet again at the rear. Hence the air over the curved top must travel farther and faster than the air along the bottom, creating lift—a lower pressure on the upper surface of the wing. Almost as important as the basic secret of lift were the secrets of *controlled* flight: a rudder and a crude form of aileron. The first aileron was simply a warping or twisting of the wing surfaces to change the lift characteristics and cause the airplane to bank in a turn. With lift and control, man could fly. From these studies the Wright brothers were able to design first a glider and then the airplane that carried Orville Wright and all mankind into a new dimension.

Writing of the event a decade later, Orville Wright described what happened on that blustery winter day, December 17, 1903:

> When we arose on the morning of the 17th, the puddles of water, which had been standing about the camp since the recent rains, were covered with ice. The wind had a velocity of twelve metres per second. We thought it would die down before long, and so remained indoors the early part of the morning. But when ten o'clock arrived, and the wind was as brisk as ever, we decided that we had better get the machine out and attempt a flight. We hung out the signal for the men of the Life Saving

Station. We thought that by facing the flyer into a strong wind, there ought to be no trouble in launching it from the level ground about camp. We realized the difficulties of flying in so high a wind, but estimated that the added dangers in flight would be partly compensated for by the slower speed in landing.

We laid the track on a smooth stretch of ground about 100 feet north of the new building. The biting cold wind made work difficult, and we had to warm up frequently in our living room, where we had a good fire in an improvised stove made of a large carbide can. By the time all was ready, J. T. Daniels, W. S. Dough and A. D. Etheridge, members of the Kill Devil Life Saving Station; W. C. Brinkley of Manteo; and Johnny Moore, a boy from Nags Head, had arrived. . . .

With all the knowledge and skill acquired in thousands of flights in the last ten years, I would hardly think today of making my first flight on a strange machine in a twenty-seven-mile wind, even if I knew that the machine had already been flown and was safe. After these years of experience I look with amazement upon our audacity in attempting flights with a new and untried machine under such circumstances. Yet faith in our calculations and the design of the first machine, based upon our tables of air pressures, secured by months of careful laboratory work, and confidence in our system of control developed by three years of actual experiences in balancing gliders in the air, had convinced us that the machine was capable of lifting and maintaining itself in the air, and that, with a little practice, it could be safely flown.

Wilbur having used his turn in the unsuccessful attempt on the 14th, the right to the first trial now belonged to me. After running the motor a few minutes to heat it up, I released the wire that held the machine to the track, and the machine started forward in the wind. Wilbur ran at the side of the machine, holding the wing to balance it on the track. Unlike the start on the 14th, made in a calm, the machine, facing a twenty-seven-mile wind, started very slowly. Wilbur was able to stay with it till it lifted from the track after a forty-foot run. One of the Life Saving men snapped the camera for us, taking a picture just as the machine had reached the end of the track and had risen to a height of about two feet. . . .

The course of the flight up and down was exceedingly erratic, partly due to the irregularity of the air, and partly to lack of experience in handling this machine. The control of the front rudder was difficult on account of its being balanced too near the center. This gave it a tendency to turn itself when started, so that it turned too far on one side then too far on the other. As a result the machine would rise suddenly to about ten feet, and then as suddenly dart for the ground. A sudden dart when a little over 100 feet from the end of the track, or a little over 120 feet from the point at which it rose into the air, ended the flight. This flight lasted only twelve seconds, but it was nevertheless the first in the history of the world in which a machine carrying a man had raised itself by its own power into the air in full flight, had sailed forward without reduction of speed, and had finally landed at a point as high as that from which it started.

They made several more flights that day, and that evening sent a wire to their father, Bishop Wright in Dayton, Ohio, requesting that the press be informed. A Norfolk, Virginia, paper had picked up the story but printed an inaccurate account of the event. On January 5, 1904, the Wright brothers issued a statement to the Associated Press, but few editors believed the story and few newspapers reported the event.

The first flight lasted only twelve seconds.

**(U.S. Air Force)**

In May, the Wright brothers, with an improved craft, assembled the press at a cow pasture near their home in Dayton to witness a flight. *The New York Times* carried a short report, their first mention of the memorable December 17, 1903, flight under a May 26, 1904, dateline.

> The Wright flying machine, invented by Orville and Wilbur Wright, brothers, which made a successful flight at Kitty Hawk, N.C., last December, had another trial near this city today, which the brothers said was successful. Great secrecy was maintained about the test and but few witnessed it.
>
> The machine after being propelled along a track for the distance of a hundred feet, rose twelve feet in the air, and flew a distance of thirty feet, when it dropped. This was due, the inventors say, to a derangement of the gasoline engine that furnishes the power. In the fall the propellers were broken and the test could not be repeated.

By the fall of 1905 the Wright brothers were making flights for as long as thirty minutes and for distances as far as twenty-four miles. Although they were as yet the only men to have achieved aerial flight, there was no acclaim for their attainment. They offered their invention to the War Department and were turned down.

Across the Atlantic men were still struggling to unlock the secrets of flight. In France a small, dapper, moustached, society darling, Alberto Santos-Dumont, had turned his attentions away from his dirigibles, which had already won him aerial fame, and had built a strange box-kitelike airplane with the wings in the back and the tail in the front. And he flew his airplane standing up. The wings did not utilize the cambered airfoil of the Wright plane and hence had little lift, but the engine had great power and the flat, V-shaped dihedral of the wings gave the flying box kite stability.

On October 23, 1906, Santos-Dumont remained airborne for a distance of 197 feet at Bagatelle Field in Paris and was acclaimed throughout Europe as the first man to fly a heavier-than-air craft. Communications were of such a nature at the time that he believed he was. On November 12 of the same year, he flew a distance of 733 feet to capture another French Aero Club prize, this one

Santos-Dumont believed he was the first to fly.

for being the first man to fly a heavier-than-air craft more than a hundred meters, although the Wright Brothers had already surpassed this record.

Aviation was on its way.

In May of 1908, Wilbur Wright demonstrated the Wright machine for European observers, and the beautiful gliding ease and graceful maneuverability of the American's machine immediately outclassed by comparison all of the more awkward European powered kites and other unmanageable flying contraptions. This European acclaim opened the previously closed doors in America, and the Wright brothers were soon receiving the recognition earlier denied them.

The Wright brothers' accomplishment was noted by a man who would himself one day be listed among aviation greats: Igor I. Sikorsky, a young man with an inventive mind and a deep yearning for the sky.

"During the summer of 1908, I again went abroad with my father, spending about six weeks in Germany," he later wrote. "Almost every day I read about the flights of Count Zeppelin in one of his early dirigibles. It was during that summer that I saw for the first time a reliable and accurate newspaper account of a successful flight made by one of the Wright brothers. This information impressed me considerably. The newspaper writer, an eye witness of the flight, apparently did not realize the immense importance of this event. He wrote about a flying machine that rose gracefully into the air, making a flight of several minutes, and then landing not far from where the flight began. It surprised me not to see big editorials in the papers of the world declaring that the age-long dream of giving wings to man, a possibility which was predicted and expected by some and positively denied by others, finally had become a fact.''

The words of the visionary young man were typical of the early believers in the future of the airplane. By 1909 man's awkward and budding adventure in flying had come to full bloom. The years of public skepticism surrounding the early flights of Wilbur and Orville Wright were gone, and the pioneers were enjoying full recognition for their triumph. President Taft received them and their countrymen honored them. The brothers were awarded the first Langley Medal, an aviation award named for the professor who had vainly sought the success for which the medal was given.

The Wright brothers had organized an aircraft company, and Wright airplanes were widely sought in the avalanche of enthusiasm for flight that now promised to propel the awakening world into a new air age. In Europe and in the United States, men were designing and building airplanes that really flew. They were machines that would carry aviators at their will beyond the perimeters of the cow pasture.

In London, the *Daily Mail* offered one thousand pounds to the first man to fly an airplane across the English Channel. Two men dared to meet the challenge, Hubert Latham and Louis Blériot. Latham, one of the first of the new breed of aviators attempting to set new records in speed, distance, altitude, and endurance, had tried once before and failed. Louis Blériot, who at the turn of the century attempted flight in a flapping-wing device had built, flown, and wrecked more aerial contraptions than any of his contemporaries. But crashes did not daunt Blériot, who seemed determined to achieve aviation fame.

On the night of July 24, 1909, both men were camped along the coast of France. A strong onshore wind effectively grounded both pilots, as neither plane was sufficiently powerful to buck a strong head wind.

Shortly after midnight, Louis Blériot wakened from his uneasy sleep to notice that the wind has subsided. He drove to the field and in the darkness before the dawn pondered the feasibility of starting out for the English coast. At 4:35 A.M. he decided that conditions were right for the flight; with a tank full of gasoline and his three-cylinder, twenty-five horsepower Anzani engine roaring healthily, he took off and headed for the English Channel.

The aircraft he flew was the eleventh airplane he had built. It was a monoplane twenty-five feet long and it had a wingspan of twenty-five and one-half feet. The wings were round-tipped, made of a single wooden center spar and curved ribbing, and covered with a double layer of stretched and treated linen. The fuselage was a long, thin crate, four long poles vertically braced with diagonal wires, tapering back to a small empennage. The fuselage was covered a little more than halfway back and the swarthy, moustached aviator Blériot controlled his machine from a perch precariously situated midway atop the wing, with the wind whipping against his helmeted head. There were no instruments of any kind to guide him over the open water, only dead-reckoning navigation with the rising sun "held" at fixed positions over his wing tip.

Louis Blériot recounted his flight in a special dispatch to *The New York Times:*

> Ten minutes are gone. I have passed the destroyer, and I turn my head to see whether I am proceeding in the right direction. I am amazed. There is nothing to be seen—neither the torpedo-boat destroyer nor France nor England. I am alone; I can see nothing at all.
>
> For ten minutes I am lost; it is a strange position to be in—alone, guided without a compass in the air over the middle of the Channel.
>
> I touch nothing, my hands and feet rest lightly on the levers. I let the aeroplane take its own course. I care not whither it goes.
>
> For ten minutes I continue, neither rising nor falling, nor turning, and then, twenty minutes after I have left the French coast, I see green cliffs and Dover Castle, and way to the west the spot where I had intended to land.
>
> What can I do? It is evident the wind has taken me out of my course. I am almost at St. Margaret's Bay, going in the direction of Goodwin Sands.

Now it is time to attend to the steering. I press a lever with my foot and turn easily toward the west, reversing the direction in which I am traveling. Now I am in difficulties, for the wind here by the cliffs is much stronger and my speed is reduced as I fight against it, yet my beautiful aeroplane responds still steadily.

I fly westward, chopping across the harbor, and reach Shakespeare Cliff. I see an opening in the cliff. Although I am confident I can continue for an hour and a half, that I might, indeed, return to Calais, I cannot resist the opportunity to make a landing upon this green spot.

Once more I turn my aeroplane, and, describing a half circle, I enter the opening and find myself again over dry land. Avoiding the red buildings on my right, I attempt a landing, but the wind catches me and whirls me around two or three times. At once I stop my motor, and instantly my machine falls straight upon the ground from a height of seventy-five feet. In two or three seconds I am safe upon the shore.

Soldiers in khaki run up, and policemen. Two of my compatriots are on the spot. They kiss my cheeks. The conclusion of my flight overwhelms me.

Thus ended my flight across the Channel—a flight which could easily be done again. Shall I do it? I think not. I have promised my wife that after a race for which I have already entered I will fly no more.

An eyewitness to the historic moment described his arrival:

Very early in the morning a wireless message was received from Calais that Blériot intended to make the flight. Then in quick succession came the news that he had left land, that he was flying high and was fast making Dover. It was expected that he would land west of Dover, but from the direction taken it was soon evident that he would alight to the eastward. Only a few minutes after the wireless announced the start the laconic message "out of sight" was received at Dover. Hardly had this been transcribed when the coast guard scanning the sea with his telescope shouted that Blériot was within sight.

Hastening to the cliff east of the bay, I was fortunate enough to arrive just a moment before the airship, which was flying fast, like a gigantic hawk. The craft approached the cliff, growing larger every instant. The noise of the engine was audible in a moment, so swiftly did he come. Blériot swooped overhead, glancing from right to left, and then turned his machine to the east and came to the ground in the meadow. He circled with consummate ease and made the landing gracefully, but even though the monoplane touched the ground lightly it was slightly damaged.

An editorial in the London *Daily Mail* noted that "Great Britain's insular strength is no longer unchallenged; that the aeroplane is not a toy but a possible instrument of warfare, which must be taken into account by soldiers and statesmen, and that it was the one thing needed to wake up the English people to the importance of the science of aviation."

As the news was flashed around the world, Wilbur Wright told newsmen: "Blériot's successful flight was splendid. I know him well, and he is just the kind of man to accomplish such an undertaking. He is apparently without fear, and what he sets out to do he generally accomplishes. This recklessness makes him anything but a good aviator, however, for he lacks entirely the element of caution. His speed was excellent, and his machine made faster time than I thought it capable of negotiating."

To this his brother Orville added: "I'm glad Blériot won the prize offered for the first aeroplanist to cross the Channel, but I can't for the life of me understand how he ever managed to do it with the flier he has. His motor struck us both as being well nigh impossible, while he seemed to lack control over his machine. The great number of accidents in which he figured with his flier disclosed this lack of control, while his engine never could be depended on."

On the morning of Blériot's successful flight, Hubert Latham also attempted the passage, only to crash into the treacherous water of the Channel, nearly losing his life and receiving deep facial wounds for his effort.

The crash of Hubert Latham gave added significance to the success of his rival. The spirited astronauts of 1969 who ventured to the surface of the moon were better trained and prepared and better equipped for the relative unknowns of the solar system than were those 1909 adventurers for the chopping swells of the English Channel. But if men were to fly higher, faster, and farther, the Channel flight, as symbolic of the capabilities of the airplane, had to be made.

# CHAPTER 2

# The Airplane
# Goes Faster

By 1909 the growing enthusiasm for aerial flight was international in breadth. All over the world men not yet accustomed to horseless carriages dared to look at the sky, watch the birds in flight, and dream. The first international air meet was scheduled at a race-track at Rheims, France, as a special feature of the annual champagne-week festivities. From August 22 through August 29 most of the renowned aviators and their assorted flying machines were assembled for aeronautic tournaments of endurance, altitude flights, and—most spectacular—air races.

The contest attracted thirty-eight contestants and over a quarter of a million spectators, including government and military leaders from most of the European nations, to watch and to consider the current and potential value of these aerial vehicles.

The winner of the speed race, the grand finale, was to receive the Gordon Bennett Cup, a special prize offered by the publisher of the *New York Herald,* James Gordon Bennett. The entrants comprised most of the names in aviation, including a young man named Glenn Curtiss as the representative of the Aero Club of America.

Curtiss was clearly the most remarkable of the competing young aviators. Although he had learned to fly only the year before, he had already achieved a considerable reputation both in flying and in the construction of airplanes.

One month before the contest at Rheims, he had gone to the Aero Club in New York and sought to be its representative in France. The club accepted his offer only to learn that he had neither the plane nor the engine for the event.

With less than a month available, Curtiss began building the airplane, a bi-wing, linen-and-frame craft with an eight-cylinder engine which would generate, he hoped, fifty horsepower. If he miscalculated, time would not permit a correction. Together with his mechanic, "Slim" Shriver, Curtiss worked virtually around the clock without waste of time or movement.

It was finished in time to be loaded on shipboard for the voyage to Le Havre. At Le Havre Curtiss learned there was a train that would get him to Rheims in time to enter the air meet on August 22, but it was a passenger train with no freight cars to carry the airplane. It required some persuasive pleading, but finally the railroad permitted the disassembled airplane to be recognized as part of Curtiss's personal baggage and, as such, to be loaded in the baggage cars to accompany the pilot to the air race.

It was a colorful and exciting contest. Save for the Wright brothers, virtually every other important aviation pioneer attended the momentous air meet. The fact that aerial machines could actually compete in a controlled sporting event had focused world attentions on the affair.

One journalist of the day wrote prophetically of the events:

> To say that this week marks an epoch in the history of the world is to state a platitude. Nevertheless, it is worth stating, and for us who are lucky enough to be at Rheims during this week there is a solid satisfaction in the idea that we are present at the making of history. In perhaps only a few years to come the competitions of this week may look pathetically small and the distances and speeds may appear paltry. Nevertheless, they are the first of their kind, and that is sufficient.

Henri Farman of France flew to a victory in the endurance race, sustaining continuous flight for three hours, fifteen minutes over a distance of 118 miles, and thrilled the crowd by carrying two passengers in his machine.

Hubert Latham, still bearing vivid scars from his near-fatal crash in the English Channel, claimed the altitude record, climbing to the dizzy height of 508 feet.

The climactic event, the Gordon Bennett Cup race, was scheduled for the seventh day. The favorite was Blériot, the dean

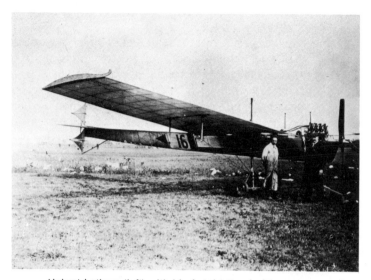

Hubert Latham (left) with his Antoinette airplane.

of the new young breed of airmen, who had for this event a new, lightweight monoplane powered by an eighty-horsepower engine.

The American, Curtiss, had entered only the speed event, the final race, and for this was criticized by his countrymen, who doubted he was any match for the superior French machine and the more experienced pilot. They felt he should have competed in some of the earlier events, in order to secure at least some of the minor prizes for the United States. Curtiss steadfastly refused, not wishing to risk possible damage to his fragile machine before the major race.

By August 29 Curtiss's determination had already won a few rewards. The field of real contenders had been narrowed: only Louis Blériot, Hubert Latham, and Eugène Lefebvre of France, G. B. Cockburn of England, and Glenn Curtiss of the United States remained. (A week after the races, Lefebvre became aviation's first pilot to die in a crash, the victim of a stall.)

The air races were run against the clock. Each contestant was entitled to a trial flight and then one competing flight anytime during the day from 10:00 A.M. to 6:00 P.M. Glenn Curtiss decided to make his bid as early as possible in the morning.

Promptly at the stroke of ten, his *Golden Flyer* was rolling along the pasture at Betheny and into the air. The flights were at low altitudes, usually just barely above the ground. Curtiss wanted to get a feel for the air turbulence near the ground surface created by the temperature and terrain variations. Upon the completion of this trial run, he was satisfied with the reaction of the airplane to the turbulence.

"I felt that it was time to make the start for the Cup," reported Curtiss, "despite the boiling air conditions, which I had found existed all over the course and made flying difficult if not actually dangerous. We hurriedly refilled the gasoline tank, sent official notice to the judges, carefully tested the wiring of the machine by lifting it at the corner, spun the propeller, and the official trial was on." The engine roared at its full power as the *Golden Flyer* climbed to an altitude just under five hundred feet before coming over the starting line. Curtiss had gone to his maximum altitude so that he could maintain a gradual descent over the course and gain additional speed.

"The sun was hot and the air rough," wrote Curtiss, "but I had resolved to keep the throttle wide open. I cut the corner as close as I dared and banked the machine high on the turns. I remember I caused great commotion among a big flock of birds which did not seem to be able to get out of the wash of my propeller. In front of the tribunes the machine flew steadily, but when I got around the back stretch, as we would call it, I found remarkable air conditions. There was no wind, but the air seemed fairly to boil." Along the back stretch the changing terrain created convective currents—hot air rising, cool air descending—that could be catastrophic to the fragile aircraft caught in the invisible drafts. The *Golden Flyer* pitched wildly in the turbulence.

"My machine pitched considerable, and when I passed above the 'graveyard,' where so many machines had gone down and were smashed during the previous days of the meet, the air seemed literally to drop from under me. It was so bad at one spot that I made up my mind that if I got over it safely, I would avoid that particular spot thereafter. Finally I finished the twenty kilometres in safety and crossed the line in fifteen minutes and fifty seconds. My average speed had been forty-six and a half miles per hour." (Officially timed as 43.38 m.p.h.)

Glenn Curtiss with one of his early biplanes.

As he crossed the finish line a wild cheer went up from the few attending Americans. But Curtiss, once his time was posted, modestly pointed out that Blériot had not yet made his flight and there were no times with which to compare his own.

During the course of the day his competitors fell by the wayside as they failed to top Curtiss's record of forty-three and one-third miles per hour. But Blériot kept his own counsel, and as the afternoon lengthened Blériot simply sat near his machine and waited. The clock swept to five. The air had begun to die down into an evening calm when the sleek-looking monoplane bearing the proud numerals "22" was rolled into a starting position. The Frenchman mounted his airplane and his mechanic gave the propeller a swift pull. Curtiss sadly listened to the throaty roar of eighty horsepower.

"He started off," wrote Glenn Curtiss, "with what seemed to be a terrific burst of speed. It looked to me just then as if he must be going twice as fast as my machine had flown; but it must be remembered that I was very anxious to have him go slow. The fear that he was beating me was father to the belief.

"As soon as Blériot was off, Mr. Cortlandt Bishop and Mr. David Bishop, his brother, took me in their automobile over to the judges' stand. Blériot made the first lap in faster time than I had made it, and our hearts sank.

"Again Blériot dashed past the stand, and it seemed to me that he was going even faster than the first time. Great was my surprise, therefore, when, as he landed, there was no outburst of cheers from the great crowd. I had expected a scene of wild enthusiasm, but there was nothing of the sort. I sat in the automobile, wondering why there was no shouting, when I was startled by a shout of joy from my Friend, Cortlandt Bishop, who had gone over to the judges' stand.

"'You win! You win!' he cried, all excited as he ran toward the automobile. 'Blériot is beaten by six seconds.'

"A few moments later, just at half-past five o'clock, the Stars and Stripes were slowly hoisted to the top of the flagpole, as we stood uncovered while the flag went up. There was scarcely a response from the crowded grandstands; no true Frenchman had the heart to cheer. A good, hearty cheer requires more than mere politeness. But every American there made enough noise for ten ordinary people, so that numbers really counted for very

Védrines in an early Morane, the year before he broke the 100 M.P.H. mark in a Deperdussin.

*(U.S. Air Force)*

little in the deep feeling of satisfaction at the result of the first great contest in the history of aviation.''

It was not until 1912, however, that airplanes were going faster than automobiles. On February 12, 1912, at Pau, France, Jules Védrines broke the 100 m.p.h. mark, flying a Deperdussin, a radically new airplane designed by a young French engineer, M. Béchereau. The Deperdussin that Védrines flew was a monoplane with a fuselage shaped like a cigar, plus streamlined cowling over the engine, solid disc wheels, and landing gear without the usual bracing of wires and struts. The plane was the product of Béchereau's belief that the reduction of drag—streamlining the aircraft—could be of as much significance in producing speed as the addition of added horsepower for the engine.

In the same plane, Védrines later made the record official with a clocked speed of 108.18 m.p.h. over a thirty-lap, 124.8-mile course to win the Gordon Bennett Cup at the races held that year in Chicago.

His record was in turn overtaken by others in other races as aviators sought the honor of being fastest and the other rewards of winning the air races.

The assassination of an archduke plunged the European continent into a war that put a temporary end to the international speed competitions. The military needs of the warring nations shifted emphasis to the more deadly uses of flying machines, as war gave giant impetus to the development of speedier aircraft. Engines with more power and reliability mounted in airplanes that were sturdier and better designed brought to an end that era of frail craft and daring men. The airplane that began in the war as an auxiliary tool for observation ended as a primary weapon for destruction. The field of aviation, which prior to the war had been the private domain of a handful of pioneers, was now swelled by hundreds of young enthusiasts. The war not only trained airmen but more important, created public heroes.

After World War I, when military interest in aviation fell to a characteristically low postwar ebb, peacetime aviation heroes were again created at the air races. National and international interest in air racing—long distance and closed course—reached an almost fever pitch.

During the score of years between the two World Wars, it was possible for private individuals or groups to built airplanes to compete for the fame and the glory and the attractive prizes offered for racing without the need for military or governmental subsidy.

The earlier Gordon Bennett Cup races faded from the scene, and in their place were others: the Pulitzer Cup, the Schneider Trophy races for seaplanes, the Thompson Trophy for closed-circuit racing, those exciting pylon-circling contests of the National Air Races, and the Bendix Trophy races, exciting, long-distance, cross-continent competitions.

It was during this brief era of the late Twenties and early Thirties that the air races had their most spectacular hour. The planes that won the races were generally the fastest planes that man could build. Although the speeds attained in the races were not specifically clocked according to F.A.I. rules and hence not official, they represented the best that airplanes could attain.

The aeronautical developments growing out of the efforts to win—developments in design, streamlining, retractable landing gear, supercharged engines, canopied cockpits—provided the foundations for the development of the fast fighter planes of World War II, which in turn produced airplanes too fast for air races. Air racing, of course, continues today, supported by the enthusiasm of a new generation of airmen, but record flights have now reached speeds in the thousands of miles per hour, and have passed into a new domain.

In 1922, however, the threshold of speed to be crossed was two hundred miles per hour, and in the Pulitzer Cup race several U.S. Army fliers reached the magic number flying Curtiss, R-6 Racers. Lt. Russell L. Maughan, flying one of these airplanes, averaged 248.5 m.p.h. to capture the Pulitzer Cup, and unofficially to set a new world speed record. It remained unofficial because it had not been timed or supervised in accordance with F.A.I. regulations.

Two days later, on October 13, 1922, after the air meet was over, General "Billy" Mitchell in the same Curtiss Racer flew an officially clocked course in the presence of the F.A.I. observers, and recorded an official world speed record of 222.97 m.p.h. The snap of the wind through the cockpit tore apart the seam of General Mitchell's leather helmet, marking even then the beginning of the end of the airman's symbolic headgear, the leather helmet with chin straps.

Along the waters of Bay Shore Park near Baltimore, Maryland, the 1925 Schneider Trophy race for seaplanes produced a new record and introduced a new name to aviation—Lt. James Doolittle of the Army Air Service. Only five aircraft started in this race; a Gloster-Napier III flown by the British aviator Capt. Hubert Broad, an Italian Macchi flying boat flown by Giovanni de Briganti, and three Navy Curtiss Racers equipped with pontoons. The three Curtiss seaplanes were flown by Lieutenants Ralph Oftsie, George Cuddihy, and James Doolittle.

Although the weather had been squally and blustery for two days, the dawn of the scheduled race day broke with clear skies and crisp freshness brought in by an arctic high-pressure air mass. It was a perfect autumn day. A mild breeze of ten to fifteen miles per hour blew across the Chesapeake Bay, and a few scattered cumulus clouds punctuated the clear blue sky. A crowd

Lt. James Doolittle with his Curtiss racer.

**(U.S. Air Force)**

had gathered along the shore and on the pier a small knot of newsmen and spectators stood beside the judges' stand.

The three Curtiss Racers made swift takeoffs from the mildly chopping waves, and almost at once those who watched the black-and-gold Racer flown by Doolittle knew that they were witnessing a special performance. Jimmy Doolittle was, as the history of aviation was later to record, one of those special men born for the air. There was the touch of the eagle in the flight of his plane.

Around the first pylon Doolittle snapped his seaplane into a steep bank and held the vertical position as he sliced around the turn to roll out with graceful ease on the straightaway while the other planes were still making their turns. Around the triangular course he raced—seven laps, twenty-one turns, each neatly and perfectly executed by the skillful aviator as he gained giant leads in each turn.

A newsman standing at the judges' station described the final moment:

> A tiny speck out over the water could be seen, flying low and with great speed to the home pylon at one side of the pier. It was Doolittle, streaking his way through the air at 223 miles an hour. Just before he reached the pylon he banked sharply, holding his machine far on her side and keeping her in tightly to the course.
>
> His skill was shown here, for instead of trying to level his vessel out as soon as he got around he held her on her side until he had almost reached the pier, so that the ailerons would not drag and prevent him from recovering the speed he lost in banking.
>
> When those on the end of the pier were able to duck the black thunderbolt that was being hurled at them, Doolittle slowly straightened his plane up to a level position and gave her a slight lift to increase his margin of safety in clearing the pier, but he came so close that those below him had the thrill of their lives and got some idea of what a speed of 223 miles an hour means. The ship approached as fast as the eye could follow, and when it reached a point fifty feet away all details of it were lost. It was just a black shape crashing by and vanishing, the sound of it hitting the ear almost as a blow.

By the time the race was half over it was seen that Doolittle was running away with it. His speed jumped from 223 miles an hour to 228, 230, 231, and then 232. His motor was running with an even song that did not seem loud until it went by 30 feet away.

As he came by the pier on his last lap, having flown faster than at any other time, he pulled back on his stick and sent the little craft zooming almost straight up, her momentum carrying her to 2,000 feet in a few seconds.

Doolittle circled around and came down in a long glide that landed him far out in the bay. He turned and taxied back in a shower of spray. When he got nearly into the pier he shut off his motor and climbed down on a pontoon. A rope was thrown to him and made fast to the plane as it was towed toward the pier.

There was a burst of cheering when Doolittle got near enough to hear, and the boyish looking pilot smiled as he took off his leather cap and bowed somewhat shyly.

The following day, an official timer, Otis A. Porter of the National Aeronautic Association, was on hand while James Doolittle put the same craft through the prescribed course to set an official seaplane speed record of 245.72 miles an hour.

During the next several years, spectacular flights over the poles and across the oceans and the continents helped to stir national and international interest in airplanes. By 1929 the National Air Races at Cleveland were important events, for air racing was a big business.

In 1930, Clifford Henderson, the originator and promoter of the National Air Races, approached wealthy industrialist Vincent Bendix and sold him the idea of sponsoring, along with the National Air Race Committee, a cross-country air race that would be an annual free-for-all speed race testing the competing pilots' abilities as navigators, pilots, and meteorologists. At the same time the airplanes they flew would have to be swift, durable, and consistently reliable. The proposal was that Bendix match the prize money of the committee, to create the purse plus a special trophy bearing the magic name of Bendix.

As Don Dwiggins described the event:

> From the start, the Bendix classic would be wide open, a contest with a substantial cash incentive to make it worth while

for the little guys to gamble on their dreams, and for the best
qualified airmen to pit their skills against one another, skills
needed in the most grueling of all races.

Unlike the closed-course pylon races—the Thompson, Greve
and other dazzling duels performed annually at the National
Air Races—the Bendix would demand of each pilot the utmost
in ability as a navigator, meteorologist and flight-planner; and
of the ships themselves, the cleanest, most efficient design,
the fastest speed, and the most rugged endurance.

The race was to be flown from Burbank, California, to the
Bendix pylon at the National Air Races at Cleveland. The first
race was scheduled for September 4, 1931, and it was not surpris-
ing to find that Jimmy Doolittle—ex-bantamweight boxer who
later took an aeronautical-engineering degree from the Massachusetts Institute of Technology, now out of the Army Air
Service and an executive with the Shell Oil Company—had
entered the lists for the competition.

Eight planes were prepared for takeoff that cloudless September
evening. At Union Air Terminal hundreds gathered around the
assembled airplanes at the end of Runway 15 to watch the preparations for the dash to Cleveland. Six of the competing airplanes
were Lockheed "Vegas," monoplanes with a high degree of reliability and a fuel capacity that permitted nonstop flight from California to Cleveland. One flown by Art Goebel, winner of the Dole
race from California to Hawaii in 1927, was a Speed Vega, reliable
but not as fast as the other Lockheeds. Two of the Lockheeds
were of the "Orion" class: low-winged with retractable landing
gear, permitting speeds up to 225 m.p.h. Harold S. Johnson and
Beeler Blevins each were flying one of these craft. Three
Lockheeds were low-winged, two-place sport planes, of the
"Altair" class, with hand-cranked retractable gear and clean lines
for speed. Captain Ira C. Eaker, James Goodwin Hall, and Lou
Reichers each flew an Altair. A seventh racer, the Travel-Air
S Mystery, was flown by Walter Hunter, and a squat green-
and-yellow Laird Super Solution named the *Sky Buzzard* was
flown by Doolittle. Doolittle's airplane had the fastest air speed
but its short range required frequent stops.

The race was supervised by the National Aeronautic Association. Larry Therkelsen, the official timer, was on the runway

to flag the planes off. The competitors were launched in tandem, racing the clock but not each other. Each chose his own route, some selecting the straight line from Burbank to Cleveland, and others making deviations to take advantage of terrain, prevailing winds, and available landing fields. Each selected his own method of navigation, using radio-range navigation, pilotage, or in some cases dead reckoning.

Doolittle, a perpetual optimist, had little doubt that he would win the Bendix, and indeed he intended to continue to Newark, New Jersey, to snatch an additional prize for the fastest cross-country flight. He would fly by dead reckoning along a route carefully planned in advance and marked in ten-mile increments, stepladder fashion, across his flight chart. As he flew his predetermined compass course he would check his path across the ground. His relationship to his predetermined position would tell him whether he had a tail wind, head wind or crosswind, and he could compensate accordingly. In instrument weather conditions he would maintain his course by time and speed alone. This was a method as old as the sailing ships and as effective in 1931 as it had been centuries before.

As Blevins' Orion went off ahead of him, Doolittle snapped closed his cockpit, rechecked his engine instruments, firmly hitting the panel with the edge of his hand to free sticking instrument needles, caged his gyro compass, set it according to the known 150-degree heading of the runway, uncaged it, and slowly began to ease his throttle forward, holding his brakes tightly locked. He nodded his readiness, and Therkelsen flashed the starter flag. Doolittle released his brakes, and his Super Solution roared down the runway. The tail came up and at the end of a four-hundred-foot run the little racer lifted from the ground and headed out on course. Overtaking and passing Blevins, Doolittle wagged his wings in salutation and disappeared into the east.

Wrote Don Dwiggins:

> At 5,000 feet he dropped his plane's nose to pick up speed, then climbed on toward rugged San Gorgonio Pass and the giant peaks that lay to either side. At 11,000 feet he leveled off, retrimmed the biplane, and settled down on his compass heading zero-seven-five magnetic, a course that would give him an easterly track over the ground. He scanned the panel, set

his gyro compass, then brought altimeter, air-speed, bank and turn, and artificial horizon instruments into alignment.

Doolittle flew with fanatic precision. When his flight profile called for 11,000 feet, it was not enough to fly 50 feet above or below the altitude. He knew from past experience that one tiny error added to another tiny error made compound problems that could become serious to a pilot in an emergency, with many things on his mind. He had been the first man in the world to fly an airplane from takeoff to landing completely "blind," back on September 24, 1929.

Early dawn lighted the sky as Doolittle's racer crossed the Colorado River and he picked up the snow-capped San Francisco Peaks on the horizon. The sky became a roseate glow, his propeller disk a fiery pinwheel as he bored into the morning. He now had altitude to spare; the high peaks were behind him. He began a shallow dive, picking up more speed, letting gravity pull him along faster and faster, like a speedboat riding on its step.

Like an auto racer at a pit stop, Doolittle put down at Albuquerque, New Mexico, in a quick, short landing, slammed his throttle and mixture closed, clicked off the magnetos, leaped from the cockpit, and opened the fuel tanks. The trucks, already waiting, began to pump gasoline into the airplane. In a few minutes he was once more airborne, winging eastward.

His flight to Albuquerque, a distance of 674 miles, had been made at a speed of 228 m.p.h. Doolittle was pleased. If he could continue at this rate he could stretch his flight to Newark to beat Frank Hawk's transcontinental speed record and win an additional $2,500 in prize money to add to the $7,500 Bendix first prize.

Dwiggins continued:

Crossing Oklahoma at 5,000 feet, in order to pick up a tail wind, Doolittle streaked over the Canadian River and dropped into Kansas City 3 hours 6 minutes after leaving Albuquerque. There the gasoline crew swiftly refueled his plane, and within minutes he was airborne. Storm clouds appeared ahead.

Meanwhile, it was raining at Cleveland, and the crowd was small. Pylon race events had been cancelled. But at the white finish line stood Jimmy's wife, Jo, and their two sons, James, ten years old, and John, nine. There was no doubt in their minds who would win.

Rather than swing off course to go around a massive squall line ahead of him, Doolittle settled down in the cockpit, steadied the wings and went on instruments. Lightning stabbed the black sky. Big raindrops began to pelt the cowling with a deafening tattoo that all but drowned out the engine noise.

The plane bored through the squall line into clear sunshine. Ahead lay the green fields and autumn-red trees of Ohio. In the distance Doolittle could see Cleveland Municipal Airport, and the tall, red and white pylon emblazoned with the name: BENDIX.

Doolittle had won the race, but he did not pause for the plaudits. Instead, he refueled his craft and raced toward the east. The *Sky Buzzard* streaked over the Allegheny Mountains and into a second storm line. Rain poured over the canopy in blinding sheets. Doolittle held his course, his eyes sweeping his flight instruments in easy, rhythmic sequence—needle, ball and airspeed, altimeter, climb indicator, gyrocompass, flight indicator —as the washing rain pelted the cockpit.

When he passed through the storm, he had crossed the mountains. Now he started his final, gradual letdown toward the airfield at Newark. He landed in a flashing 360-degree overhead approach, and as he chopped his throttle, the timer marked him in. He had set a new coast-to-coast record—11 hours, 11 minutes—and had won two prizes in a single flight.

Although never a world speed-record holder under F.A.I. rules, Roscoe Turner was a pilot whose name became virtually synonymous with fast airplanes and air racing. Born in the steamy flatlands of Corinth, Mississippi, in 1895, he leaped into the twentieth century with a flair and a dash that has always since been considered typical of the "dashing aviator." Turner's leather helmet, flying goggles, waxed moustache, and flashy uniform of a colonel in the Nevada National Guard were his hallmarks. He appeared often with a parachute tossed casually over his shoulder as he walked the streets of Los Angeles with a toothless lion cub named Gilmore trailing him on a leash. As Roscoe later remarked, "The lion liked to fly. The Humane Society made me build him a parachute, but he never used it."

A pilot in World War I, Turner had not been in the service long enough to reach combat when the war ended. After the war he was successful as a lion tamer, a parachute jumper, and a Hollywood stunt flier. He did all the flying for the Howard Hughes movie *Hell's Angels*. When he undertook air racing, it was with the same zest and dash; and he enjoyed the success of his victories, prizes, and trophies.

As Roscoe Turner himself described a Thompson Trophy race:

Ten... Nine... Eight... Seven... seconds, the clock on the dash panel says, ticking them off. And you sit in there the cramped cockpit and sweat. Waiting for the starter to drop the flag.

The tiny racing plane trembles. The propeller clatters. The skin throbs.

You're in No. 2 position, next to the orange job with the taper wing, second from the end of the line. There are nine others, wing-tip to wing-tip, all rarin' to go. Stinging, snorting little hornets.

And you've got to fly each one of them besides your own. Because you never know what the other guy is going to do.

This is the Thompson Trophy Race. The big one. The National Air Races. The one that really counts. Aviation's "Kentucky Derby." You've got to win. Everything you own is wrapped up in this trim and powerful little racer. Everything. Even your spare watch is in hock.

For 365 days, since the race last year, you've been getting the ship ready. Wings clipped to cut through the air faster. Engine souped up to get more power. One thousand two hundred horsepower in your lap and a feather in your tail. That's what it amounts to. Enough to make any aeronautical engineer beat himself to death with his slide rule.

For what? For fame and glory and headlines and the prize money. So you can pay off your debts and come back next year.

Check your instruments, fuel gauge. Pressure gauge. Oil temperature. Tachometer. Cylinder head temperatures. Glance at the chronometer. The clock has stopped. No, it's still running.

Six ... Five ... Four ... Why is a second a year? Tick, tick, tick, it sounds like the bong of Big Ben in your ears. Tension, nerves, fear. It drowns out the roar of the crowd.

The grandstand; a kaleidoscope of colors. It'll be a blurred ribbon the next time you see it flash by.

See that black and yellow job down the line? Keep your eyes on him. He's the guy to beat. Get out in front of him and try to stay there. No. 8, that's him. *Number Eight ... Number Eight ...* Beat him ... Beat him ... The engine sings it. A battle cry. Remember what your mechanic said—"They're ganging up on you. Look out! They're going to try and box you in." Just like they do at a horse race.

Three ... Two ... One second now to go!

Why won't your feet be still? They're jumping up and down on the rudder pedals. Dammit! You can't stop them. And your hands? Sticky, trembling on the stick and throttle. Shaking like you've got the Dts. Goggles streaming with perspiration. Your clothes are soaked. They're soggy. Itchy. Hell fever, that's what you've got. Scared-to-hell fever. You always catch it about now—with one second to go. It'll go away. As soon as ... There's the flag.

Slap the throttle. Werrummm! The ship leaps forward. Your feet stop jumping. Hands? Cold and steady. Now, crouched in the cockpit, this is your world. Nothing else matters. It's up to you.

Faster, faster, faster, shooting across the field. Pull back on the stick. Not too fast. Easy does it. You're free. The ship leaps forward again, like a shot from a gun. No more ground drag. Too much speed. You'll rip the wings off if you don't slow down the propeller.

Where are the others? Count 'em ... one ... two ... three ... they're all up. Don't get too close. One error and it's curtains for both of you.

You're no longer human. You're a machine. Every move is timed to the split second ... There's the red roof. Pylon coming up. Left rudder. Left stick. Wing up. Wing down. You're around. The straightaway. More throttle. The wind whistles in your ears.

Brown roof. Big tree. Another turn. Here come the others. Who's that on the left wing? He's cutting in too close. You'll get his prop wash on the next turn ... Here it comes, boy ... Hang on!

Too sharp. Take 'em wider next time. Don't try to cut so short. Let the other guy kill himself. You're doing all right. There's the grandstand again. Swoosh!

Pull off a strip of tape from the dashboard. That's how you count the laps. Thirty laps. Thirty pieces of tape. Twenty-nine now ... Check it the next time you go by the crowd. The guy will have the big numeral card out. It should read *28*.

Where is No. 8? You can't see him. Red roof again . . . turn . . . straightaway . . . throttle . . . brown roof . . . big tree . . . pylon . . . the grandstand. Okay, it says *28*.

There he is! Just ahead. You're gaining on him. Faster, faster . . . Pour it on. Pray this thing will hold together . . . Red roof coming up . . . Try to cut it real short this time . . . Take the chance . . . Maybe you can get him on the turn . . . NOW . . . Wing down deep . . . Snap back . . . Jerk . . . Shake, tremble, roar! But you made it. There's nobody in front of you.

If you could only look back and catch that number card for a recheck. It was so blurred. Maybe you missed a pylon. Maybe they'll disqualify you. No, not that, please. And let 'er hang together another two minutes.

It's over.

You won!

You're shaking again. You can hardly control the ship after she's on the ground. Your heart beats louder than the engine. Uniform soaked, sopping wet. Hands tremble. Knees buckle as you climb out to meet the reporters and photographers with a big forced smile . . . Headache. Muscle ache. Exhaustion. Oh, for a great big soft bed.

Air racing is like that. It's the toughest test of all on men and machines. I know. For ten years I was pushing pylons in the Thompson. For ten years I was smashing records across the country in the big Bendix Transcontinental. Three times winner of the Thompson, many times loser. But it gets in your blood, and it stays.

Roscoe Turner won the Bendix Trophy in 1933 with a flight across country in 11 hours, 30 minutes, and the following year he won the Thompson Trophy. In the 1934 Thompson Trophy race, Turner and Doug Davis, an Eastern Airlines pilot, each in a Wedell-Williams racer, were the front runners. Davis was the favorite having already been the winner of the first Thompson in 1931, and Roscoe Turner, with the Bendix Trophy in hand, was a promising contender.

The start was quick and in the early laps Davis and Turner pulled away from the pack. Like darting bees, airplanes flashed around the pylons and roared wide open down the straightaways. As he approached the turns, each man cut tighter and tighter to the upright. Doug Davis had the lead and was holding his position four hundred yards ahead of Turner.

The crowd was yelling wildly as the planes spun past at speeds over 200 m.p.h. In the eighth lap the two Wedell-Williams racers roared toward the pylon, with Davis still in the lead. Turner was inching closer. Davis began his turn as close as he could to the pylon, easing into the turn with gradual pressure on the left rudder and a flick of the stick to hold the plane tightly through the turn. The familiar G-forces pressed him into the seat and he tightened his stomach to hold pressure in the swing around the pylon. Looking along his low wing, Doug Davis could see the ground spinning dizzily past as the plane whirled by the axis of the pylon. Then, in a careless moment, the nose of the plane dropped. Davis added top rudder. The plane was in a tight, steep bank, and Davis pressed harder on the right rudder to lift the slipping nose. The airplane was in a dangerous cross-controlled condition. Rudder and aileron were pressed in opposite directions. Davis felt the plane snap, then whip violently upside down in a high-speed, cross-controlled stall that slammed the plane into the earth to explode in a yellow blossom of gasoline-fired flame. Doug Davis was dead.

Roscoe Turner and his Wasp-powered Wedell-Williams Special Racer.

**(National Air and Space Museum, The Smithsonian Institution)**

Turner finished the race to take the trophy, but he was shaken by the sudden tragedy before him. He overflew the finish by three additional laps around the course, and broke off only when he saw the others circling away for landing.

During the 1935 Bendix race Roscoe Turner barely escaped death himself, when he miraculously landed his flaming airplane with a broken oil line. On the last lap, with black smoke rolling from the racer, Turner chandelled from the course to an altitude where he could bail out. As he struggled for altitude, he thought about the payments still due on the racer and reconsidered his decision. Man and airplane dove for the landing field, smoke and flames streaming behind.

As Turner recalled that moment: "I stuck with it. You don't want to see your ship go, if you can help it. And there was a chance. I headed down. Fast. Leveled off. The wheels hit. Wham! I thought sure the whole bottom fell out. The little ship bounced 50 feet. Slam! She hit again. Hung on. Rolled to a stop. I was down and safe.

"'Tough luck, Turner,' said a reporter racing up to the ship. 'That's the damnedest luck we've ever seen.'

"'What do you mean, tough luck,' I said, trying to be calm and making a mess of it. 'Anytime you can get down and walk away from it, that's good luck. I'm just as happy as if I had good sense.'"

In 1938 and again in 1939 Turner won the coveted Bendix Trophy; the three-time win was a feat never matched by another pilot.

After his third victory in 1939, the colorful Roscoe Turner, foreseeing the end of the era, announced his retirement from racing. Many others associated with aviation were also beginning to divorce themselves from the closed-course races. Planes were now too fast, and the dangers to the pilots were disproportionate to the rewards.

An editorial in *The New York Times* best summarized the changing views: "The Roman holiday sport of whipping high-powered little planes around a pylon-studded race course joins with transatlantic solo flights and other such colorful exploits in the fast-moving cavalcade of an industry that has outgrown its swaddling clothes."

The cross-continent Bendix Trophy races continued in later years, but in 1940, probably because of the war in Europe, the air races in Cleveland were canceled.

It is of significant note that Roscoe Turner's winning speed of 283.4 m.p.h. in the 1939 Thompson Trophy race was a long way from the world speed record made by a German test pilot, Fritz Wendel, in the same year, at Augsburg, Germany. On an officially clocked course, Wendel flew his Messerschmitt Me. 209 at 469.22 m.p.h. (It was not a Messerschmitt B.F. 109R as it is listed in the F.A.I. records.)

"With its tiny wing and, for those days, horrifying wing loading, the '209' was a brute," Fritz Wendel recalled. "Its flying characteristics still make me shudder. It had a dangerous tendency to nose down without any reason or warning, and it touched down on the runway like a ton of bricks. Even on the ground its characteristics were no more ladylike, as it would suddenly swerve off the runway without any provocation. In retrospect, I am inclined to think that its main fuel was a highly volatile mixture of the sweat from my brow and the goose pimples from the back of my neck!"

On April 4, 1939, Wendel took off from Haunstetten for a training flight in preparation for the speed-record attempt in the second prototype, the Me. 209V-a. The test plane was unwieldy and Wendel struggled with the controls. After a flight of only a few minutes he decided to return to the field. As he made his approach he lowered the landing gear over his usual landmark, the Siebentischwald, a forest near the airfield. Suddenly the lubricating system failed, the pistons seized in the cylinders, and the propeller locked stiffly in place. "With a jolt, the plane virtually pulled up in midair," Wendel later wrote, "the result of the combined drag of the lowered undercarriage and the unfeathered airscrew. The viscious little brute started dropping like a stone, and below me was the forest! I strained on the stick with all I had and, to my surprise, the plane responded. I screamed over the last row of trees bordering the Haunstettenstrasse, and was even more surprised to find myself staggering away, relatively unhurt, from the heap of twisted metal that seconds before had been an Me. 209."

Only twenty-two days later, on April 26, 1939, Wendel was

again climbing into the cockpit of a blue-painted Me. 209V1 to challenge the established speed record.

"The engine sparked into life with its characteristic roar. A very brief warm-up, a last instrument check, and I was off, searing up and down the course and screeching around the clearly marked turning points. I touched again and saw a crowd of workers and technicians racing toward the plane. I climbed out of the cockpit, and Willie Messerschmitt slapped me on the back and told me that we had 'got it.' The Me. 209, as I was to discover later, had averaged 469.22 m.p.h.''

In 1964, when a renewed interest in air racing led to the holding of the Reno National Championship Air Races, Fritz Wendel's F.A.I.-approved level-flight speed record for a piston-engine, propeller-driven airplane had remained unbroken for twenty-five years. Pilots in all kinds of modified fighters—P-51s, P-38s, F-4Us and many others—had attempted to better the record.

Darryl Greenamyer, a test pilot for Lockheed-California Company, in a modified F8F-2 "Bearcat" he had named *Smirnoff,* made an assault upon the speed record on a three-kilometer course set up during the 1966 Los Angeles National Air Races. After the second run, he was unable to maintain directional stability with his modified vertical stabilizer and was forced to abandon the runs. Three years later, on August 16, 1969, his persistence was rewarded. On a National Aeronautic Association-timed run in his Grumman Bearcat he reached 482.462 m.p.h. to establish a new world record.

The speeds of propellers and piston engines were approaching their limits when Wendel set his record in 1939. But man's quest for faster speeds had already demonstrated the need for a better airplane. The new dimension was the jet.

Back in July, 1942, Fritz Wendel had strapped himself into a propellerless airplane, the Messerschmitt Me. 262 prototype. The airplane, with twin wing-mounted jet engines, had first been flown with a piston engine and propeller mounted in the front, the reliability of the propellerless engines being uncertain.

Now the crutch had been removed and the jet was in its pure form. Three years earlier, on August 27, 1939, a *Heinkel* He-178 powered by a centrifugal-flow turbojet engine had made a brief flight at Rostock, Germany; and the English had flown a jet pro-

Wilhelm Messerschmitt, the designer of the Messerschmitt jet, congratulates Captain Fritz Wendel after his record speed flight.

**(U.S. Air Force)**

totype, the Gloster E.28/39, in England on May 15, 1941. But the jet was still a fledgling, and the flight characteristics of the Messerschmitt jet were unknown. Wendel lined up the plane with the runway at the Leipheim airfield in Germany, pressed his throttles forward. Observers standing nearby were deafened by the banshee scream of the twin jet engines winding to a painful pitch. Inside the cockpit the sound was muted, and in the muffled quiet Wendel felt the jet begin to roll. Absent was the whine of a propeller and the howl of an engine that had the throttle pushed to the fire wall. The landing roll began more slowly and increased gradually compared to the characteristics of conventional craft. No twist of torque pulled at the rudder, and the jet seemed to lift silently into the sky. Fritz Wendel then felt for the first time the noiseless but remarkably powerful thrust of the engines. He sensed through the light reaction of the controls the ease with which the aerodynamically "clean" airplane sliced through the sky with speed and easy maneuverability.

In America, test pilot Robert Stanley would feel the same remarkable characteristics of flight after he climbed into the Bell XP-59A on October 2, 1942. Across the hard red clay of the Mojave Desert, the new noise, the wail of the jet engine, replaced the more familiar throaty thunder of a reciprocating engine. The fake wooden propeller, placed on the plane so that those who saw the jet would have no cause to wonder, had been removed and the craft rolled into position for takeoff.

Miles away from the air base, those citizens who saw that first jet streaking through the sky, trailing a stream of black smoke that resulted from the combustion of the kerosene fuel, watched in wonder. The plane, high above, made a curious sound: its roar was deep and seemed to fill the heavens with an awesome power. Some observers hurried to telephones to notify the authorities of the sighting of a burning airplane, others merely watched dumbstruck at the swiftness of the darting bird; but few knew, or could have known, what historical event was flashing before their eyes.

These incidents marked the beginning of the jet airplane, whose development would be as swift and as spectacular as the advances of aviation itself in its first score of years. Propeller-driven planes had reached the limits of their capabilities, and jet engines would carry airmen into a new order of speed, with limits yet unknown.

# CHAPTER 3

# The Rocket Airplane Carries Man to Record Speeds

When speeding airplanes approached the speed of sound, there were those who believed that the sonic barrier represented the final limit of man's ability to travel through the air. They reasoned that the natural phenomenon of sound, the transmission of energy from source to receiver by the compression of molecules in longitudinal pressure waves—sonic waves—presented the ultimate restraint on the speed of flight. As airplanes approached the sound barrier, shock waves developed; a shell, invisible to the eye but steel-hard, acted like a giant hand placed before the aircraft to stop its forward motion. Airmen spoke of the sound barrier with the same awe and respect that ancient mariners had when they spoke of those mystic dragons awaiting the wandering sailor at the rim of the sea on the far corners of the flat earth.

Fighter pilots during World War II occasionally brushed close to the sound barrier in combat dives. Mysterious things happened to their planes—weakened spots of metal would puncture on the wings, or controls would lock in the iron vise of the force exerted by the compressed air of the sonic wall. Some pilots did not recover from such a final dive, others were released from the devil grip as enigmatically as they had been seized.

The precise point at which an airplane would encounter the sound barrier, the speed of sound—720.9 m.p.h. at the standard sea-level temperature of 59° F. and decreasing as a function of temperature to 662 m.p.h. in the stratosphere at a temperature of −67° F.—was known and could be easily calculated. The speed of sound is referred to in aviation language as "Mach 1." Whether an airplane could penetrate the sound barrier with its problems of high drag and marginal or nonexistent aircraft controllability was not known. There were many daring men of aviation, however, who were ready and eager to find the answer.

On December 18, 1943, air officers of the armed services, representatives of American aircraft industries, and officials of the National Advisory Committee for Aeronautics (NACA, the forerunner of NASA, National Aeronautics and Space Administration) assembled in a quiet conference room in Washington, D.C. It was at this conference that Robert A. Wolf of Textron's Bell Aerosystems Company first suggested that NACA fund and develop an aircraft to explore and probe the sonic wall to find the hole through which machine, man, and the future of aviation might plunge.

As Mr. Wolf suggested: "The opportunity was at hand to build a high-speed research airplane to provide needed aerodynamic information for aircraft manufacturers. This information is particularly needed for the high-speed range of flight that is now reached by conventional fighter aircraft in dives, but which may be attained by jet propulsion aircraft in level flight. The development and testing of this aircraft could be ideally handled by the National Advisory Committee of Aeronautics."

Wolf's proposal won the approval of the director of NACA, and by 1944 Congress had appropriated the initial funds for a series of research airplanes. If man was ever to fly beyond the speed of sound, high-speed flying laboratories would have to lead the way.

In cooperation with the Air Force and the Navy, NACA began work on the X series of experimental airplanes. Headquarters for this program was at Muroc Air Force Base (now named Edwards AFB) deep in the Mojave Desert, seventy miles from Los Angeles. There, forty-four square miles of cement-hard red mud provided a matchless landing field for some of the world's most exotic experimental aircraft. The table-smooth surface of the dry lake was ideal for the testing of airplanes whose unknown characteristics might cause their pilots to need instant elbow room for unscheduled landings.

The first aircraft designed especially for the assault upon the sound barrier was a small rocket-shaped plane 30 feet, 11 inches long, with a needle-tipped nose and stubby wings. Built for the U. S. Air Force by Bell Aircraft Corporation, it was powered by four fifteen-hundred-pound-thrust rockets capable of developing speeds between nine hundred and one thousand miles per hour. The strange orange-and-white craft did not take off from the ground in a conventional fashion, but was designed to be launched from the underbelly of a Boeing B-29 mother ship. Officially the plane was the X-1, but the project pilot, Capt. Charles E. Yeager, nicknamed it *Glamorous Glennis* in affection for his wife.

Captain Yeager, a double ace in World War II and one of the leading Air Force Test pilots, made ready for the assault on the sound barrier in cautious, programmed stages. His first flights in the X-1 were after drops from the mother ship followed by long, spiraling, powerless glides to the desert floor. Once he had mastered the subtle flight characteristics of the new airplane, he began to fly in powered flight, each mission inching by degrees toward the mysterious and magical Mach 1.

October 14, 1947, was selected as the date for the penetration of the sonic wall. As the target date approached, the increased tension among project personnel was easy to detect. Yeager himself, showing outward calm, could not deny his own increasing apprehension. The touch of fear was a familiar sensation; its twinges had ridden with him in the cockpit when he flamed eleven German aircraft in combat.

On the morning of October 14, the desert sky was a bright and brittle blue. Along the road to the air base, a dry wind rustled the Joshua trees and rolled an occasional thistle among the sagebrush. But Yeager had no mind for the desert decorations. He hurried toward the flight line where there was a bustle of activity around the Boeing mother ship and the X-1. As he walked toward the aircraft, Yeager gave an unconscious tug upon his jacket and patted his side, where he secretly nursed several cracked ribs received the night before when he was thrown from a horse at a nearby dude ranch.

"I didn't tell any of the guys." he later reported. "As I recall, it hurt quite a bit, but there's not a lot of strain in flying an airplane like the X-1, except when closing the door—you have to pull up real hard on the lever, and that was the worst part. But you're sitting in there and nobody can see you and you can grimace all you want to.''

When all was in readiness, Yeager climbed the ladder through the nose wheel into the front cabin of the B-29. Inside the cabin of the big bomber, the control panels, like individual metal tablets, stood separately within the flight deck, a greenhouse of glass in the nose of the cigar-shaped mother ship. Heavily laden in a G-suit (pressure suit), coveralls, and parachute, Yeager made himself comfortable on a seat along a wooden bench while the B-29 flight crew prepared for takeoff. Major Robert Cardenas, a leading Air Force test pilot, was at the bomber controls.

Outside, two F-80 fighters swished into the desert air to fly "chase" on the rocket airplane, and the B-29 crew chief, with the fire extinguisher at the ready, gave the signal for engine start. As the four Pratt and Whitneys roared noisily to life, Yeager tried to relax on his wooden perch. The B-29 taxied into position and, upon signal from control, rolled down the runway, lifted into the air, and began its slow, circling climb to altitude.

While the mother ship climbed through five thousand feet, Yeager started his own preparations. Squeezing through the bomb-bay entrance door behind the navigator's table, he made his way out along the catwalks toward the waiting rocket craft. Inside the dimly lit bomb bay the noise of the engines and the roar of the slipstream were deafening. Secretly favoring his tender ribs, Yeager eased himself into the X-1 cockpit and pulled the hatch closed. He put on his helmet and adjusted his oxygen mask. Yeager was back at work again, and the tension began to ease. Deft fingers snapped the toggles and pressed the switches as he swiftly moved through his checklist. He flipped on the radio.

"Okay, Cardenas, how do you read me?" he asked.

"Loud and clear," answered Cardenas from the forward flight deck.

Yeager completed his checklist. All was in order.

"Five minutes warning," called Cardenas.

Behind Yeager were thick-walled tanks of rocket propellants, alcohol and liquid oxygen (lox). All around him in the cramped cockpit were instruments, warning lights, and controls. He knew them by heart and could reach any one of the hundreds of dials, buttons, or switches blindfolded. The control stick was part stick, part wheel. It looked like the top of an H which he held by the vertical uprights.

The bomber wheeled into an easy turn at 21,000 feet of altitude. Major Cardenas' voice clicked on the radio: "Am turning on the base leg."

Yeager readied himself for the drop.

"B-29 eight zero zero to NACA radar, Muroc Tower, chase aircraft. One minute warning."

Cardenas lowered the nose of the B-29 so that it began a shallow dive to bring its speed up to 240 m.p.h., the minimum flying speed for the loaded *Glamorous Glennis*.

"Muroc Tower to Air Force eight zero zero, clear to drop."

"Roger, Muroc."

Yeager flipped the switch to activate the recording devices; if Yeager did not return from the sonic wall, the messages from the recorder would.

Cardenas began the count:

"Eight zero zero, here is your countdown. Ten—nine—eight—seven—six—five." He skipped four with an appropriate pause. "Three—two—one. Drop!"

For Chuck Yeager time was frozen in the bomb bay of the B-29. For a second that seemed an eternity there was waiting, then, with a sharp crack or snap, like the sound of a strand of wire breaking, the X-1 dropped. The sudden release created a brief zero G, and Yeager rose in his shoulder straps while his stomach seemed to float, a sensation experienced when one goes over the top of the grade in a roller coaster. As he dropped into the brilliant daylight from the darkness of the bomb bay he was blinded momentarily. Then his eyes adjusted, and from a white void dials and instruments again took their familiar form. The *Glamorous Glennis* was gliding free of the mother ship.

Yeager fired his first rocket engine. The impact slammed the plane forward, and the X-1 began to climb at a tremendous rate of speed. Following the flight profile, he fired his next rocket engines according to schedule as the airplane bolted to 37,000 feet in an almost vertical climb. The bomber and the F-80s dropped away as if they were standing still. From outside the X-1, a dot of visible white shock waves trailed the plane, turning later into the steady stream of a single telltale contrail.

Inside the X-1 there was no noise save the clicking of flight instruments, and Yeager was experiencing a strange sensation. Emotionally he could sense leaving the limits of the known and entering a region of the unknown. His earlier apprehension had disappeared with the action of flying the airplane. Now he could feel the press of the powerful rocket engines shoving him noiselessly into a realm of speed unknown to man. He had the exhilarating feeling of being suspended in space and time. He described it as "floating in motion on top of a ball that moves in every direction at once and never rests."

At 37,000 feet Yeager eased his rocket ship into level flight and watched the Mach indicator build past .8. The needle flicked slowly clockwise and Yeager waited for the impact of the sound barrier. A shock wave was building on the nose of the ship. The plane reached .97 Mach. Yeager watched. The control stick was steady in his hand. Then the needle jumped to 1.05, the shock wave on the nose was gone, and the X-1 was flying faster

"Then the needle jumped to 1.05, the shock wave on the nose was gone and the X-1 was flying faster than the speed of sound." *(NASA)*

than the speed of sound. The moment of history had come and gone almost silently. As Yeager later noted: "I was kind of disappointed that it wasn't more of a big charge than it was."

Two and one-half minutes after rocket firing, the fuel was exhausted; and the X-1 slowed and dropped back through the sound barrier with easy grace. Yeager scavenged the fuel system by pumping nitrogen through the rocket plumbing to flush away the ignitable oxygen and alcohol. The *Glamorous Glennis* began the long glide back to earth.

Approaching the lake, with a chase plane riding at four o'clock high giving instructions, Yeager touched down at 165 m.p.h. Red dust billowed as the X-1 came swiftly to a safe halt.

The phenomenal breakthrough, which was hailed by Air Force Chief of Staff General Hoyt S. Vandenberg as "the greatest achievement in aviation since the first flight of the Wright brothers' airplane in 1903," remained a closely guarded secret until it was announced by Secretary of the Air Force W. Stuart Symington on June 10, 1948. Between October and June, Charles Yeager had punched the sturdy X-1 through the wall in repeated flights.

This significant work was acknowledged by President Harry S. Truman who, on behalf of the National Aeronautic Association, presented the Robert J. Collier Trophy, one of the most prized of all American aeronautical honors, to the three men "regarded as most responsible for the achievement of breaking the sound barrier": John Stack, a research scientist who pioneered the work in determining the physical laws affecting supersonic flight, principally the concept of the X-series aircraft; Lawrence D. Bell, president of the Bell Aircraft Company, which engineered and built the supersonic craft; and Charles E. Yeager, who flew it.

An editorial writer for *The New York Times* prophetically observed: "The selection of these three men spotlights the teamwork among science, industry and skilled human daring which is required to push forward into even more eerie atmosphere the frontiers of flight.

"That man and apparatus have thus been able to crash through the transonic barrier and far exceed the speed of sound is an aeronautical triumph of the first magnitude. It opens broad, new vistas both for national defense and the peaceful flights of commerce."

Meanwhile, military jet aircraft were setting official speed records. On August 25, 1947, Major Marion E. Carl of the United States Marine Corps flew the Douglas D-588-1, the "Skystreak," to an official F.A.I. record of 650.92 m.p.h. This was a flight by a jet taking off from the ground and returning, as contrasted with the air-launched rocket flights of the X series.

In December, 1947, Marion Carl wrote, "At present I hold the world's speed record for the measured three-kilometer course, but it will be only a matter of time—probably a very short time—before it is again broken."

He was right. By the following year his record had been bettered by Major Richard L. Johnson, whose record in turn was topped within a few years.

On July 16, 1953, Lt. Col. William F. Barnes had pushed his North American F-86D "Sabre" jet to .91 Mach for a record 715.74 m.p.h., just below the speed of sound in an official run ninety feet off the deck across the burning sands of the hot desert that surrounds the Salton Sea in southern California. During the same period air-launched rocket planes were flying at almost twice these speeds. The experimental Douglas D-558-2 "Skyrocket," launched from the bomb-bay of a B-29, was flown to 1,238 m.p.h. by test pilot William Bridgeman on August 7, 1951, and to 1,327 m.p.h. by Scott Crossfield on November 20, 1953.

On October 3, 1953, Lt. Comdr. James B. Verdin of the U.S. Navy, flying a prototype Navy F4D, the Douglas "Skyray," from a runway takeoff, set a new official record of 753.4 m.p.h. streaking across the Salton basin. Reaching Mach .96, at the edge of the sonic wall, the record speed was obtainable without crossing the sound barrier because the high 98.5-degree temperature at sea level caused the speed of sound to occur at a higher true airspeed than under normal conditions.

By March 10, 1956, L. Peter Twiss had broken the thousand-miles-per-hour mark at Ford-Chichester, England. Step-by-step records were made, only to be broken by a faster ship as men and airplanes sought to attain undreamed-of speeds. The X-2 series, heavier and faster, replaced the successful X-1 and X-1A.

The sound barrier had been met and broken. Now the aeronautical pioneers were challenging the heat barrier. The X-2 was constructed of a special skin made of heat-resistant stainless steel and a nickel alloy. The new challenge, the heat barrier, was not a problem of compression like the sound barrier, with a fixed single speed or range or speeds. Rather it was a general problem in the speed zone past 1,150 m.p.h., where the friction of the air, the so-called ram temperature rise, caused temperatures to rise so high that conventional aircraft metals began to lose their strength. This zone was referred to as the "thermal thicket," and the X-2, with a potential range up to 2,500 m.p.h., was designed to explore this thicket and to pluck its thermodynamic thorns.

On August 2, 1956, Lt. Col. Frank K. Everest dropped free from a Boeing B-50 mother ship and, kicking in the X-2's powerful Curtiss-Wright rocket engines, was propelled to a record 1,900 m.p.h.

In September Capt. Iven G. Kincheloe, Jr., flew the X-2 to a record altitude of 126,200 feet. That same month test pilot Melburn G. Apt in his first powered flight in the X-2 rode the rocket airplane beyond the two-thousand-miles-per-hour mark.

The B-50 mother ship carried Apt's X-2 to drop altitude above

End of landing roll after the first Bell X-2 flight.

*(NASA)*

the desert. James Carson was flying an F-100 in high chase and Kincheloe was in low chase, flying an F-86.

Below and abeam of the giant bomber, Kincheloe was positioned to watch the X-2 drop free. The launch was good. Mel Apt flicked on his rocket engine, and the powerful rocket engine shot yellow flames from the tail and shoved the X-2 up with a smashing thrust.

"Start the nose up," radioed Kincheloe.

Mel Apt held the aircraft with needle-point accuracy at the profiled climb angle. The second rocket fired. Kincheloe, now beginning to fall back in his F-86, confirmed the burn.

"You've got her. Attaboy. Keep her coming back. Some more. You've got her. Looking real good. O.K. He's starting to climb now, high chase."

With full rocket power the X-2 swiftly left the low chase plane behind, to circle and to wait for the descent.

Apt's flight plan was designed to produce a parabolic flight path which would arch the sky to reach a maximum altitude of seventy thousand feet. At the top of the arch as he transitioned from the climbing portion of the flight to level flight, Apt and the X-2 would go from a normal 1-G condition to zero G, weightlessness. This brief period of weightlessness was the key to attaining maximum speed from the rocket aircraft. At zero G the angle of attack of the wings is low, producing minimum drag, which when accomplished in the rarefied atmosphere of near-space will permit the rocket engines to produce maximum speed per pound of thrust. At the point of entering the over-the-top phase of the maneuver it is essential that the pilot exercise extremely accurate control of the flight path if maximum speed is to be attained.

This is exactly what Mel Apt did. He held the soaring rocket exactly on course as steady and sure as if the plane were riding on a rail.

Radar control, monitoring the flight, marked him at profile positions on the flight plan. "One," announced radar.

Apt's eyes swept instantly to the Machmeter. The needle read Mach 1 and was climbing. His eyes ranged systematically over the flight and engine instruments and his highly skilled reflexes acted and reacted to the messages from the dials as he held his craft tightly on its flight path. The nearer he could hold to the projected flight path the closer he and the X-2 could come to maximum performance, and the faster the plane would go into the thermal thicket.

"Two," called radar, and Apt had reached fifty thousand feet exactly on schedule.

Carson in high chase picked up the rising X-2, flew with it for a brief time, then watched as it flashed away. Carson lost sight of the rocket plane as it climbed into the bright sun, and he did not find it again.

Coming up to seventy thousand feet, Mel Apt began the smooth pushover. Going over the top, the X-2 felt to Apt as if it were fixed in space.

The strange sensation of weightlessness flooded over him. The craft arched through zero G. The mighty rockets shoved the gleaming white airplane to speeds greater than three times the speed of sound. Mel Apt was exactly on profile.

His eyes watched the Machmeter: Mach 3, and still moving. Mel Apt pushed the X-2 to 2,060 m.p.h. Then the last of the fuel was sucked from the tanks, the rockets sputtered and fell silent. Apt had reached the end of the scheduled burn. His radio clicked on and in his usual businesslike voice he reported, "O.K. She's cut out. I'm turning."

The high-speed 180-degree turn was critical in order to glide back to the lake bed at Edwards. But in a cruel twist of fate, Captain Apt's perfect flight, in which he attained a speed never before flown by man, doomed him to a violent death. His precision in maintaining the flight profile had given the X-2 the opportunity to reach its maximum speed, a speed greater than expected and a speed at which the aircraft became directionally unstable. This meant that once the nose was moved from straight and level flight it would tend to start swinging, then whipping from side to side in ever increasing arcs. At these supersonic speeds the force of air against the side of the rocket ship would tear the plane apart.

This was the unknown; and Mel Apt, when he began his turn homeward, was only seconds away from death.

Suddenly the silence was shattered by a cry from Apt. "She goes—!" were the only words shouted before his voice rose in a scream as if he had been punched in the stomach by an invisible fist.

The X-2 went out of control, its nose rising and snapping like a wounded porpoise. At almost two thousand miles per hour the airplane whipped from side to side, pitching, yawing, rolling. Although he was strapped tightly to his seat, Mel Apt was slammed violently about. He fought the controls but could not hold them. The plane was no longer a flying machine; it was a maverick projectile buffeting the pilot within and hurtling back toward earth.

No one had ever bailed out of an airplane at those high speeds, but if Apt did not make a quick bailout, the buffeting would be likely to knock him senseless. He yanked the handle.

The explosive charge fired, separating the forward cockpit from the fuselage, projecting the pilot-capsule into the screaming stream of air. The capsule tumbled end over end, slamming Apt against the walls. He was struck fierce blows.

The drogue parachute opened, righting the capsule for the subsequent release of the larger chute. It did not come. Mel Apt

Capt. Melburn G. Apt who was killed on his first flight in the X-2.
**(U.S. Air Force)**

The X-15 under the wing of the B-52 mother ship that carried it to 50,000 feet.

was unconscious as the capsule, trailing the small drogue chute, plunged into the desert below. He died on impact.

The X series continued. A new airplane, the X-15, was designed by North American Aviation to continue the test of men and machines and to solve the mysteries of speed and of space. Three X-15s were built, each a fifty-foot, needle-nosed, stub-winged, vertical-finned test craft, half airplane and half space-vehicle. The X-15 was launched at fifty thousand feet from the wing rack of a Boeing B-52 mother ship.

On February 24, 1968, William H. Dana, NASA test pilot, described the sensations of flying the world's fastest self-powered vehicle:

> The launch itself provides the first surprise of the flight. The act of leaving the wing of the mother ship in free fall gives the X-15 pilot the sensation that he was fired off the mother ship's shackles by some hidden cannon. This sensation is not eased until the rocket engine lights one to two seconds after launch.
>
> Then begins as busy a minute-and-a-half as most pilots ever want to experience. In that short time, the X-15 accelerates

from subsonic speed to about six times the speed of sound. A myriad of events take place in this 90 seconds: the pullup to climb altitude; the maintaining of this climb angle to the designated pushover point; monitoring of speed, altitude, and air loads to ascertain that the planned flight is being flown; manipulation of switches to trigger the experiments onboard; and finally shutdown of the engine at the prescribed maximum velocity. All of these events are performed under an acceleration that presses the pilot into the back of his seat with two to four times the force of gravity.

A time deviation of one second in the performance of any of these events can mar the quality of the important data being acquired.

Engine shutdown brings some relief of physical stress, but the workload continues. If the flight is an attitude mission, that is, if it leaves the atmosphere, the pilot must operate attitude control rockets to keep the X-15 upright and weathervaned along the flight path until the atmosphere is re-entered.

On April 21, 1961, Major Robert M. White, a U. S. Air Force test pilot, flew the X-15 to 3,074 m.p.h.; in November of the same year he pressed the rocket plane to a speed of 4,093 m.p.h.

On October 3, 1967, Major William J. Knight rode the X-15

Major Robert White walks away from the X-15 after his world record flight. His son, Gregory, is on the left.

*(U.S. Air Force)*

"Nine of the 199 missions had been flown by the pilot who was to be the first man to set foot on the moon — Neil Armstrong."
**(NASA)**

to an unofficial record speed of 4,534 m.p.h., the fastest speed man has ever flown in a winged airplane.

After the 199th mission on October 24, 1968, the X-15 project was complete. William H. Dana made the final flight, successfully closing the tests which had provided information to guide the future advances of aeronautical science. And nine of the 199 missions had been flown by the pilot who was to be the first man to set foot on the moon—Neil Armstrong.

The lessons learned in the X-series aircraft were well used in the development of standard aircraft design, as military operational jets were flying faster and faster.

On December 15, 1959, Major Joseph W. Rogers in an Air Force fighter, a Convair F-106A, set a 1,524-m.p.h. record over a clocked fifteen-kilometer course, only to have his record toppled two years later by a Marine flyer, Lt. Col. Robert W. Robinson, who reached 1,605 m.p.h.

Then in 1964, the grand lady of aviation, holder of more F.A.I.

world flying records than any other pilot, winner of the 1938 Bendix Trophy race, Jacqueline Cochran, announced her intention to set new speed records. She borrowed a Lockheed F-104G, arranged use of the course at Edwards Air Force Base, and assembled the necessary N.A.A. stewards. Over a period of days occupying all of May and parts of June of that year, Miss Cochran overcame the difficulties of weather and scheduling to set three world records: the fastest speed by a woman over 15/25-kilometer, 100-kilometer, and 500-kilometer courses.

By May 1, 1965, Col. R. L. Stephens had flown a Lockheed YF-12A to an official speed of more than two thousand miles per hour.

Thus, with the knowledge acquired from the X-series aircraft —the aeronautical bridge between aircraft and spacecraft—man had flown faster than he had ever dared to dream he would go.

The X-series of experimental jet airplanes.
**(National Air and Space Museum, The Smithsonian Institution)**

# CHAPTER 4

# Balloons Study
# Space First

Airplanes were little more than a subject of academic speculation when men were first born aloft in baskets hanging by rope webs beneath great globular bladders filled with hot air. Although balloons were more spectacular than practical and their association with flight more carnival than scientific, they were for many years the only vessels available for aerial experimentation. And until recently, if scientists wished to explore in space, balloons were the only vehicles, unencumbered by the limitations of air-breathing engines, that could take them and their instruments to high altitudes.

In 1862, the Balloon Committee of the British Association for the Advancement of Science selected their most distinguished member, 53-year-old James Glaisher, to make a flight to thirty thousand feet in order to make methodical observations and recordings of the conditions that existed at great altitude. Air samples were to be gathered, temperatures regularly noted, and barometric pressures reported. An aneroid barometer had been built, and it was to be tested against the delicate, thermometer-shaped mercury barometer.

The aneroid barometer was a presealed bellows attached to a wire indicator on a premarked scale. The barometer, remarkable for its ruggedness, sensitivity, and simplicity, was successfully tested by Glaisher in 1862, and thereafter served generations of airmen in all manner of aerial machines as an altimeter, a device for measuring altitude.

To help James Glaisher reach thirty thousand feet, the Balloon

Committee secured the services of the leading English aeronaut, forty-three-year-old Henry Coxwell. A fifty-five-foot balloon bag was constructed that was to be filled with a special gas made from the distillation of coal. At Wolverhampton, England, the launch site, preparations were made for a lift-off to be witnessed by officials of the Committee.

Glaisher and Coxwell were aware of other attempts at high-altitude flights, but there was very little accurate information about the dangers involved. Their great concern was how high the aerostat could ascend—the scientists at that time failed to realize that the limitations of altitude were not those of the vehicle but of the human passengers. Hypoxia—oxygen starvation—the mortal enemy of man in space, had not yet been identified. Today pilots know that at twenty thousand feet life can be sustained only briefly without a pressure oxygen mask, and airplanes pressurize their interiors to maintain the safe pressure that exists below ten thousand feet. But unmindful of hypoxia and its deadly hazards, Glaisher and Coxwell prepared for their flight.

All was in readiness on the morning of September 5, 1862. Ignoring a threatening storm, the adventurers began to fill their bag. By noon the inflation was completed, but the dark thunderclouds were now menacingly close. If the storm struck, the balloon was likely to be destroyed in the rain and wind unless they deflated the bag and prepared to go aloft another day. However, the airmen did not want to disappoint the now impatient Balloon Committee representatives. The wind grew stronger and the taut bag snapped uneasily at the mooring ropes.

Coxwell and Glaisher were of a single mind. Heedless of the added dangers, they climbed on board their wicker basket, loaded their instruments, adjusted the sand ballast, secured a crate of six pigeons, and, just as the storm broke, ordered the aerostat cut loose.

Running before the heavy wind the balloon whisked the basket swiftly over the field. Coxwell unloaded ballast and the aeronauts shot up into the belly of the storm. In moments they had pierced the low scud and rose in clear air toward the dark mass of the angry thunderhead above them. These raging maelstroms of fierce convective currents have been known to twist metal airplanes, glaze them with ice, and tear them apart. Apprehensive of the unknown dangers above, the aeronauts braced themselves on the floor of the basket as their balloon rose swiftly upward into the base of the storm. Coxwell pulled on the valve line to test the gas-escape valve at the top of the balloon bag, the sole method of descent for the aerostat.

Suddenly they were in the storm. Torrents of water swept over the bag and filled the basket. The balloon and basket spun dizzily. Like a small cork in a frothing sea, the balloon tossed and swayed. Coxwell and Glaisher clung helplessly to the ropes in the bottom of the carriage. Lightning danced through the clouds and great claps of thunder crashed around them.

As quickly as it began, the rain stopped; the cloud lightened and the balloon lifted its passengers through the top of the storm. Above the sun was bright, the sky blue and clear: the magnificence of the panorama of the parade of rain clouds falling away below was breathtaking. The air, heavy with ozone, smelled of clean autumnal crispness in complete contrast to the sultry dampness below.

Glaisher checked his instruments: they were passing through ten thousand feet. Coxwell emptied more sandbags and the vehicle reached higher toward the sun. Both men were now unconsciously breathing harder. Glaisher continued to record his instrument readings. So innocent were the men of the real dangers of great altitudes that neither had worn gloves, and Glaisher did not have even a cap to protect his bald head. As the aerostat passed through fifteen thousand feet, the temperature had dropped to eighteen degrees Fahrenheit. A pigeon was then released to test its flight characteristics at great altitude. The bird fluttered in a vain attempt to fly in the rarefied atmosphere and, finding none, fell helplessly groundward in a plummeting spiral.

The clatter of the thunderstorms faded beneath them and around the balloon fell a shroud of total silence.

As the vehicle climbed through twenty thousand feet, Glaisher recorded the temperature as eleven degrees. Both men were breathing deeply and rapidly in the thin air. Coxwell, struggling now at his work, dropped more ballast to lift the aerostat higher and higher. By now the two men were unknowingly suffering the beginning stages of hypoxia. More pigeons were dropped—one fell straight down, the other struggled to the high ropes to lock his talons on a perch beyond the astronauts' grasp. Ice glazed the balloon, instruments, and men. Above them the gas-release-valve line had entangled itself in the shroud lines—out of reach.

As Glaisher later wrote of the onset of his hypoxia:

> When at the height of 26,000 feet I could not see the fine column of the mercury in the tube; then the fine divisions on the scale of the instrument became invisible. At that time I asked Mr. Coxwell to help me to read the instruments, as I experienced a difficulty in seeing them. At that time he had to leave the car, and to mount into the ring above to adjust the twisted valve line. I then had no suspicion of other than temporary inconvenience in seeing. Shortly afterwards I laid my arm upon the table, possessed of its full vigour; but directly after, being desirous of using it, I found it powerless. It must have lost its power momentarily. I then tried to move the other arm, but found it powerless also. I next tried to shake myself, and succeeded in shaking my body. I seemed to have no legs. I could only shake my body. I then looked at the barometer, and whilst I was doing so my head fell on my left shoulder. I struggled, and shook my body again, but could not move my arms. I got my head upright, but for an instant only, when it fell on my right shoulder; and then I fell backwards, my back resting against the side of the car, and my head on its edge. In that position my eyes were directly aimed towards Mr. Coxwell in the ring. As in the case of the arms, all muscular power was lost in an instant from my back and neck. I dimly saw Mr. Coxwell in the ring, and endeavoured to speak, but could not do so. In an instant intense black darkness came over me, and the optic nerve lost power suddenly. I was still conscious, with as active a brain as whilst writing this. I thought I had been seized with asphyxia, and that I should experience no more, as death would come unless we speedily descended. Other thoughts were actively entering my mind when I suddenly became unconscious, as though going to sleep. At that time we were between six and seven miles high.

The balloon still climbed.

Coxwell realized that if he didn't reach the release-valve line they would ascend until the balloon burst, or they froze to death, or died of lack of air, or met "whatever other fate awaiting in the deepening blue sky above."

With great effort he pulled himself up into the ropes toward the base of the bag where the rope webbing holding the top of the balloon was drawn together around a metal hoop. From this ring he could grasp the ensnared release-valve line. Drawing himself up on two ropes, he slowly lifted his legs over the hoop until he sat upon it, as a man would sit atop a fence. His breath was labored from the brief exertion and his hands were numb from the biting cold. Carelessly, he placed his bare hands on the exposed iron hoop and they froze to the metal.

The balloon was now passing through thirty thousand feet.

The aeronaut turned to his companion in the basket for help, but the older man had passed out. Coxwell struggled, but could not release his hands. The initial agony of the pain in his hands began to ease as he started to experience a pleasant exhilaration that is now known by those who penetrate the great altitudes as the mind's warning of approaching hypoxia. Coxwell shook off the euphoria and lunged for the cord with his mouth. After several trips, he succeeded in catching the line in his teeth. The first tug failed to open the now frozen valve, so Coxwell desperately pulled harder. A tooth broke; his lip split, and he was fast losing sensibility.

In a mighty effort, holding the rope tightly in his bloody mouth and painfully clenched teeth, he threw himself backward. The valve cracked open as he pivoted away from it. The sudden liberation of the line carried him backward in an arc so that he was upside down with his legs around the hoop and his head in the basket. The force of the semisomersault tore his frozen hands from the ring and dropped him into the bottom of the carriage.

Escaping gas hissed from the tip of the bag, the balloon apexed and started its descent. Coxwell looked at the barometer. It was reading seven inches of mercury—35,000 feet. Glaisher described the next few minutes:

> Whilst powerless I heard the words "temperature," and "observation," and I knew Mr. Coxwell was in the car, speaking to me, and endeavouring to rouse me; and therefore consciousness and hearing had returned. I then heard him speak more

emphatically, but I could not speak or move. Then I heard him say, "Do try; now do!" Then I saw the instruments dimly, next Mr. Coxwell, and very shortly I saw clearly. I rose in my seat and looked around, as though waking from sleep, and said to Mr. Coxwell, "I have been insensible." He said, "Yes; and I too, very nearly." I then drew up my legs, which had been extended out before me, and took a pencil in my hand to note my observations. Mr. Coxwell informed me that he had lost the use of his hands, which were black, and I poured brandy over them and ministered to his torn lips.

Glaisher and Coxwell had now been higher than any man before them; and although they made many subsequent flights together, they were not so foolish as to try to reach so high again. Their record-breaking achievement, however, was another important steppingstone in the upward procession of aeronautics. It was now realized that if men were to rise to 35,000 feet and beyond, they would need special equipment.

By the turn of the century crude pressure masks and tubes had been developed; and on July 31, 1901, two German scholars, Artur Berson and Reinhard Süring, made an ascension from Berlin, reaching 35,433 feet. Their pressure breathing apparatus did not function well and a hurried descent was necessary. During the next two decades, men and balloons made many altitude flights but none approached the record set by the two Germans. Still, the continued assaults upon the upper air, along with the aviation developments of World War I, helped advance the art of pressure masks and oxygen-breathing mechanisms to a practical and useful level.

Capt. Hawthorne C. Gray of the United States Army was one of the men who made significant contributions to the development of pressure masks and the pressure breathing systems as he reached up in his giant balloons to poke and probe into the stratosphere. A skilled balloonist, he twice scaled the lofty elevation of 42,470 feet.

The first occasion was on May 4, 1927, when he was launched from Scott Field in an Army Air Corps balloon. For the ascent Gray's face was protected by a glass-fronted mask and he was heavily suited, gloved, and helmeted against the chill of the upper air. His large, open wicker basket contained two cylinders of oxygen under pressure, recording instruments, and equipment innovations devised by Gray himself.

The balloonist rose easily through the 1901 German record of 35,000 feet, and he watched the details of the earth below dim and haze into indistinguishable objects. For companionship in the silent world that is balloon flight, Gray kept a radio playing. The music had a strange, ethereal quality in the muffled stillness of the rarefied atmosphere.

At forty thousand feet the balloon seemed to have peaked and it would rise no higher. All ballast had been cut away, and the face mask had frosted over, leaving only the smallest nickel-sized opening from which the captain could see. Gray wanted to reach 42,000 feet, so he jettisoned one of the oxygen cylinders and then watched the balloon inch slowly to 42,470 feet. At this height he began to sense his own approaching dizziness and quickly pulled the hydrogen-release valve.

Immediately Gray began to descend, at first slowly, then at an ever accelerating speed. As the balloon dropped through thirty thousand feet the bag began to flutter, and after descending a few thousand more, it collapsed. Down from the heavens spiraled the balloon and basket. Captain Gray had no ballast to drop and no way to brake the dive. At eight thousand feet he jumped over the side of the basket and, when he had cleared the plunging balloon, pulled the rip cord on his parachute. As the silk canopy snapped open above him, the balloon quickly fell past him to the earth below.

This flight to 42,470 feet had placed Gray higher than any balloon man had been before; but because he did not return to earth in his balloon, the National Aeronautic Association was unable to give recognition to his achievement.

Undaunted by this failure, Gray began to plan for his next flight into the stratosphere.

Using vacuums created in ground chambers, he worked with mice to determine the effects of the lack of oxygen and atmospheric pressure upon life systems. His experiments clearly defined the need not only for oxygen but, more important, for oxygen under pressure for the continuation of life in the thin upper atmosphere. He developed mixer valves and pressure masks and special moisture-free instrumentation to prevent freezing water crystals from destroying the effectiveness of his equipment.

By November 4, 1927, Gray was ready once again to be lifted to the edge of the stratosphere in his newly designed and improved balloon.

Captain Gray's equipment had been greatly modified since his first flight in May, but he still carried a radio for companionship. The sound of music, he believed, helped ward off the unsettling sensation of being separated from earth, a psychological phenomenon not fully understood at that time. The radio provided music until Gray reached 34,000 feet, but then he accidentally broke off the antenna while moving an oxygen bottle. Thereafter there was only silence.

The unsteady and ever enlarging handwriting on his flight log tells how Capt. Hawthorne Gray met his end. Lulled into a sense of wellbeing by that siren of death, hypoxia, who leads her victims into a feeling of excited overconfidence and then into gentle unconsciousness and finally eternal sleep. Captain Gray reached his desired height of 42,000 feet and began slowly to valve his craft for an easy descent—too slowly to save his life.

The final entry on the captain's log reads: "Sky ordinary deep blue, sun very bright, sand all gone."

The barograph showed that after this entry the balloon gentled itself up to his earlier mark of 42,470 feet before beginning a steady downhill descent.

The balloon with Gray lying dead in the basket was found where it had settled to an easy landing at Sparta, Tennessee. Because of the barograph, there is no question that Captain Gray had once again reached a record altitude, but this time death had robbed him of official recognition. The rules require that a balloonist remain in command of his craft until the end of his flight. Nevertheless, Captain Gray had significantly advanced man's preparedness for exploring the outer rim of the earth's atmosphere and had attained an altitude never to be reached again by man in an open basket.

If man wished to go higher still, a better carriage than a simple open basket would have to be used. The Swiss physicist Auguste Piccard's contribution was the space gondola, a spherical chamber instrumented, mechanized, and pressurized to retain a life system within, while a giant balloon lifted it into the hostile world of the upper atmosphere. With this important scientific advance, man would in a brief span of years triple the heights to which he could climb.

On May 27, 1931, Piccard and his assistant, Paul Kipfer, in a space gondola rose to 51,775 feet over the mountains of Bavaria. They established a new record, but the number of feet they ascended was not as important as the fact that they had demonstrated the feasibility of the gondola and at the same time had penetrated into that strange and mysterious place in the sky—the stratosphere. (It is now known that the gaseous envelope that surrounds the earth is itself layered. The troposphere is that primary layer lying next to the earth wherein all of the climatic activities take place—the clouds, the winds, the storms, the ever-stirring convective currents, and the laterally flowing rivers of air.) Above the troposphere Piccard and Kipfer found a strange and hauntingly serene aerial province. Beyond the weather, above the clouds, out of reach of weather agitation, in a region where the temperature itself tended to stabilize, they reached the stratosphere. Although in today's jet world, airliners ply the wakeless seas of the stratosphere in tranquillity, the early adventurers into this unknown arena stirred the attentions of the civilized world, and man eagerly sought to learn more of that mysterious territory.

Professor Piccard made another ascent the following year. With him went a new assistant, Max Cosyns. The two left Dubendorf airfield outside Zürich, Switzerland, on August 17, 1932, and twelve hours later they landed safely in an open field near Volta Mantovana, south of Lake Garda, Italy. In the course of the ascension, Professor Piccard dispatched the first radio message ever originated in the stratosphere. "All is going well," the message said. "Observation good. Our altitude is from 14,000 to 15,000 meters." On this ascent Professor Piccard broke his own altitude record and reached a height of 53,152 feet, or 10.1 miles.

In August, 1933, America decided to try her hand at piercing the stratosphere. Lt. Comdr. T. G. W. Settle of the United States Navy was chosen to pilot a giant balloon, named *A Century of Progress,* in honor of the Chicago World's Fair. The balloon and gondola were of the same type as that used by Professor Piccard, with a larger gas capacity, but the balloon failed to live up to its name, as its progress was but a feeble mile into the sky. It came down on the tracks of the Burlington Railroad, two miles from its starting point near Chicago, without having completed any significant aerial achievement.

Lieutenant Commander Settle made another attempt in November of the same year. With Major Chester L. Fordney, of the Marine Corps, he ascended from Goodyear Field, Akron, Ohio, at 9:30 A.M. on November 20. Their gigantic bag had a gas capacity of 600,000 cubic feet and was inflated with 110,000 cubic feet of hydrogen. This time there was no hitch. The great bag soared easily and began drifting toward the east, taking a zigzag course high over Ohio, Pennsylvania, Maryland, and back to Pennsylvania. Over Pennsylvania the balloon reached its greatest height of 61,237 feet, to set a new world's record.

A few months before this record-breaking flight, another successful attempt had been made to enter the stratosphere, this time in Russia. On September 30, 1933, the Russian Red Army balloon *Stratostat* left the ground near Moscow and climbed to a height of 60,694 feet, carrying the commander, Georgi Profkoviet, and his two companions, Ernest Birnbaum and Konstantin Godunow, to an altitude almost ten thousand feet higher than Professor Piccard had reached. However, the record is not official, as Russia was not recognized at that time by the Fédération Aéronautique Internationale. This splendid flight lasted eight hours and nineteen minutes, and there was no trouble going up or coming down. The balloon landed about sixty miles southeast of Moscow, in Kolomna. As a courtesy, the F.A.I. mentioned this achievement in its annals. The Russians refused to supply any scientific data regarding the flight except that the balloon was built of rubberized percale; its gas capacity was over 860,000 cubic feet but was inflated to only about 125,000 cubic feet at the takeoff. They wanted world recognition for the record, but they refused to allow the world to share in their scientific knowledge.

Another Russian vessel made an even higher trip into the stratosphere four months later. The Soviet civil balloon *Osoviakhim I* lifted off from its launch site in Moscow on January 30, 1934.

In command was Paul Fedossejenko, one of the Soviets' best-known aeronauts. With him were Llya Oussyskine of the Institute of Physical Science as vice-commander and Andrey Vassenko, the craftsman who had built the balloon.

The triumvirate reached a record height of 72,200 feet, but as they began their descent ground control lost radio contact. A search was begun and on the following day the wrecked balloon was found in Potisky Ostrog, 150 miles east of Moscow. All three balloonists were dead amid the shattered pieces of the gondola, which had not been adequately adjusted and had apparently broken loose, plunging the brave airmen to the snow-laden earth below.

The tragedies and the near-tragedies give emphasis to the hazards of these pioneering ventures. In the United States on July 28, 1934, Capt. Orvil Anderson, Capt. Albert W. Stevens and Major William E. Kepner barely escaped from the torn balloon of their *Explorer I* by parachuting from the falling gondola. The Explorer series of balloons resulted from the efforts of the National Geographic Society in Washington, D.C., and the

Capt. Albert W. Stevens, Major William E. Kepner, and Lt. Orvil Anderson, who escaped by parachute from the falling gondola of *Explorer I*.

**(U.S. Air Force)**

United States Army Air Corps, which combined their resources to build the complicated equipment needed to lift men and machine high into space in order to make meaningful explorations in this new domain.

Undaunted by the near-disaster of their first attempt, Captain Anderson and Captain Stevens on November 11, 1935, boarded the gondola of *Explorer II*, a mammoth balloon 192 feet in diameter and 315 feet high. This second balloon bore the airmen aloft to an altitude of 72,395 feet, a record that stood unmatched for two decades. Again, it was not the number of feet alone that gave the flight special significance, but rather the important new scientific data collected by the two military officers.

Because they made their balloon ascent while safely within a gondola, Anderson and Stevens were able to remain at peak altitude for an hour and a half—long enough to answer the often asked question: What was it like to be in that strange and exciting place, the stratosphere?

Captain Stevens, the commander of the expedition, answered

*Explorer II* before lift-off from Strato Bowl near Rapid City, South Dakota.

**(U.S. Air Force)**

that question for the readers of *National Geographic Magazine* in an article he wrote for them in the January, 1936, issue:

I suppose our questioners think one should be in a state of tingling excitement, as in a racing car going at highest speed. But my impression of the stratosphere was that of being in a profound calm, as we hung suspended nearly 13¾ miles high, motionless in air, although we were drifting with the air at a considerable speed. Our balloon even refused to turn, and my side of the gondola constantly faced toward the sun.

Outside I could see, through one of the ports, our fan for turning the balloon revolving at the rate of 5,000 times a minute. But the ammeter, in circuit with the motor of the fan, showed that less and less power was required to turn it over, and the fan blades were now turning in air so thin that the propelling action was nil. At lower altitudes the fan had been effective in rotating the balloon, but we were now floating in the nearest approach to a natural vacuum in which man has ever placed himself.

To look directly at the sun through one of the portholes was blinding. The sun's rays were unbelievably intense. Through the upper porthole we looked often at the vast bulk of the balloon, upon which the sun beat fiercely.

Observations of the earth and sky were made at the top of the flight, 13.71 miles above sea level.

The earth could be seen plainly underneath through the lower porthole and hundreds of miles in every direction through the side portholes. It was a vast expanse of brown, apparently flat, stretching on and on. Wagon roads and automobile highways were invisible, houses were invisible, and railroads could be recognized only by an occasional cut or fill. The larger farms were discernible as tiny rectangular areas. Occasional streaks of green vegetation showed the presence of streams.

Here and there water could be seen in the form of rivers or lakes, especially if the sun was reflected from the water's surface. No sign of actual life on the earth could be detected. To us it was a foreign and lifeless world. The sun was the one object that commanded our attention; we were temporarily divorced from Mother Earth.

The horizon itself was a band of white haze. Above it the sky was light blue, and perhaps twenty or thirty degrees from the horizon it was of the blue color that we are accustomed to. But at the highest angle that we could see it, the sky became very dark. I would not say that it was completely black; it was rather a black with the merest suspicion of very dark blue.

In the years that followed, military men continued to climb higher and higher in balloon and gondola. It was from these journeys in the stratosphere that a vast store of knowledge became available for aircraft development and space travel. The ability of the balloon to reach and, more important, to remain at great altitudes for long periods of observation made the contribution of the men who manned them crucial to the future of space travel.

In the late 1950's, Lt. Col. David G. Simons, an Air Force doctor, helped pave the way for U. S. manned space programs by flights in the Man High capsule which was lifted aloft by a balloon. The Man High program was organized to find, define, and solve the physical and psychological problems that man might encounter in space. From the flights the U. S. Air Force and NASA acquired information that was utilized in the selection of astronauts and in the design of equipment for space survival.

Lt. Col. Simons in front of a Man High capsule.

**(U.S. Air Force)**

In August, 1957, Colonel Simons rode the capsule to a record altitude of 102,000 feet and then remained there for thirty-two hours, taking observations from that invisible demarcation line where the earth's atmosphere ends and space begins.

The launching of the flight took place in Minnesota, from an open mine pit. The pit protected the balloon so that surface winds would not interfere with the inflation. The teardrop balloon after launch rose in a 2-hour, 18-minute steady ascent through the 100,000-foot mark. Inside the cramped capsule, Colonel Simons, his hands numb with cold, took frequent readings and photographs of his instruments during the climb.

As he neared his mark, Colonel Simons clicked on his radio with a foot-pedal switch: "I'm pretty close to the top now, Otto. The balloon is almost full and my rate of ascent has dropped off sharply." For Otto Winzen, the president of the small research company that had developed the capsule, this was an exciting message.

Colonel Simons later recalled that moment of success:

> The altimeter faltered, then stopped. I noted the time: 11:40. It had taken me two hours and eighteen minutes to bump against the earth's ceiling. Slowly the needle dropped then rose again. The balloon was gently bounding like a basketball being dribbled in slow motion in an upside-down world. It had ascended as high as it would go.
>
> My radio earphones crackled.
>
> "N-C-A Three Eight, this is Three One." Otto's voice sounded jubilant. "The radio beacon altitude is 102,000 feet, I repeat, 102,000 feet. Congratulations, Dave. That's a record."
>
> Too excited to care about the hazards of living where no man had tarried before, I looked around me. The earth's familiar blue atmosphere was easily discernible around the entire horizon. If you consider an arc drawn from the eastern horizon up through the sky overhead and down to the western horizon as 180 degrees, the band of blue that represents the sky to an earthbound viewer reached up about ten degrees, beginning at the horizon with a washed out whiteness and gradually changing to pale blue that grew even deeper until it merged with the intensely deep but dark bluish purple of space. This was the earth and its atmosphere as the pilots of the X-15 would see it during their searing, hot glide down from 100 miles up.

As the day wore on the balloon and gondola bobbed up and down above and below the 100,000-foot mark, while Simons continued to make his important observations of space, man, and capsule. Difficulties with the radios plagued the flight, and the ground crew below in trucks were obliged continually to drive to new posts in order to keep up with the drift of the balloon.

By nightfall, the cooling effects of darkness had caused the balloon to begin a descent. Below, thunderheads of a fast-moving cold front began to build. Simons dumped ballast to retain altitude above the dangerous storms. Gradually the balloon leveled at seventy thousand feet. Simons continued his observations, but a full day in the hot, cramped gondola had brought on a numbing fatigue. His mind clouded and he began to be inaccurate in his recordings from his instruments. Recognizing his own fatigue, he radioed control:

"N-C-A Three One, this is Three Eight. I'm just too tired to go on for a while. With your permission I think I'll try for a half hour's sleep."

"Roger, Dave," came the reply. "Better to spend some time resting than fighting yourself. You'll be able to accomplish a lot more after some sleep."

"Thanks, Colonel," replied Simons.

"One other thing," radioed Col. John P. Stapp, Man High flight surgeon. "In case you haven't already done it, you'd better eat another candy bar to keep your blood sugar up."

He did and then the exhausted aeronaut lay back on a small net hammock and dozed. At a little after 12:30 A.M. he was awakened with a start. Colonel Simons described the next few frightening minutes:

> Suddenly the inside of the capsule flashed with a bright light.
> "My God, it's lightning," I cried.
> Had it hit the antenna? Was there fire?
> Outside I could see the active pulsations of lightning in the thunderheads below, and they looked menacingly closer than they had before. But still I had no way of knowing whether the thunderheads were 1,000 feet or 15,000 feet away.
> The flash was the color of lightning. But if it hit the gondola it would have left some evidence. Probably it would have started a fire. Where was it?

Quickly I checked the capsule. Nothing was out of order.

But how close would a bolt of lightning have to be to light the capsule so strongly? Surely no more than a few hundred feet. With that proximity, why had I heard no thunder? Perhaps the thinness of the atmosphere muffled it.

I checked my altimeter. Down almost to 70,000 feet now. I had dropped more than I thought, cutting into the comfortable margin of safety that had left me unconcerned by the storm before.

For the first time during the flight I was genuinely afraid. Could it be that the thunderheads rose higher than the 55,000-60,000 feet altitudes most meteorologists always had thought to be a storm's limit?

"Good God," I cried as another bright flash flooded the capsule with light.

Now I was verging on panic. If I was that close to the storm, and lightning had reached upwards twice to lash at me, sooner or later it would hit. My capsule had become a trap instead of an observatory. And there was nothing I could do but sit here and wait for the last crashing flash that would hit and

The Strato-Lab High balloon being inflated before the flight.

*(U.S. Navy)*

leave fire or total destruction in its wake. I had no more available ballast to drop away so I could rise above the storm. I could cut into my live power reserves to drop ballast, but that would offer only temporary respite. For without power, I would have to come down soon and I could not descend through the storm.

Forcibly, I calmed myself. Panicky thoughts of dire possibilities will get me nowhere. The first and most important thing I must do is determine my true altitude and try to figure out how much space remains between me and the storm.

As I studied the clouds below, the gondola flooded with light again.

I slumped back in my seat with relief.

If strength had remained, I would have laughed at this colossal practical joke the *Man High* capsule was playing on me.

Above Colonel Simons' head an automatic camera, preset to light a photoflash strobe light every five minutes to record dial settings, had malfunctioned early in the flight and had been out of order. Suddenly it was working again, lighting the interior of the gondola with a blinding flash every five minutes. The thunderstorm was safely twenty thousand feet below.

With daylight the balloon rose once more to the ninety-thousand-foot altitude, and once again the sun warmed the capsule, sending the interior temperatures to uncomfortable levels. At noon Colonel Simons began his scheduled descent, and within a short time he was in a C-47 winging his way back toward Minneapolis with the valuable taped data from the flight in his bag and a new altitude record under his belt.

Comdr. Ross and Lt. Comdr. Prather in their gondola moments before lift-off.

*(U.S. Navy)*

Four years later, on May 4, 1961, in a gondola and balloon launched from the deck of an aircraft carrier, Comdr. Malcolm D. Ross and Lt. Comdr. Victor A. Prather attained a new record altitude of 113,700 feet, gathering still more answers to man's questions about the enigmatic regions above him. After a successful landing, Prather lost his life in a fall from the strap lift of a recovery helicopter.

The fact that in the 1970's, the age of rockets and spacemen, scientists still find significant needs for sending man and balloon higher and yet higher up to the very edges of the earth's vesture gives continued usefulness to the spherical bladders of gas that rise silently aloft and hang majestically buoyed to the top of the sky. The United States Air Force, for example, maintains the 1110th Balloon Activities Squadron to investigate regions high above the earth. In order to gather data about cosmic radiation, water vapor, temperature, air pressure, chemical content, and infrared transmissibility an inexpensive platform is necessary, one that can climb above 100,000 feet and remain for a fixed period for prolonged readings and sample collections. That platform is the balloon.

Lift-off from the carrier.

*(U.S. Navy)*

# CHAPTER 5

# The Airplane Reaches Outer Space

During the emerging days of aviation, the men who flew learned to balance their craft by its response to the controls, much as cyclists learn to balance their bicycles. Manned flight was at a level where speed and altitude were measured against the familiar components of the landscape.

While pioneer pilots believed that flying at high altitudes was more hazardous because of the frailty of the craft, the experienced Louis Blériot, one of aviation's earliest birds and holder of the first F.A.I. pilot's license, viewed the matter entirely to the contrary. It was Blériot's belief that the very frailty of the aircraft that some pilots feared in fact provided an additional margin of safety that would save their lives. As the survivor of frequent crashes, his opinion carried authority. In 1911 he wrote:

> More than once, owing to lack of skill, I have seen a pilot send his aeroplane upwards at such a steep angle that the machine first came to a standstill in the air, and then, losing all steerage-way, slid back tail-first towards the ground.
>
> Such a well-known pilot as Mr. Hubert Latham has—as an example of immunity from injury—had some dreadfully serious-looking falls without breaking a limb or suffering anything more than a temporary shock. This ability to come crashing to the ground without hurting oneself does not lie in any special cleverness on the part of the pilot. It lies in what one might well term the elasticity of the aeroplane.
>
> What happens, when an aeroplane strikes the ground, is this:

First some wooden rod or strut breaks, and then another, until perhaps half the machine has been either crushed or beaten in. The breaking of these parts, one after another, absorbs the shock of the impact with the ground. Thus a very bad shock is gradually damped, as it were, until it has lost the greater part of its violence by the time it has reached the pilot.

Thus the very frailness of the aeroplane has proved its pilot's salvation.

The real aerodynamic problem he was describing without recognizing was the problem that greater speeds and altitudes would soon reveal, the stall and the tailspin. Without identifying the problem, he did recognize the absolute necessity of greater knowledge and skill. "Certainly, however," he wrote, "one must prepare for a far greater solidity in the construction of aircraft. The progress of this wonderful industry would be sadly limited were building to be always restricted to the production of aeroplanes of wood, canvas, and wire.

"At present, it is true, while we are finding out new facts every day about engines, and the effect of the speed of machines, and are exploring unknown heights ... we must aspire first to learn to control all unmanageable positions of the machine."

It was fitting, perhaps, that record altitude flights began first with the Wright brothers. On November 13, 1908, Wilbur Wright demonstrated a Wright craft for French officials at Auvours, France, and climbed to an altitude of eighty-two feet, to establish the first official world's altitude record. On the same day, Henri Farman, at Issy, France, climbed to the same record altitude of eighty-two feet in a Voisin, unknowingly matching the record flight of Wilbur Wright. The next month, Wright climbed his airplane to 361 feet and the competition was on.

That summer at the Rheims aerial festival, Hubert Latham won the altitude competition by ascending to 508 feet. If the Wright brothers were cautious, businesslike, and scientific in their valuable contributions to aviation, Latham was the opposite. He had already launched a successful business career when he fell strangely ill. Although the doctors disagreed, Latham believed that he had contracted tuberculosis and he feared that he was doomed to an early and painful death. Having long been an advocate of powered heavier-than-air flight, he took up aviation with total abandon, assuming that his death would come from the sky and be swift and merciful.

Latham obtained the ninth pilot's license issued by the F.A.I. and sought to win every airman's prize that his time and skill would permit. Twice he had plunged into the English Channel in a Levasseur Antoinette monoplane while trying to capture the ten-thousand-pound prize offered by the London *Mail*. Both crashes were the result of a stall and tailspin.

After winning the altitude competition at Rheims he toured Europe, making exhibition flights wherever crowds could be gathered, and there was never a shortage of eager spectators.

By December of 1909 Latham had climbed to an altitude of 1,486 feet, and then he topped his own record by moving the mark to 3,445 feet on January 7, 1910.

When early airmen gathered in the cluttered comfort of their hangars in the midst of pipe tubing and canvas to swap tales of flying, they described how, at the dizzy heights of fifteen hundred feet and above, the sensation of forward movement disappeared, the earth became pleasantly fixed below, and the horizon

Hubert Latham took up aviation with total abandon.
**(Library of Congress)**

leveled into a distant division between earth and sky. Level flight from such a height, they claimed, required keeping the airplane's wings in a steady position in relation to the horizon. Speed could be determined by judging the velocity of the wind sweeping past the pilot.

By the end of 1910, the altitude record had been pushed above the ten-thousand-foot mark by Georges Legagneaux at Pau, France, and Archibald Hoxsey in Los Angeles. The two airmen reported that at altitudes of ten thousand feet and above, the usually clear details of houses, people, trees, and moving vehicles faded from definitive view in the general haze below.

Hubert Latham did not have the airplane to top their mark. He was determined to try, but he never had the opportunity because he lived but two more years. He died not of the dreaded tuberculosis, or in the anticipated crash of a diving aircraft, but of a strange jungle disease contracted while on a hunting safari in Africa.

In one of the early expositions on the subject of altitude flight, aviators Gustav Hamel and Charles C. Turner wrote:

> What the aviator who ascends to great altitudes has to face is the strain upon his physique when flying in air that is very attenuated, and the possible danger incurred in descending in a very brief space of time to the earth where there is a barometric pressure of some thirty inches. No matter how gently he takes this descent, he will almost inevitably feel its effects in temporary deafness. Coming down from about 10,000 feet in twelve minutes the authors have experienced a buzzing in the ears, and afterwards have had slight headache. These distress signals showing themselves, it is clear that the faculties have been to some extent impaired, and landing the machine, in which accurate judgement of the distance from the ground and delicate manipulation of the controls are necessary, should be done with care.

But man and machine went ever higher. On a hot, muggy August day in 1911, Lincoln Beachy, who in the few years of the aviation explosion had made a name for himself as a stunt pilot and an aviator's aviator, corralled the necessary Aero Club officials, climbed into a *Curtiss,* and spiraled up to cooler regions, setting an altitude record of 17,573 feet.

The following autumn he made an even greater contribution to aviation when he conceived and accomplished a method of recovering from the dreaded stall and tailspin.

Beachy, the master of the loop-the-loop, had noted unhappily that some of the young pilots who attempted to emulate his own aerobatic maneuvers got their aircraft in awkward positions and fell spiraling to a fatal crash. In his mind's eye he retraced these falling machines over and over, trying to visualize the actions and reactions of the aviators as they spun to their doom. He wondered, too, why it was that he had never been a victim.

One evening just as he was about to fall asleep, Beachy's aerial experience and his mental reenactments of the stall and tailspin converged into a logical explanation of the deadly dives.

The tailspin, he reasoned, was a partial stall condition that occurred when a pilot, in flying through some maneuver, inadvertently got in a nose-high attitude at too slow an airspeed. The aircraft's position caused a single wing to stall, dropping the plane into a spinning dive. The average aviator, spinning toward earth, would pull back on the controls for recovery. According to Beachy's theory, however, this would only aggravate the stall, since a stalled wing was not a *flying* plane. To recover, he reasoned, it was necessary to stop the spinning through rudder control and dive the airplane to make the wing fly. Then a simple dive recovery would return the plane to level flight. Beachy further reasoned that he himself had never experienced an accidental tailspin because his experience was such that from the sound of the rushing wind and the feel of the plane he could always tell when his own aircraft was approaching an inadvertent stall condition.

The following morning he flew his plane to a safe five thousand feet, held the nose in a climbing attitude, cut the throttle, and waited with stick back for the sound of the wind to cease and the plane to mush and roll off on a wing into a tailspin.

It happened quickly. The craft snapped over and he was looking down the nose of the airplane toward the ground, watching the earth spin crazily below. He felt as if the plane were diving, spinning straight down, but he knew that it was not. He kicked his opposite rudder; the plane responded, the spinning slowed, then stopped. He pulled back on his stick, in the natural fashion, and the plane continued to fall. Now he reversed his control, pushing his stick forward. The plane lurched, the dive steepened, and suddenly he was in a power dive, with the familiar rush of air pushing by the windshield.

He hauled back on the stick, pulling Gs. The airplane responded and rose in a graceful climb.

Lincoln Beachy had come back from the tailspin. Soon all who would listen and learn could also make the tailspin a controlled maneuver and not a spiral of death. Beachy's technique for spin recovery, simple and effective, has remained unchanged throughout the years of aircraft development and is today a lesson learned by all fledgling aviators.

By the end of 1911, airmen and airplanes were advancing aviation at a rapid pace. So quickly were records made and broken that an early aerial historian, E. Charles Vivian, was moved to comment, "It was the year in which flying may be said to have grown so common that the 'meetings' which began with Rheims were hardly worth holding, owing to the fact that increase in height and distance flown rendered it no longer necessary for

Lincoln Beachy, in a 1913 Curtiss Pusher.

**(U.S. Air Force)**

a would-be spectator of a flight to pay half a crown and enter an enclosure. Henceforth, flying as a spectacle was very little to be considered."

On September 17, 1912, Georges Legagneaux recaptured the altitude record, reaching 17,891 feet, only to lose it quickly to others. He regained it on December 29, 1913, by a flight to 20,080 feet. Legagneaux wrote about the accomplishment:

> The best means for training for flights for altitude is to fly high. Thus if I fly to Villacoublay or the neighborhood, it is never at less than 3,000, 4,000 or 5,000 metres [9,000 to 16,000 feet]. If I go from Villacoublay to Chartres I pass over the 80 Km. which separates them, rising continually. It is, besides, much more agreeable, especially when the weather is clear.
>
> When I set out from Fréjus to pass the 6,000 metres, I had one clear idea—to beat the record which was held by Perreyon with 5,880 metres [Édouard Perreyon, who set a world's record of 19,325 feet at Buc, France, March 11, 1913]; for it was necessary to exceed this figure by more than 150 metres, that is to say, to do at least 6,035 metres, in order that it might be passed by the F.A.I. On my barograph I marked a line at 6,150 metres. It was necessary that my needle should reach that point to succeed. I took on my machine a bottle of compressed oxygen.
>
> At the aerodrome the temperature was 12 degrees above zero [centigrade]. I rose, describing a circle above Antibes and L'Esterel. Here I noted a curious thing—when I was over the land the machine mounted well; above the sea it had much more difficulty in rising. Therefore, contracting my circles, I no longer left L'Esterel.
>
> Another curious fact—and I am not the only one to have noticed it—was that over the Gulf of Antibes, the higher I rose, the more clearly could I distinguish the bottom of the sea. Many details remain fixed in my memory.
>
> I took twelve minutes to go from 4,000 to 5,000 metres; seventeen minutes to go from 5,000 to 6,000 metres. At 6,000 metres it was 22 degrees below zero—a difference of 34 degrees since the start.
>
> My barograph was covered with a layer of ice so thick that I could not distinguish the diagram; every second or two I rubbed it against me to see the movement of the needle. From time to time I used the oxygen; that saved me from the semitorpor into which I fell again and again.

When the 3,000 metres were reached for the first time by aeroplane, by the way, it was related that blood came from the nose, ears and nails of the aviator. I confess that, happily, I did not feel any of these unpleasantnesses. But, instead, I felt as though my head were empty. I could no longer think of anything, even of the record to beat. But I wished to see the needle arrive at the mark I had put on my diagram. The motor "knocked" badly and made an infernal noise. The time seemed to me extraordinarily long—at last, the needle reached 6,150 metres.

Then I had only one thought, to free myself from this position, not exactly painful, but fatiguing. I had not the slightest wish to go 100 metres higher.

The motor stopped completely as I descended. Twelve minutes later I touched the ground.

During World War I the development of aircraft for altitude flying spurted ahead. In the United States, Dr. Sanford A. Moss made important improvements in French inventor Professor Auguste C. E. Tateau's engine booster to create the turbine supercharger for American aircraft. Moss, working in the General Electric Company turbine and compressor plant at Lynn, Massachusetts, developed the turbine supercharger to operate with the Liberty 12 engine.

It was the development of the supercharger that made further altitude flights possible. The supercharger in its simplest form is a series of turbine fins that are rotated by hot exhaust gases. The fins in turn spin a centrifugal air blower to compress the thin air at high altitude into a density comparable with atmospheric pressure at lower altitudes. Thus the aircraft engine is able to operate as if flying at a lower altitude. In a later development, superchargers were also used to provide a compressed-air system for cabin pressure in altitude aircraft.

Major Rudolph W. Schroeder was one of the first to make significant use of the supercharger. On February 27, 1920, he flew a supercharged airplane, an open cockpit, bi-winged Packard Le Père, to his third altitude record.

Those who watched from the ground saw the spiraling contrails as he corkscrewed through altitudes no airplane had ever reached before. Lester J. Maitland, himself a record-holding pilot and one of aviation's pioneers, described Schroeder's flight to the record altitude of 33,114 feet:

> When Schroeder on his altitude flight reached the 33,000 foot level he found he had enough gas left for another ninety minutes of flying. He continued his climb. After struggling one hundred feet or so higher he discovered with horror that his oxygen supply was exhausted. Gasping for air, like one who had been breathing poison gas, Schroeder tore off his mask—the worst thing he could have done. The deadly carbon-monoxide gas from the engine poured over him. He inhaled it in hasty gulps. He felt himself go. It grew dark before his eyes. He knew he was fainting. He pushed the stick forward to put the plane in a glide, put his hand on the switch that cut off the engine and passed out.
>
> Through the frozen strata of the upper air where nothing can live, Schroeder's plane plunged toward earth in swoops, circles, and sudden darts. Men on the ground saw its crazy maneuvers and wondered what had happened. It came closer and closer. Presently it would crash, and no one would ever know what had taken place. Then, when only 2,000 feet above the ground, the plane straightened out, came down in a gentle dive, described a circle, nosed into the wind, and landed. Officers and men on the field rushed toward the plane and found Major Schroeder, apparently lifeless, slumping over the side of the cockpit, staring at the ground with frozen, sightless eyes. He was rushed to the hospital, where he soon recovered consciousness, but it was some time before he could see, as he had frozen his eyeballs. Afterward Major Schroeder reported how, at the end of his five-mile fall, he had regained consciousness just long enough to realize his predicament and save himself and his ship from a crash. Major Schroeder set a record that day, but he came uncomfortably near paying a top-notch price for it.

In 1921 an improved Moss supercharger was installed in another Packard Le Père at McCook Field at Dayton to be test-flown by Lt. John A. Macready.

It was a warm December day—December 9, 1921—when Macready made the final check on his Le Père. The aircraft preflight completed, he buckled himself into a leather-skinned feather-quilted suit for altitude flying. He wore this over his uniform, which was in turn worn over a heavy suit of woolen underwear. His feet, hands, and head were covered with appropriate fur-lined outerwear. His goggles were separate and had been smeared inside and out with a film of gelatin as an ice preventive.

Six flasks of oxygen were on board, but all unnecessary equipment had been stripped away to lighten the craft. An oversize propeller had been added to give extra bite in the rarefied atmosphere.

Since the primary purpose of the flight was to test the Moss supercharger, no N.A.A. officials were present for the event.

The airplane rose steadily over the field, climbing in easy circles until it was only a tiny speck in the blue sky to those observers on the ground.

Inside the open cockpit, Macready felt confidence in himself, his equipment and the airplane.

"I was not worried at any time until I reached 39,000 feet," he remembered. "At this altitude ice from my breath within the mask must have clogged the oxygen pipe for the reason that I felt the force become diminished and began to feel very bad effects from its lack. I tried to blow this out and did succeed in getting a taste of ice but could not act quickly enough to clear the entire tube, so swung over onto the emergency flask. I tore a small plaster from the side of my mask, placing the tube through this aperture directly into my mouth within the mask, and in an instant I was feeling comparatively normal."

The Le Père continued to climb as the supercharger compressed the rarefied air to sea-level pressure. Above 40,800 feet the supercharger could no longer maintain sea-level conditions and the engine power rapidly decreased. For a long time the airplane struggled to climb but a few hundred feet higher. Then it faltered and would climb no more.

"At an indicated altitude on the dial of 41,200 feet, the plane swung and rolled," remembered Macready, "and I could obtain very little action on the controls. The controls were almost useless, as there was not enough sustaining surface to move the plane in the desired direction. It hung at this point practically without control, and I held it there for almost five minutes before I was absolutely certain I could go no higher. When assured of this, I pulled the throttle slightly back in order to glide down, but even with this small movement the bottom seemed to drop out of the plane and down it quickly went toward the earth."

Macready spiraled downward. His goggles, gelatin notwithstanding, were coated with ice and he was groggy and weak, teetering on the brink of unconsciousness. The plane dropped until it reached practically 20,000 feet, where Macready leveled his descent and remained for twenty minutes in order to regain his senses and reorient himself.

When his mind was clear, Macready nosed over and returned to the field. The test of the supercharger had been a complete success, a mechanical method of providing more air for the airplane engine had worked well, and an unofficial altitude record had been established. "A pool had been made in the hangar,"

Lt. John A. MacReady and the plane he flew to a record altitude.
*(U.S. Air Force)*

Macready wrote, "with the different mechanics betting on the altitude. Dr. Moss, inventor of the supercharger, won the pool with a guess of 41,000 feet. The actual calibrated altitude of the flight as indicated on the barograph charts was 40,800 feet, which is the highest altitude any living being has yet made."

Macready in his open cockpit airplane had reached the practical limits of man's ability to fly high. Although Capt. Hawthorne C. Gray went higher in 1927 in an open basket suspended from a balloon, he perished from oxygen starvation after attaining his record altitude. Clearly, if man was to operate at extreme altitudes in any meaningful way, better equipment had to be devised. Oxygen alone was not the answer. Air pressure was needed to supply the lungs with the proper percentage of usable oxygen and air pressure was necessary to keep the body itself functioning. Without sufficient pressure at levels above 35,000 feet, nitrogen comes out of solution in the bloodstream, causing pain, possibly paralysis, and sometimes death.

Two methods of supplying atmospheric pressure to high-altitude flyers were considered. One was the pressure suit, the other the pressurized cabin.

Wiley Post, famous as a round-the-world flyer, was an early proponent of the pressurized coveralls. For his 1933 world flight, he had supercharged the engine in his *Winnie Mae* and now a year later he proposed to add an additional supercharger to pressurize a flying suit. The pressure suit Post built resembled a deep-

Wiley Post (left) with the high altitude pressurized suit that he designed and built.
**(National Air and Space Museum, The Smithsonian Institution)**

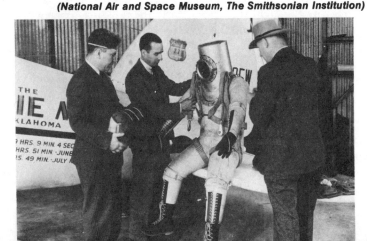

sea diver's gear. The cylindrical aluminum helmet looked like a large tomato can, but it was cleverly rigged with two valves, one of which admitted air under pressure from the supercharger while the other admitted oxygen, making it possible for the aviator to mix and regulate the percentage of oxygen in the compressed air. The helmet was fastened tightly to a rubber suit which encased the pilot's whole body in sea-level pressure. Excess pressure could be exhausted through a valve in the boots.

Post made his first flight in the pressurized suit on December 3, 1934, from Bartlesville, Oklahoma, but he lost his bearings at altitude and landed, out of gas, ninety miles away. On December 7, 1934, he tried again.

"I headed into the wind which I estimated was blowing about 200 miles an hour," said Post after landing. "From then on I could see without difficulty Oklahoma City 110 miles away and Elreno 150 miles west of my landing field. The thermometer outside registered 70 degrees below zero, yet I was comfortable. The flying suit worked perfectly after I had fastened the facepiece on my helmet and turned on the supercharger at 20,000 feet. They hang floral offerings on good race horses. I would like to hang one on that Wasp engine of mine. It ran like a clock, and that is the same engine that won the Los Angeles-New York race and then flew around the world twice, not counting the regular flying I have been doing. It has gone so far I would not even estimate how many miles have passed under it. As a result of this flight I am convinced that airplanes can travel at terrific speeds above 30,000 feet by getting into the prevailing wind channel."

Post's flights did not establish F.A.I. records, but his experiments with the flight suit, particularly the pressure-oxygen mixer and regulator, advanced the development of pressure and oxygen systems for aircraft.

It was the idea of Major Carl F. Greene, an Air Corps officer stationed at Wright Field in Ohio, that an airtight airplane could be built that could fly in the substratosphere without special oxygen equipment for the fliers. Macready had blacked out at 38,180 feet; Schroeder had frozen his eyeballs at 40,800 feet; Hawthorne C. Gray had died at 42,470 feet. Greene was determined to find a safe way to fly high.

"We knew we had to operate at high levels," Greene said

later, "and we knew that it was up to us to find all the answers. It was too easy for men to die the way Gray did."

The pressure cabin was clearly the answer.

During the summer of 1932, the XC-35, built by Lockheed with a new monocoque design in place of the older, square, box-kite airplane body frame, was delivered to Wright Field and readied for its maiden pressure flight into the substratosphere. Major Greene was among those who flew on the test flight with Capt. Alfred H. Johnson, the pilot. At twelve thousand feet Johnson turned on the XC-35's superchargers. Slowly the airplane climbed to 33,000 feet, but the pressure within the cabin remained that of an altitude below nine thousand feet, and no oxygen supplies were required. Tests on the XC-35 continued throughout the summer and fall. The airplane, with its hermetically sealed cabin, made its most important flight the following winter, on February 3, 1933, when it carried Assistant Secretary of War Louis A. Johnson from Chicago to Washington, flying at 22,000 feet, above some heavy storm clouds, without the use of oxygen.

The practicality of altitude flying within a sealed compartment was established, and designers of aircraft took cognizance of the important innovation.

By October 22, 1938, Mario Pezzi at Montecello, Italy, had flown to a new record of 56,046 feet.

World War II added further dimension to flying higher than before. High-altitude flying in supercharged airplanes became commonplace. American heavy bombers, Boeing B-29s, operated at great heights with engines and cabin pressurized by super-chargers. The ceiling of the B-29 was high enough to operate beyond the range of most enemy ground guns or fighters.

After the war, aviation looked first to the jets to carry man higher and then to the great rocket power of the X-series aircraft.

It was in an X-2 carried aloft by a Boeing B-50 mother ship that Captain Iven C. Kincheloe, Jr., reached an altitude of 126,200 feet on September 7, 1956.

Dropping from the underbelly of the B-50, the Bell X-2 scorched skyward, leaving its contrail print across the sky. At 65,000 feet the rocket was only partially through its burn; at 85,000 feet Kincheloe experienced mild buffeting of the wings, but the altimeter continued to wind up.

"Ten," radioed radar control, denoting the final mark in the preplanned flight profile. Kincheloe was on his schedule as the rocket ship sliced past ninety thousand feet, moving at a speed of fifteen hundred miles per hour. The X-2 reached 100,000 feet and shot out of the earth's atmosphere into the vacuum of space. The rocket engines behind Kincheloe rumbled. Then the tubes consumed the final drops of fuel and fell silent. Now the ship was coasting away from earth in an eerie silence.

The first spaceman glanced away from his instruments. Through a small window he could see the brown desert below. To the west was the azure blue of the Pacific Ocean and above was the black void of space.

When the X-2 reached 126,200 feet, it arced over and twisted to the left to begin its fall back toward the earth. It traveled as a projectile now because its control surfaces were useless above the earth's atmosphere. Kincheloe simply rode with his craft as it dropped in a twisting vertical dive. The Mach needle began to climb—Mach 2 . . . 2.5 . . . 2.6.

G forces of reentry began to build, and as air again rushed

Capt. Joe B. Jordan in the high-altitude pressure suit he wore on his record flight.

**(U.S. Air Force)**

Joseph Walker in the X-15 he flew to an altitude of sixty-seven miles.
**(U.S. Air Force)**

past the X-2's wings, control returned. Kincheloe eased back on the stick to flatten his dive. The rocket plane slowed, and he gently inched the craft into a turn toward Muroc Dry Lake.

A new altitude record had been set. When Kincheloe, the first man to fly to the top of the sky, filed his report with the test center, he concluded with a trenchant comment: "The aircraft was pleasant to fly throughout the flight and the achievement was as anticipated."

Military jet aircraft were also setting F.A.I. altitude records —records for airplanes taking off and landing under their own power. On December 14, 1959, Capt. Joseph B. Jordan flew a Lockheed F-104C out of Edwards Air Force Base in California to an altitude of 103,389 feet. This record was topped on April 28, 1961, by Russian aviator Gueorgui Mossolov in an E-66-A at Podmoskovnoe when he reached an altitude of 113,890 feet. But neither of these records could touch the heights reached by the half-airplane, half-spacecraft X-series airships.

On August 12, 1960, thirty-six-year-old test pilot Major Robert M. White floated weightless for almost a minute at the top of the arc as the X-15 reached a record 131,000 feet.

Glimpsing a view of the sky and earth that TV audiences have now come to accept with less wonder, Major White observed: "It was a very deep blue, but not exactly like night. There was distinct contrast. Your view encompasses three distinct bands —the earth, the light blue of the sky and then the very deep blue of extreme altitude. It was very impressive."

Larger engines were being prepared for the X-15, whose ultimate goal was to reach a speed of four thousand miles per hour and an altitude of one hundred miles. There were those who feared that at one hundred miles the X-15 might enter earth orbit, but the rocket plane lacked the necessary orbital insertion speeds now familiar to space-age citizenry.

The X-15 pushed the altitude record higher and higher until on July 19, 1963, test pilot Joseph A. Walker reached 354,200 feet—sixty-seven miles above the earth, a feat which remains the unofficial altitude record flight for an airplane. New horizons were forecast when the U. S. Air Force awarded astronaut wings to those who had flown the X-15 to an altitude above fifty miles.

The record flights by these airmen seem to pale before the fantastic space voyages that have now carried men to the moon itself. However, the successes of our astronauts are due in a large measure to the knowledge of the upper atmosphere and space acquired by the pilots who reached upward in their aircraft for the top of the sky. Likewise, the passengers who travel in the quiet comfort of high-flying jets owe much to the men who dared the mysterious regions above us and who cared to find the answers.

# The Balloon Answers
# the First Challenge
# of the Sky

Edmond Rostand, the author of *Cyrano de Bergerac,* wrote about an aerial locomotion process whereby a man was wrapped with glass vials filled with "morning dew." According to Rostand, when the sun rose in the morning the strangely equipped aviator would be lifted skyward by the power of the sun "drinking the mist of dawn." (Nothing was said as to how the process was reversed and the airman returned safely to earth.) This novel method of flight was but one of many imaginative notions advanced by the quixotic poets and fruitless inventors who had pursued the miracle of flight for more than fifty centuries.

Francesco de Lana, an Italian Jesuit priest, wrote a book in 1670 that proposed the use of vacuum balloons. The airless vacuum, he reasoned, being lighter than air, would levitate copper balloons and carry with them a boat in which man could ride. Once aloft, he suggested, the aerial craft would be propelled through the sky by a light mast bearing a strong sail.

This was a reasoned application of Archimedes' principle dealing with density and displacement, but in practice it would not work. If the copper spheres could be made light enough to achieve buoyancy from their internal vacuum, they would also be crushed by atmospheric pressure. Father de Lana had, however, been moving in the right direction, for it was the lighter-than-air balloon that first lifted man into the sky.

It was to an adventurous physicist, Jean François Pilâtre de Rozier, and his friend the Marquis François Laurent d'Arlandes, a young infantry officer, that fell the honor of the first manned flight. Their journey was made in a Montgolfier, a hot-air balloon invented and perfected by the Montgolfier brothers, Joseph Michel and Jacques Étienne.

The Montgolfier brothers had noticed that paper cubes, when folded together and allowed to fill with heated air and smoke, would float up the chimney. It began as a game but led to man's first excursion into space, for they reasoned logically that a larger cube made of paper or a paperlike material, similarly filled with smoke or heated air, should carry a payload aloft. In November, 1782, Joseph Montgolfier succeeded in constructing a large cube of strong, lightweight, silken fabric that rose to the ceiling. During the following months the brothers worked to build a balloon, spherical and considerably larger. On June 5, 1783, they sent an unmanned balloon skyward at Annonay, France, while government observers watched. The brothers then worked to develop a system of fire pots and grates which, when filled with straw, would generate a continuous supply of smoke and hot air to maintain the prolonged lift necessary for manned flight.

Accounts of the Montgolfiers' experiments spread through Paris and another physicist, Jacques A. C. Charles, conceived a method of using a basic Montgolfier in conjunction with the lighter-than-air gas, hydrogen, discovered in 1766 by the English scientist Henry Cavendish. On August 27, 1783, before amazed spectators, Charles launched from the Champ de Mars his small, thirteen-foot hydrogen balloon, made of thin silk varnished with a rubbery gum. It rose to an altitude of three thousand feet and traveled in the air currents for over fifteen miles. Frightened peasants promptly hacked the rubbery, globular monster to pieces when it fell at Gonesse.

On the nineteenth of the following month, in a demonstration for the court at Versailles, the Montgolfier brothers used a larger Montgolfier and sent three animals—a lamb, a rooster, and a duck —aloft in a wicker carriage fastened beneath the balloon. The animals ascended to fifteen hundred feet and after eight minutes of flight drifted gently back to earth, unharmed save for the rooster's broken wing, an injury caused by a kick from the lamb.

The Montgolfiers were now ready to construct an aerostat for human flight. Not for themselves—they were builders, not aeronauts—but for their friend Pilâtre de Rozier, who had enthusiastically volunteered. De Rozier was patently aware of the significance of the adventure he was about to undertake.

The balloon the Montgolfiers built was of a linen-and-paper material—strong, light, and pliable. When fully inflated it was pear-shaped, towering seventy feet high and stretching forty-six feet in diameter through the thickened middle. The bag was magnificent, dyed an elegant blue and ornamented with elaborate and intricate gold decorations. Great, ornate monograms and fleurs-de-lis honoring the King of France emblazoned it. Circling the upper portions were signs of the zodiac and around the bottom festoons of red-and-gold-accentuated theatrical masks and giant eagles. If this was to be an aerial first, it was also to be a colorful beginning.

The base of the balloon narrowed to a small opening which by a series of ropes was secured to a woven wicker carriage. The carriage was a circular, doughnut-shaped veranda with a three-foot wicker banister. The balloon's appendixlike lip passed through the hole of the doughnut and opened over the flue of a small furnace to contain a continuous fire, suspended below the carriage. A brick platform served as a launch pad. During inflation billows of black smoke poured into the balloon, which was tethered between two poles.

The Montgolfier brothers were careful craftsmen. They made several test runs during which de Rozier ascended a short distance into the air while the balloon remained anchored by a stout rope.

Having satisfied themselves that de Rozier might safely be sent up in a free flight, the Montgolfier brothers announced the impending first flight of man. However, the air age almost died aborning; King Louis XVI decided that human beings were not meant to fly and directed that the flight not take place.

It was at this point that de Rozier enlisted the aid of the Marquis d'Arlandes, who in exchange for an invitation to share the moment of glory secured the reluctant but all-important sanction from the King.

Thus it was that on the morning of November 21, 1783, two

gentlemen, elegantly attired, appeared at the gardens of La Muette to demonstrate, hopefully, that man could fly above the earth.

Manning the bellows, smudge-faced stokers fanned the straw fire, sending dense smoke into the yawning mouth of the giant balloon. As it filled, the skin stretched smooth and taut. A crowd of onlookers had gathered at the moorings in the gardens. Included among them were the Dauphin and other representatives of the King. Police and soldiers guarded the swelling balloon. At one-forty-five in the afternoon the bag was in readiness.

Today astronauts begin their space voyages atop towering rockets surrounded by hissing vapor, silvery tubes, blinking lights, and the clicking and humming of electronic components. The air age itself began with regal grandeur. Preceded by guards, the aeronauts pushed through the crowd toward the balloon's wicker carriage, its sides gaily decorated with red draperies.

The two men were resplendent in blue velvet with white stockings, black patent-leather shoes, and plumed hats. They mounted the brick platform, bowed deeply to the Dauphin and other royalty, shook hands with the Montgolfier brothers, waved solemnly to the excited assemblage, and climbed over the three-foot railing into the basket. Their aeronautic gear was already stowed on board: straw, pitchforks, water buckets, sponges, and extra matches. The fire was lit in the onboard furnace. The firemen stoked the straw-fed flames and smoke billowed from below. Upon order the handlers let go of the restraining ropes and the giant balloon slowly and gently lifted from the ground.

In a letter to a friend, the Marquis d'Arlandes described the historic journey:

> Because of your questions and that of the public about our aerial voyage I will describe as best I can this first journey in which man attempted to fly through an element which seemed, prior to the discovery of the MM. Montgolfier, so little fitted to support them.
>
> We went up on the 21st of November 1783, at near two o'clock, M. Pilâtre de Rozier on the west side of the balloon, I on the east. The wind was nearly northwest. The machine, say the public, rose with majesty; but really the position of the balloon altered so that M. Pilâtre de Rozier was in the advance of our position, I in the rear.

"The machine rose with majesty."
**(National Air and Space Museum, The Smithsonian Institution)**

I was surprised at the silence and the absence of movement which our departure caused among the spectators, and believed them to be astonished and perhaps awed at the strange spectacle; they might well have reassured themselves. I was still gazing, when M. Pilâtre de Rozier cried to me—

"You are doing nothing, and the balloon is scarcely rising a fathom."

"Pardon me," I answered, as I placed a bundle of straw upon the fire and slightly stirred it. Then I turned quickly, but already we had passed out of sight of La Muette. Astonished, I cast a glance toward the river. I perceived the confluence of the Oise. And naming the principal bends of the river by the places near them, I cried, "Passy, St.-Germain, St.-Denis, Sevres!"

"If you look at the river in that fashion you will be likely to bathe in it soon," cried Pilâtre de Rozier. "Some fire, my dear friend, some fire!"

We traveled on; but instead of crossing the river, as our direction seemed to indicate, we bore toward the Invalides, then returned upon the principal bed of the river, and traveled to above the barrier of La Conférence, thus dodging about the river, but not crossing it.

"That river is very difficult to cross," I remarked to my companion.

"So it seems," he answered, "but you are doing nothing. I suppose it is because you are braver than I, and don't fear a tumble."

"I stirred the fire, I seized a truss of straw with my fork; I raised it and threw it in the midst of the flames. An instant afterward I felt myself lifted as it were into the heavens.

"For once we move," said I.

"Yes, we move," answered my companion.

At the same instant I heard from the top of the balloon a sound which made me believe that it had burst. I watched, yet I saw nothing. My companion had gone into the interior, no doubt to make some observations. As my eyes were fixed to the top of the machine I experienced a shock, and it was the only one I had felt. The direction of the movement was from above downward. I then said—

"What are you doing? Are you having a dance to yourself?"

"I am not moving."

"So much the better. It is only a new current which I hope will carry us from the river," I answered.

I turned to see where we were and found we were between the Écoles Militaire and the Invalides.

I now heard another report in the machine, which I believed was produced by the cracking of a cord. This new intimation made me carefully examine the inside of our habitation. I saw that the part that was turned toward the south was full of holes, of which some were of a considerable size.

"It must descend," I cried.

"Why?"

"Look!" I said. At the same time I took my sponge and quietly extinguished the little fire that was burning some of the holes within my reach; but at the same moment I perceived that the bottom of the cloth was coming away from the circle which surrounded it.

"We must descend," I repeated to my companion.

He looked below.

"We are upon Paris," he said.

"It does not matter," I answered. "Only look! Is there no danger? Are you holding on well?"

"Yes."

I examined from my side, and saw that we had nothing to

fear. I then tried with my sponge the ropes which were within my reach. All of them held firm. Only two of the cords were broken.

I then said, "We can cross Paris."

During this operation we were rapidly getting down to the roofs. We made more fire, and rose again with the greatest ease. I looked down, and it seemed to me we were going toward the towers of St. Sulpice; but, on rising, a new current made us quit this direction and bear more to the south. I looked to the left, and beheld a wood, which I believed to be that of Luxembourg. We were traversing the boulevard, and I cried all at once—

"Get to the ground!"

"But the intrepid Pilâtre de Rozier, who never lost his head, and who judged more surely than I, prevented me from attempting to descend. I then threw a bundle of straw on the fire. We rose again, and another current bore us to the left. We were now close to the ground, between two mills. As soon as we came near the earth I raised myself over the gallery, and leaning there with my two hands, I felt the balloon pressing softly against my head. I pushed it back, and leaped to the ground. Looking round and expecting to see the balloon still distended, I was astonished to find it quite empty and flattened. On looking for Pilâtre de Rozier I saw him in his shirt sleeves creeping out from under the mass of canvas that had fallen over him.

The flight had carried the men a distance of eight miles for a duration of twenty-five minutes. Although on occasion they had soared up to three thousand feet, most of the flight had occurred at one to two hundred feet above the ground. This historical first was witnessed by thousands of Parisians and world notables, including that thoughtful American, Benjamin Franklin, who on January 16, 1784, reported the event to his government in Philadelphia and proposed the development of airborne troops.

Public reaction to the success of the first balloon flight was instantaneous and overwhelming. The world acclaimed balloons, and merchants decorated everything—plates, dishes, furniture, clothes, paintings, banners, even knobs for canes and buttons for clothes—with balloon replicas. So great was the enthusiasm for balloons that by the spring of 1784 the French government had to promulgate its first flight-safety ordinance: "Being an Ordinance Prohibiting the Launching of Balloons and Other Aerostatic Machines." It established certain minimum safety requirements.

Only ten days after the Pilâtre de Rozier flight, an even more remarkable balloon ascent was made by J. A. C. Charles and M. N. Robert, in a hydrogen balloon built very much like modern balloons. Their aerostat was a gum-varnished silk sphere covered with a net. From it hung parallel ropes gathering the net to a ring fastened below, from which hung a wicker basket. At the top of the balloon was a valve to release hydrogen for descent, and at the bottom was an appendixlike lip used in filling the balloon. The basket contained sandbags of ballast to aid lift, and carried the world's first aeronautical flight instrument, a mercury barometer. Their balloon rose from the Tuileries Gardens in Paris to a height of ten thousand feet. They traveled twenty-seven miles and stayed aloft for two hours and five minutes, ending the flight with a perfect landing at Nesle.

And thus the race was on.

Men in balloons began to float farther and farther over mountains and seas.

As early as January 7, 1785, less than a year and a half after the first ascension, French balloonist Jean-Pierre Blanchard, and a prosperous American surgeon practicing in London, John Jeffries, set out to float across the English Channel. Dr. Jeffries reported in his diary that he had flown with Blanchard on one previous occasion "in consideration of one hundred guineas presented him for that purpose."

The earlier flight took place on November 30, 1784, with Jeffries and Blanchard being "toasted off by the Prince of Wales and other royal persons who were interested in lending their presence to the cause of aerial development." Jeffries recorded that he carried aloft with him a "mariner's compass, thermometer, barometer, hydrometer, electrometer and a timepiece . . . to make meteorological discoveries."

The balloon ascension lasted one hour and twenty-one minutes, during which the aeronauts floated into the county of Kent, a fair distance from Rhedarium in London where they began. So awed was Jeffries by the silent aerial journey and the spectacular view that he made no meteorological observations. He praised Blanchard's expert manipulation of the aerial oars which, according to Jeffries' inaccurate observations, "appeared materially to influence the course, ascent and progress of the Balloon."

The so-called oars consisted of four wide, wooden-handled, fabric-covered blades which Blanchard had affixed to the basket in order to row and guide his craft through the air. Since the balloon floated in the air currents, the four oars, resembling the wings of a stubby dragonfly, were useless.

From this successful ride, however, Jeffries became convinced that a balloon could safely carry two passengers across the English Channel. The American doctor, whose medical practice in London grew out of the fact that he had served as a British surgeon major during the Revolutionary War, now totally abandoned medicine in his passion for ballooning. His new ambition was to become "engaged in another Aerial Experiment, designed to fly from the Royal Castle of Dover, across the British Channel into France."

Jeffries suggested this adventure to balloonist Blanchard, who agreed at once although the thought promptly occurred to him that, since it was he who had the aeronautical skills, he ought, perhaps, to make the journey by himself instead of sharing the honors. However, Blanchard found that the cost of the necessary aerostat was more than his own finances could support and he reluctantly agreed to permit the doctor to accompany him, attaching to the consent as many restrictions as he could negotiate. As Jeffries observed in his diary, one of the conditions of the flight was that "in case of necessity on our passage, I would get out of the Car for his preservation."

Even after the bargain had been struck and Jeffries had advanced the necessary funds, Blanchard tried several times to persuade the doctor not to accompany him. On a test flight in which the balloon, anchored by a rope, was inflated and allowed to rise, Blanchard donned a girdle with weights sewn into the lining so that it would appear that the aerostat did not have sufficient lift to buoy both men. But Blanchard did not reckon with the tenacity of his companion; and whatever the artifice, Jeffries found a solution that would enable him to make the flight. The wiles of Blanchard caused Jeffries to note that he was "a petulant little fellow, not many inches over five feet, and physically well suited for vaporish regions."

The wrangling between the men continued until flight time,

when on the seventh of January, 1785, they awoke to find the skies cold but brilliantly clear with a strong, biting wind driving steadily out of the northwest. Then quarreling ceased and in the shared excitement of high adventure they began the task of inflating the hydrogen balloon.

"The balloon being filled a little before one o'clock," he later wrote in his diary, "we suffered it to rise, so as to be disengaged from the apparatus, etc., for filling it, and to be drawn down again right to the edge of the cliff, where we attached the oars or wings with the moulinet and gouvernail [a rope and pulley device] to the car. Exactly at one o'clock we rose slowly and majestically from the cliff, which being at the time of ascent from it almost covered with a beautiful assembly from the city, neighbouring towns and villages, with carriages, horses, etc., together with the extensive beach of Dover, crowded with a great concourse of people, with numbers of boats, etc., assembled near the shore, under the cliffs, afforded us, at our first arising from them, a most beautiful and picturesque view indeed."

The fearless aeronauts had floated a third of the way across the Channel when the balloon began to drop rapidly toward the churning sea. Blanchard in a frantic reaction valved the balloon, dumping valuable hydrogen, and they sank faster. To compensate both men began cutting and dropping ballast. They leveled off. Next they threw overboard half of the pamphlets they had carried to distribute among the receiving French to advertise their journey. Gradually the balloon began to rise again, and as they rose they could make out the hazy pencil line of the French coast. Within a few minutes the coast loomed large before them, but the aerostat again began to sink.

"At about half past two," wrote Jeffries, "I found we were descending very rapidly. We immediately threw out all of the little things we had with us, such as biscuits, apples, etc., and after that one of our oars or wings; but still descending, we cast away the other wing and then the gouvernail; having likewise had the precaution, for fear of accidents, while the balloon was falling, partly to loosen and make it go easy. I now succeeded in attempting to reach without the car, and unscrewing the moulinet with all its apparatus, I likewise cast that into the sea. Notwithstanding all which, the balloon not rising, we cut away

"Threatening at any moment to plunge the passengers into the wintery waters."

all of the lining and ornaments, both within and on the outside of the car, and in like manner threw them into the sea. After which we cast away the only bottle we had taken with us."

Having no experience in judging height above the water, the doctor was shocked to observe how quickly the bottle hit the water. They were much nearer the rolling waves than they had believed. Jeffries hastily removed his overcoat and cast it over the side. Blanchard took off his heavy wool breeches and pitched them into the sea.

Both men quickly donned cork life jackets and waited for the car to strike the water.

The wind held steady, and their ground speed of twenty knots became more noticeable as they dropped closer to the surface of the sea. Now the bottom of the basket was being splashed as the aerostat skipped along the tops of the rolling waves. Frantically they ripped off everything, including parts of the gondola that could be chopped, cut, or removed, and pushed the debris into the sea. Then they removed their outer clothes and tossed them overboard.

Teased by the wind, the balloon with the basket hanging below bobbed and bounced, threatening at any moment to plunge the passengers into the wintery waters. Soon they reached the invisible rising currents along the coastline, and the aerostat was suddenly buoyed up to one thousand feet. The men in their underwear shivered in the January chill as they looked down upon the coast of France, but as they hung unceremoniously to the ropes beneath the soft globe they knew that the triumph was theirs.

At three-forty-five Jeffries and Blanchard began a slow descent into the forest of Guines, twelve miles inland. In a short time they were skimming the tops of trees, and as they did, they reached out to grab branches. They could only clutch the limbs briefly because the wind blowing against the balloon pulled them away; but this awkward landing procedure slowed the aerostat in its course until it passed over a clearing. In that instant Blanchard yanked the valve to dump the remaining hydrogen, and the aerostat, heaving an elephantine sigh, deflated over the gondola and the scantily clad heroes.

At first there were no crowds to greet the aeronauts because of the uncertainty of the time and place and even the likelihood of their arrival. But soon men on horseback and later people on foot began to arrive. The citizens of nearby Calais feted them royally, and Jeffries modestly wrote of this, "We are receiving honors and attentions much above our merit."

King Louis XVI summoned the airmen to Versailles, where he awarded Blanchard a gift of money plus a lifetime pension. He enrolled Jeffries as a founder and perpetual member of the new Paris Museum.

The excitement resulting from the daring adventure continued in both England and France for many months. One of the men significantly influenced by the journey was the pioneer aeronaut Pilâtre de Rozier, who had received a large grant from the French government to perform an important and significant feat in a balloon to match or surpass the Channel crossing of the English pair. Long before the Blanchard-Jeffries flight, he had announced his intention to cross the Channel. Now, faced with their success, he knew that he had to better their feat, by crossing the Channel the hard way—from France to England, contrary to the prevailing winds.

For his voyage de Rozier designed a radically new aerostat. Instead of choosing between a Montgolfier hot-air balloon that maintained ''controlled'' lift by use of an on-board fire, or a hydrogen balloon that depended solely upon the very efficient hydrogen gas to produce tremendous lift, he used them both. He reasoned that the hydrogen balloon would provide the basic lift and stability for flight, while the hot-air balloon would provide, through regulation of the fire, a means of controlling ascent or descent without the need for cumbersome ballast.

In spite of the success of Blanchard and Jeffries, de Rozier's

An artist's conception of the first ballooning fatality.

**(U.S. Air Force)**

friends begged him not to undertake the venture. To this he bravely responded, "For God's sake, don't mention such a thing; it is now too late. Give me encouragement, for I would rather take a knife and pierce it to my heart than give up the attempt which I have engaged in although I was certain of meeting with death."

Patiently de Rozier waited for the proper wind. It was not, however, until the fourteenth of June, 1785, that a steady wind blew out of the southeast, promising the necessary force to carry an aerostat across the Channel. Throughout the day the favorable winds held constant, and when they were still blowing the following morning, the aeronaut ordered the inflation of the balloons.

The Marquis de Maisonfort, who greatly desired to share the adventure and the glory of the Channel crossing with de Rozier, offered money for the opportunity; but the owner and manufacturer of the balloon, M. Pierre-Ange Romaine, insisted upon his own right to ride with the famous aeronaut, and de Rozier agreed.

By seven o'clock in the morning all was in readiness. De Rozier and Romaine entered the basket of the double balloon. A cannon fired to announce the launch and slowly the machine began to rise, two majestic globes in the cloudless sky. Gracefully the aerostat floated upward and out toward the Channel.

Among the spectators that morning was de Rozier's beautiful fiancee, who had joined his friends in begging him not to attempt the flight. She considered the success of Blanchard and Jeffries a piece of remarkable good luck. Unfortunately, her worst fears were realized. The balloon was not aloft for thirty minutes when it began to sink and to reverse its direction. De Rozier added fire for lift. Ten thousand spectators saw only the result of this final act. A spark drifted to the supplemental hydrogen balloon which was floating above the hot-air balloon. In that instant the horrified onlookers saw a burst of flashing flame and a puff of smoke, followed a few seconds later by the report of a muffled explosion. Both balloons collapsed, and the airmen plunged helplessly to earth. De Rozier died instantly, and Romaine lived but a few minutes after the crowds reached the demolished basket and the broken men.

Pilâtre de Rozier, the first man to fly, was also the first to die in man's quest to go higher, faster, and farther.

# CHAPTER 7

# The Balloon
# Goes Farther

The most daring proposal for balloon travel was advanced by Salomon Andrée, a Swedish engineer and explorer who proposed to cross the North Pole in an open balloon. He ultimately received financial backing for his enterprise, and after several unsuccessful attempts at an arctic launch, finally sailed out from Danes Island, Spitsbergen, on July 11, 1897, on a northward course toward the Pole. The arctic cold soon deflated the balloon and gently deposited Andrée and his two companions on the polar ice. They made their way to White Island, where their bodies were found August 6, 1930, thirty-three years later.

The most fancied ambition of balloon men was to cross the Atlantic Ocean. Because it was there, it was a challenge too great to be denied. There was an ocean to be crossed and men in free-flying balloons were determined to cross it.

On the morning of April 13, 1844, New York City was aroused by a fantastic news story in the New York *Sun:* "The Atlantic Crossed in Three Days! Signal Triumph of Mr. Monck Mason's Flying Machine!!!"

Monck Mason, a native of Ireland and an accomplished musician, writer, and aeronaut, had in the company of seven others, according to the report, crossed the Atlantic Ocean from Great Britain to a safe landing in South Carolina after three perilous days.

The newspaper claimed to have the text of Monck Mason's daily journal of the adventure and offered an exclusive report to its readers. The *Sun's* exuberance, however, was short-lived, for the voyage was a hoax. It was invented by a hungry and gifted Virginia poet who needed the fifteen dollars he was paid for writing the story. His name was Edgar Allan Poe.

As Poe told the story, Monck Mason and his companions decided that fate had decreed they should travel westward. They set their aerial rudder accordingly and continued on the surprise journey across the Atlantic Ocean. The airmen acquired great skill at aerial navigation. They learned to operate their propeller device to travel even into a headwind and they survived a boiling gale encountered in the mid-Atlantic. The final entry in the contrived diary recounted their final triumph: *"We are in full view of the low coast of South Carolina.* The great problem is accomplished. We have crossed the Atlantic—fairly and easily crossed in a balloon! God be praised! Who shall say that anything is impossible hereafter?"

The initial enthusiasm for the heroic crossing by Monck Mason and his companions was great, but the public anger and resentment were even greater when the exploit was exposed as pure fiction. As amusing as the story is in retrospect, it did have a decided effect upon the real balloon men of the day, particularly the barnstorming balloonist and showman John Wise.

John Wise, then recognized as one of America's most knowledgeable aeronauts, had long been anxious to challenge the Atlantic Ocean in a balloon. Although he was an exhibitionist and aeronautical daredevil, he was also a thoughtful and level-headed airman who approached ballooning scientifically and carefully. He knew, for instance, that neither Monck Mason nor anyone else could have flown the Atlantic at that latitude from east to west, because the prevailing winds were from west to east. He also knew that to achieve his ambition he needed to build a balloon capable of sustained flight.

Wise formed the Trans-Atlantic Balloon Company and after fifteen years of stubborn persistence obtained the necessary financial support to build a balloon that was fifty feet in diameter and sixty feet in height. The balloon carried a wicker basket with a lifeboat hanging below. The boat was accessible by a rope ladder fixed to the side of the basket. Appropriately, the massive aerostat was christened the *Atlantic*.

To test the aerostat, Wise planned a flight from St. Louis to

New York City, from where the voyage across the ocean would begin. The flight from St. Louis was to serve two purposes: it would be a shakedown flight for the balloon and it would serve to prove the validity of Wise's theory that there was indeed a great sea of air that flowed steadily eastward. Wise's crew for the flight consisted of John Lamountane, who had supervised the construction of the craft; O. A. Gager, the promoter of the aerial adventure; and a reporter from the St. Louis *Republican,* known only to history as Mr. Hyde. The voyagers had been provisioned with sandwiches, cold chicken, lemonade, and a hamper of champagne. The *Atlantic* also carried a half ton of sand ballast and a mailbag for New York.

By the evening of July 1, 1859, all preparations were complete. Throughout the day gas had been pumped into the giant bag. At six-forty-five all was in readiness and a restless crowd of paying spectators clamored for the event to begin. Wise, carrying the lunch basket, climbed into the wicker carriage where he would handle the valving and ballast while the three passengers made themselves comfortable in the lifeboat, fifteen feet below.

On an order from Wise, the restraining ropes were cut and the mammoth balloon lifted majestically into the air. The ground breeze, blowing in a westerly direction, carried them toward the afternoon sun, but when they had attained a slight altitude, the wind direction changed and, high above the crowds, the aerostat headed eastward toward New York.

"The city of St. Louis, covering a large area, appears to be gradually contracting its lines and has finally hid itself under a mantle of smoke," John Wise wrote at this triumphant moment. "We gazed upon the fading outlines of the country with sentimental yearning as we recurred to the parting farewell of the kind friends we left behind, while at the same time our hearts are filled with joy upon the prospects of a glorious voyage to our good friends in the East, to whom has already been announced the fact of our coming."

As if pressed along by a gentle hand, the *Atlantic* glided silently along its course. In the lifeboat the three novice aeronauts enjoyed a round of manly banter and a light supper of sandwiches and fried chicken. John Wise, in the basket above, dropped off into an untroubled sleep. The men in the boat witnessed, in awe, the magnificent sunset from aloft. Gradually the gently rolling countryside darkened while the sky, in contrast, retained its ebbing light long after the sun fell from view in the west. The vessel was drifting several hundred feet above the terrain. Occasionally the sound of a voice, a slamming door, a barking dog, or footsteps would drift up to the voyagers. The free-floating balloon was serenity itself. The three passengers were overwhelmed by the strange combination of omnipotence and humility that filled them. As part of the wind, the balloon gave no feeling of motion. The sounds from below, unmuffled by ground interference, seemed almost amplifed in the transmission from ground to balloon, like sounds heard across open water; yet all around them there was a heavy mantle of total silence.

Darkness fell, and the aeronauts could make out the concentrated lights of an occasional town below and sometimes the flickering of a burning fire.

"The balance of the night," wrote Wise, "was employed in various experiments and observations. We had learned that the country watch-dogs were very ready to respond to any inquiries in the shape of 'halloos' from above. The paucity or copiousness of their answering bow-wows served as indices of the sparseness or fulness of habitations in the locality over which these demonstrations took place. Sometimes a hundred canine voices would come up at once, and then a village or thick settlement was indicated below. At another a single bow-wow told us of the lone log-cabin in the wild woods; and again the adjacent farms of the prairie were indicated by a medley of canine choruses."

When they crossed the meandering Wabash River, the aeronauts drifted above a midnight fisherman hauling his nets by lantern light. "We hailed him as we passed over," related John Wise, "and congratulated him upon his good luck. He betrayed a great deal of amazement, looking this way and that way, then into the water, and again his eyes were directed toward the shore. He looked every possible way but upward; and as we were pleasantly discussing his consternation in his hearing, it is no wonder that he felt perplexed and surprised."

Throughout the night the balloon wafted along in the easterly current. Early the next morning Wise aroused his companions so they could observe the approach to Lake Erie. In the misty light of dawn, the travelers gazed ahead at the shimmering waters. Near Toledo, Ohio, the *Atlantic* passed over the lake. In full daylight Wise was able to observe their ever increasing ground speed. He calculated that they were being carried above the water at better than sixty miles an hour—a fantastic speed in the 1880s —but the balloon as part of the air current sailed along almost motionlessly. The three men in the lifeboat below, inexperienced in air travel and at too great an altitude to fully appreciate their actual speed, were aware only that they easily overtook and passed steamboats plying the waters below.

"Air travel is the only way to go," observed Mr. Hyde.

John Wise was not so pleased with their progress, for he had noticed storm clouds gathering on the horizon. He also observed that the surface of the lake was growing choppy and whitecaps were snapping off the tops of the waves. The wind velocity was increasing, but as the balloon moved with the wind, its relative speed maintained the pleasant sensation of safety and security. Wise understood the phenomenon and the dangers, but his companions did not.

During the morning the *Atlantic* had covered a distance of 250 miles and was fast approaching Niagara Falls. Its present course would more likely carry it toward Boston than New York, but the navigational problem was not what troubled Wise.

The storm was now building rapidly and the balloon was dipping lower and lower toward the surface of the lake. Its ground speed remained close to sixty miles an hour, however. A landing at that speed could tear the *Atlantic* apart. Wise ordered all ballast dumped, and when that failed to lift the balloon, everything went overboard: food, luggage, mail, and all but one bottle of champagne, which Wise held back for medicinal purposes.

The balloon continued to sink. Gager and Hyde, now aware of the danger, climbed the rope ladder to the higher basket while Lamountane grabbed a hatchet and started flailing away at the bottom of the lifeboat, which was skipping and bouncing over the slapping waves at a breathtaking speed. Suddenly the bottom fell free, Lamountane scrambled to the car above, and the balloon, freed of the extra weight, eased skyward. At one hundred feet it leveled.

The storm clouds thickened around them. Above the wind grew

and rain began to fall. Below the angry waves foamed and surged. Although they were one hundred feet above the lake, it appeared to be within reach of the basket.

"I see a steamer in the distance crossing our track," Wise shouted to his frightened passengers. "Let's swamp the balloon, and trust to the chances of being rescued by it. What say you to this, gentlemen?"

"No, no, no!" they responded without hesitation.

"If we are to die, let us die on the land if we can reach it," said Hyde.

"We will try and rough it through," agreed Gager, who also viewed the churning waters with great fear.

Wise, however, knew that a greater danger was ahead among the trees and rocks at sixty miles an hour. Water, at least, would provide some cushion.

Wise noted:

> All eyes were now gazing intently forward—all hoping, almost against hope itself, that some relief might come to hand; anything else than black clouds and foaming billows would relieve the intense anxiety of the past hour. Minutes seemed to the mind as ages. It was like a dream that was not all a dream, and yet in the next moment we might wake up in another world. In another moment something was seen to emerge from the thick mist. The propeller steamer, *Young America,* hove in sight. As she neared us, my heart throbbed with emotion at the thought of losing the golden opportunity. In swamping, our boat would have filled with water and formed a dead drag, and with our car in the same plight, we might easily have been fished up with a line thrown us by the steamer. I had experienced that kind of rescue before by being picked up by a brig on Lake Erie. I said, "Well, boys, if you will not be saved in the water, let us get ready to return the salute of the steamer," for by this time its bell was ringing out in lusty peals, its steam-whistle was piping its shrillest notes, and all its passengers were paraded on the forward deck to cheer the aerial craft. The ladies waved their handkerchiefs and the men began to hurrah. This cheered me up, and I said, "Now, boys, for a hearty hurrah, if it should be the last one of our lives."
>
> We made the effort, but such a sickly hurrah I never heard before. Indeed, it sounded to me like the death-notes of a forlorn

hope. The people on the boat thought without doubt that we were going along nicely enough. Little did they dream that we were sailing with death-warrants in our hands.

We had now drifted for a hundred miles or more just above the tempest-tossed water, occasionally thumping against its angry billows, and no land to be seen yet. Going with a velocity of at least a mile a minute, the idea of striking the shore seemed to afford but little hope of our safety.

Suddenly, through the rain squall land appeared.

"I see land," cried Hyde, "but it seems a million miles off."

"Too near for our comfort," replied Wise.

It was Wise's plan to swamp the balloon some hundred yards before it reached the shore. He appointed one of the men to jump from the car as soon as it touched the land, so that the lightened ballon would rise above the treetops through the storm and hopefully land the *Atlantic* safely on the shores of the St. Lawrence River.

Wise continued:

But fate willed it otherwise, and before I could bring the air-ship down to the water level, it thumped with a violent crash upon the margin of the shore. Instantly I threw out the grapnel. This was made of bar iron, and an inch and one-eighth thick.

The balloon rebounded from the earth and shot up over the tree-tops; the grapnel caught in a tree, but it was like Leviathan tied to a fish-hook. A sharp jingle of breaking metal followed, and in another moment the balloon was dashing along through the tree-tops like a maddened elephant through a jungle.

Our grapnel was made useless, and as the balloon went crashing through the forest the iron-rimmed hoop cut away the branches. It now became evident that a balloon has a tremendous power when propelled by a swift wind. Limb after limb was torn from the trees in which the rigging happened to become momentarily fastened. Bound upon bound went our air-ship. It would plunge from one point of the forest to another, and ever and anon we would all be thrown in a heap to the bottom of the car. It appeared almost past belief that we could survive this dashing and crashing process for a minute longer, but still onward plunged this furious enginery of the air. Once the car had become fastened in the fork of a tree, and there the silken demon was held, swaying to and fro like a meteor of destruction.

The folds of the half-emptied balloon were cracking and flapping most fearfully. The wind was piping its shrill notes through the cords and network. Not a word was uttered by any of the crew while this fearful suspense lasted. Each one was holding on with a desperate grip for life.

In another moment a limb of the tree seven or eight inches thick was torn from its trunk, and was swinging in the rigging of the balloon. Another squall, and the air-ship bounced out of the woods and lodged in the side of a high tree, with the limb still hanging to it, and then collapsed.

The basket dropped into the top of a tree, slid downward, and came to rest at a sharp angle, nestled snugly between strong branches sixty feet above the ground.

Inside the basket the shaken men gathered their wits, discovered that no one had been injured, and, using the grapnel line, slid down to safety below.

Inhabitants who had witnessed the strange craft bouncing and crashing through the forest came running.

"An elderly lady with spectacles," remembered Wise, "made the remark that she was really surprised and astonished to see so sensible-looking a party, as we appeared to be, ride in such an outlandish-looking vehicle. She anxiously inquired where we came from; and when told from St. Louis, she wanted to know how far that was from there, and when informed that it was over a thousand miles, she looked very suspiciously over the top of her spectacles, and said, 'That will do now.'"

John Wise still clutched his bottle of champagne. He now popped the cork, took a long draw, and passed the bottle to his companions. Wiping his mouth with the back of his hand, he asked the nearest onlooker where they were. When told, he eased himself onto a stump, took a pencil, and immodestly noted:

"July 2, 1859, 2:35 P.M., landed in a tree on the place of Truman Whitney, in the township of Henderson, in the county of Jefferson, in the state of New York. Thus ending the greatest air voyage ever made."

Wise had set a world distance record of 809 miles, not to be topped by man in a free balloon for more than a decade. It was in the end John Wise's greatest flight. His designs upon the Atlantic Ocean deflated with the gas bag on Whitney's farm and his transoceanic dream was never to be realized. Even to this day no one has conquered the Atlantic in a free-floating balloon.

John Wise the balloon man became a legend in his own time. At the age of seventy-one he still was commanding his ships of the air when, on September 29, 1879, he set sail with novice companions on a long balloon voyage. Crossing Lake Michigan the balloon lost buoyancy and all perished in the icy waters of the lake.

Germany has dominated ballooning in the twentieth century. In 1913 the official F.A.I. record for duration of flight in a free balloon was captured by a German aeronaut named Hans Kaulen who remained aloft for eighty-seven hours. Another German balloonist, Emile Berliner, set the present official record with a long-distance two-day flight of 1,896.85 miles, completed on February 10, 1914. His closest competitor is a Russian aeronaut, Boris Nevernov, who, on March 13, 1941, in a USSR-VR 73 balloon, completed a flight from Dolgoproudnaia to Novosibirsk, a distance of 1,719.21 miles, in 69 hours, 20 minutes.

Although free ballooning in hot-air balloons and gas balloons is a skill and a sport enjoyed by many modern-day aeronauts throughout the United States and Europe, the first hundred years of ballooning were the most spectacular. In that bygone era aeronauts were honored as astronauts are today and the public followed their attempts to travel higher and farther with the same interest and excitement that it now follows the progress of journeys in outer space.

# CHAPTER 8

# The Dirigible Goes Around the World

On June 1, 1863, a balloon with three cylindrical bags filled with hydrogen carried aloft Dr. Solomon Andrews, a physician-turned-inventor. This aerostat relied upon gravity and wind resistance to give the pilot directional control of the machine. More flights followed, and on September 8 of the same year the New York *Herald* declared Andrews' craft "the most extraordinary invention of the age, if not the most so of any the world ever saw. . . ."

The doctor continued to work on his flying machine, and on May 25, 1865, he launched a new model, now with a single, lemon-shaped bag supporting the control basket. With three passengers—George Trow, C. M. Plumb, and G. Waldo Hill—Andrews flew out over New York City in his airship, which he had named the *Aereon*. The citizens of the city were understandably agog at the sight of the vessel speeding effortlessly above them. Hundreds rushed into the streets, whereupon Andrews tossed overboard small cards that fluttered downward in the sunlight like so many falling leaves, carrying the message "*Souvenir* of her trial trip from the car of Andrews' *Flying Ship*."

Press coverage of the flight was enthusiastic. Declared the New York *World*: "Navigation of the air is a fixed act. The problem of the centuries has been solved." In spite of the enthusiasm, there was little financial interest in the vehicle; and caught in the depression following the Civil War, Dr. Andrews' aerial adventure, though scientifically successful, was a financial bust. Bankruptcy wiped out the Aerial Navigation Company and sent

Alberto Santos-Dumont excited all of Paris.
**(National Air and Space Museum, The Smithsonian Institution)**

the doctor back to his medical practice in Perth Amboy, New Jersey.

In 1898, on the other side of the Atlantic, the dapper Brazilian inventor, Alberto Santos-Dumont, excited all of Paris with a flight in a gas dirigible powered by a small, two-cylinder gasoline motor. The flight itself ended in a crash that almost took the aeronaut's life, but not before he had successfully demonstrated controlled flight in a powered dirigible balloon. In spite of Santos-Dumont's crash, the attempt to match power to balloons was the direction in which long-distance lighter-than-air flight was moving at this point in aviation history.

"My first impression of aerial navigation was," reported Santos-Dumont, "I confess, surprise to feel the airship going straight ahead. It was astonishing to feel the wind in my face. In spherical ballooning we go with the wind and do not feel it. True, in rising and descending the spherical balloonist feels the friction of the atmosphere, and the vertical oscillation makes the flag flutter; but in the horizontal movement the ordinary balloon seems to stand still while the earth flies past under it.

"As my airship plowed ahead, the wind struck my face and fluttered my coat as on the deck of a transatlantic liner, though in other respects it will be more accurate to liken aerial to river navigation with a steamboat. It is not like sail navigation; and all talk about 'tacking' is meaningless. If there is any wind at all, it is in a given direction, so that the analogy with a river current is better.''

By the turn of the century several airminded Frenchmen were working on airships, or dirigibles. To encourage this development, M. Deutsch de la Meurthe, a wealthy member of the Paris Aero Club, offered a prize of 100,000 francs to the ''first dirigible driver to rise between the years 1900 and 1904, from Parc d'Aéro-station at Saint-Cloud, circle the Eiffel Tower and return to land at the starting point within a half hour.'' The distance was only seven miles, but the dirigible had to fly over a fixed course in a set time. Some members of the Aero Club thought that M. Deutsch might as well have selected the moon as the turnaround point.

Shortly thereafter Santos-Dumont announced that he would make an attempt for the prize in a modified version of his recently wrecked dirigible. When his dirigible was ready, he called in the judges and attempted the challenge.

The flight preparations—inflating the balloon, starting the engine, conferring with the officials—were all well attended by an enthusiastic and usually impatient crowd. The attempt, however, ended in a crash, almost in slow motion, as the fledgling dirigible crumbled into nearby trees as it lost its directional control and lift.

In the weeks that followed, Santos-Dumont made two more attempts and climbed from the dirigible wreckage on each occasion. Since the excitement of tragedy is as compelling as triumph, the crowds grew larger with each new flight.

Finally, on October 18, 1901, Santos-Dumont made plans for his last attempt at the record flight.

With a dash of the theatrics that were his trademark, he called on M. Deutsch, chairman of the judging committee for the prize, at two o'clock in the morning. Angrily the older man demanded to know why he had been aroused from his slumber. In a voice of all innocence the airman explained that he contemplated a flight at two o'clock on the afternoon of the nineteenth of October and was giving the required twenty-four-hour notice. Santos-Dumont's arithmetic was bad, but his spirit was lively.

The Central Meteorological Bureau predicted unfavorable

weather for the nineteenth, but the dashing aeronaut was undaunted in his preparations.

Grudgingly, M. Deutsch appeared at the air station early on the appointed afternoon. The threatening clouds had begun to disburse, and Santos-Dumont ordered the filling of the gasbags. At half past two the great barn doors were pulled open. Several strong young men maneuvered the inflated dirigible onto the field. Santos-Dumont sat inside the basket in a dramatic pose, his straw hat forward at a rakish angle. As the judges drew near, he tipped his hat jauntily, and flashing the smile that gladdened female hearts, he leaned forward to shake the judges' outstretched hands. The gathered crowd of onlookers responded with great shouting.

A soft wind was blowing across the field and the dirigible bag, not fully filled, flapped slightly in the breeze. An assistant suggested more hydrogen for the balloon, but the spectators were becoming restive. He climbed from his basket, wrapped the starter strap around the flywheel, and with a dramatic gesture gave a hearty yank. The engine started but with a certain amount of roughness. Santos-Dumont let it warm for a moment, and after checking the sand ballast and the guide rope rigged to the rudder, he mounted the basket for takeoff. He waved his hand and the ropes were released. The balloon rose quickly as the race against the clock began and a helpful quartering wind carried it swiftly toward the Eiffel Tower. As Santos-Dumont described it:

> The official start took place at 2:42 P.M. In spite of the wind striking me sidewise with a tendency to take me to the left of the Eiffel Tower, I held my course straight to that goal. Gradually, I drove the airship onward and upward to a height of about ten meters above its summit. In doing this I lost some time, but secured myself against accidental contact with the Tower as much as possible.
>
> As I passed the Tower, I turned with a sudden movement of the rudder, bringing the airship around the Tower's lightning conductor at a distance of about fifty meters from it.

The Eiffel Tower was crowded with spectators who jammed the spiral staircase and the balconies and who cheered deliriously as the strange aerial machine approached. When the balloon and basket circled around and slightly above them, the exuberant

Parisians broke into a frenzied roar. But in the next instant the roar of the crowd became a startled gasp as the motor sputtered and popped dangerous backfires. With its engine choking and faltering, the dirigible lost momentum, drifted to a stop, and began slowly to sink down.

Then, as the throng of people watched in spellbound silence, Santos-Dumont, high above the Parisian rooftops in a fragile balloon-and-basket contrivance, stepped from his control basket and, catlike, walked along the metal bracing to the motor. The balloon, now subject to the wind, began to drift back toward the Eiffel Tower. Standing on a brace, Santos-Dumont bent over his motor, seemingly unaware that he was about to be dashed against the tall steel structure. Suddenly the motor came alive with a resounding roar. Billows of exhaust smoke thick with oil swirled around the aeronaut. The canvas-covered propellers whirred through the air and the dirigible lurched forward.

With acrobatic grace Santos-Dumont crossed back to the basket and dropped into the driver's seat. He flashed a smile and tossed a heroic wave toward the spectators into whom he had almost crashed. Their response was a thunderous cheer. He opened full throttle and his little engine responded with an energetic vibration. Trembling fiercely in its mount, it drove the airship toward Saint-Cloud. In a storybook finish, the dirigible crossed over the heads of the judges, with only one-half minute to spare. A record had been made, a prize won, and a hero acclaimed.

In the years to follow, however, the seven-mile closed-circuit run by Santos-Dumont would prove to be but a small step in the development of lighter-than-air ships. At the same time Santos-Dumont was gathering his accolades, a sixty-three-year-old German count, Ferdinand von Zeppelin, was working on a rigid-frame airship that was a giant by comparison with Santos-Dumont's craft. By 1908 Zeppelin's great dirigible balloons had been clearly successful, and by the end of World War I they were acknowledged worldwide as the aerial vehicles of the future.

All the great powers of the world quickly produced dirigibles of varying sizes and descriptions, but it was a zeppelin that carried man farthest in the most celebrated voyage of a lighter-than-air vessel. Count Zeppelin died on March 8, 1917, twelve years too soon to see his invention reach the moment of its greatest triumph and twenty years before its greatest tragedy and the end of an era.

In spite of the fact that by the late 1920's airplanes had captured the attentions of more and more of the airminded generation, the dirigible—gas within bags within a ribbed cage—was considered the practical method for aerial travel. The great majesty and serenity of the conveyance and the apparent stability of the lighter-than-air mammoths impressed the general public, despite a history of tragic accidents and failures.

It was in this general atmosphere that the most spectacular of all dirigible flights was launched. The voyage has almost faded from the memory of man, but in 1929, the round-the-world flight of the *Graf Zeppelin* was universally hailed as a milestone in aviation and the beginning of a grand new era of air travel.

Dr. Hugo Eckener, the German airship captain and protégé of Count Zeppelin, had directed the construction of the luxury airship intended for commercial air travel. Christened the *Graf Zeppelin*, the dirigible was 776 feet in length, longer than two football fields. It carried over three and one half million cubic

The *Graf Zeppelin*, with a longitudinal section and the plan of the car for navigating officers and passengers.
**(National Air and Space Museum, The Smithsonian Institution)**

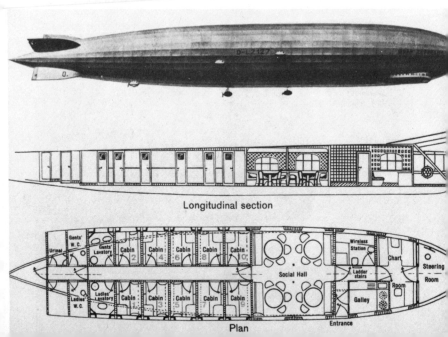

Longitudinal section

Plan

feet of hydrogen. Tucked under the front of the massive semirigid balloon was an ornate and comfortable car much like a railroad car. The front of the car was the bridge, or control room. Behind this was a chart and radio room, followed by a kitchen, then a dining room and lounge, five staterooms, lavatories, and finally a baggage compartment. A caboose area containing an emergency steering room faced rearward.

Behind the car, near the lower stern of the dirigible frame, hung five engine gondolas, each housing a 550-horsepower engine and propeller plus a control station within the gondola. One man rode at each control station to operate the engine, which in turn was commanded from the bridge. These gondolas were entered by ladders from the dirigible bag, the crewmen passing along girders and longitudinal catwalks to reach the gondolas and the bridge.

The *Graf Zeppelin* carried a crew of forty-one and had passenger space for twenty.

In November, 1928, the airship, piloted by Dr. Eckener, had set a world record for distance flight in a straight-line course

One of the five engine gondolas that were hung from the dirigible frame.
**(National Air and Space Museum, The Smithsonian Institution)**

for a lighter-than-air vehicle by flying from Lakehurst, New Jersey, to Friedrichshafen, Germany—a distance of 3,967 miles. This record, officially recognized by the F.A.I., stands unbroken to this date, as well as the duration record of 71 hours and 7 minutes for the same flight.

Because the airship was thus accredited, the announcement by Dr. Eckener that the *Graf Zeppelin* would make a special flight completely around the earth with paying passengers generated pandemic excitement. The trip was boosted and largely financed by the newspaperman William Randolph Hearst, who paid handsomely for the exclusive American rights to the story of the global journey.

In 1924, the earth had been circumnavigated by air for the first time by eight U.S. Army fliers. Their flight was a daring adventure filled with physical hardships and extraordinary dangers. It was a journey that could only have been made by skilled and fearless men—professional airmen. In 1927, the world had acclaimed the New York-to-Paris flight of Charles A. Lindbergh. It, too, was the deed of an expert aviator. By striking contrast, Hugo Eckener's magnificent dirigible was offering an adventure without danger, a round-the-world flight in virtual Pullman comfort. The passengers were ordinary people, people without aviation expertise, people whose only prerequisite was $2,500 apiece for their luxury fare.

The fact that the *Graf Zeppelin* would carry passengers around the world in armchair comfort was the extraordinary feature of the voyage and produced glowing superlatives in the newspaper that sponsored the voyage.

The Hearst papers sent Karl H. von Wiegand and Lady Drummond Hay on the trip as reporters to chronicle the epic voyage. On August 6, 1929, Lady Hay wrote:

> "How do you feel?" everyone asks me curiously these days. Even in this age of marvels it is a superlatively great adventure to circle the whirling earth in the air like a man-made satellite of a planet, in defiance of the law of gravitation and God-begotten elements.
>
> The very idea itself is colossal, presumptuous in a way, if you look at it from the Almighty's point of view. I am not the least bit nervous, firmly believing in a successful outcome

of the epoch-making expedition which comet-wise will blaze
a glittering trail for all the lighter-than-air craft now under construction and for future experiment.

There were those who believed that dirigibles were possessed
of too many natural limitations to have any meaningful future
and that the airplane would be the vehicle of the air age. But
advocates of lighter-than-air craft argued that airplanes were too
uncertain while the dirigible had proven its stability and capacity.
Neither group paid the slightest attention to an obscure scientist
named Robert H. Goddard, who was building a liquid-fueled
rocket engine, as an even more exciting means of aerial locomotion. But in 1929, the rocket was only a toy. The giant balloon
held the center of the stage.

In the early hours of August 8, 1929, the *Graf Zeppelin,* floating
gently in the still air, was moved from the hangar at Lakehurst,
New Jersey. It was loaded and ready for flight. Brilliant
searchlights flooded the area, turning night into day. Ten thousand
spectators had waited late into the night to witness the historic

This photograph of Dr. Hugo Eckener, the captain of the *Graf Zeppe-lin,* was taken at his control position in the bridge.
**(National Air and Space Museum, The Smithsonian Institution)**

launching. Upon command, the ropes were released and the silver airship rose, nose first, into the darkness and headed in the direction of New York.

The next few minutes were described by Karl H. von Wiegand:

> It was at 12:40 o'clock, eastern standard time, when New York's millions of gleaming lights spread out below us, and the towering buildings appeared like an inverted firmament. All the passengers were fascinated by the roar of whistles and sirens by which the mighty city bade Godspeed to the majestic airliner. All were thrilled by the roar that swelled up and overwhelmed us.
>
> Dr. Eckener, his face wreathed in smiles and beaming as I have rarely seen him, comes up to me from the bridge, slapping a strong, firm hand on my shoulder, and says:
>
> "Isn't that great!"
>
> We passed the starting line, the Statue of Liberty—her torch gleaming out in the light-dotted darkness of the harbor—at 12:45, and entered upon that epic of the air, the round-the-world cruise. Dr. Eckener was visibly in an intense emotional mood as we went out over the harbor. In almost a whisper, he confided:
>
> "At 12:45 we made our curtsy to the guardian goddess. We are off around the world—off on our greatest trip!"
>
> We started right up the coast, traveling close to seventy miles an hour.

The *Graf Zeppelin* passed through the air with a remarkable smoothness. During daylight hours the inside of the cabin was brilliantly lit by large windows that gave the passengers an observation-tower panorama of the passing scenery. The *Zeppelin*'s passengers enjoyed a far more exciting and detailed view of the landscape than do today's air travelers, as the airship seldom flew more than a thousand feet above the water or ground surface. In the bravado and camaraderie of the common adventure, the passengers and the ship's officers were a happy and genial group. As Lady Hay noted, "It is like going to a party three times a day in a small town—we meet the same people all the time and chat over delicacies that no home kitchen provides for work-a-day occasions."

By the afternoon of August 10, the *Graf Zeppelin* had passed above England and France and reached Friedrichshafen. Passing through low clouds and mist rising from the surrounding hills, the silver ship headed down toward the waters of Lake Constance and the airfield nearby. Hundreds of young German boys had gathered at the site to aid in landing the dirigible. As it drifted slowly over the field, the ropes were grabbed and the ship pulled to the ground. The troop of boys then marched the dirigible into the hangar. Huge crowds surged forward. Once inside the hangar, Dr. Eckener emerged from the ship to a great ovation from the happy throng.

After a four-day layover in Germany, the *Graf Zeppelin* was ready for the next and longest leg of her trip: eastward to Tokyo.

Special Russian representatives were taken aboard, a necessary condition for permission to cross that vast nation. By the early dawn of August 15, the *Zeppelin* was once again ready for flight.

Through the early dawn the ship sailed eastward, toward Berlin, the Baltic countries, and Russia.

"Rapidly the mists and fogs melted away from the earth and the sphere became clear in detail as a vast relief map," wrote von Wiegand. "Medieval towns, with walls, towers, isolated castles and clusters of peasant dwellings with red-tiled roofs, stood out picturesquely against the green background. We began breakfast over the beautiful city of Nuremburg at 6:45. Captain Lehmann, Lady Hay, Sir Hubert Wilkins and Colonel Iselin and I sat together. A little later, Commodore Eckener came in from the bridge and ordered one egg and coffee."

In two days the silver airship had reached the wastelands of Siberia.

Von Wiegand continued:

> Flying at the rate of seventy-five miles an hour, it took us a full sixty minutes to pass through the dense smoke of vast forest fires after crossing the Ural Mountain chain this afternoon. Even the leaping flames and glowing forests were visible in the distance through the pall.
>
> When we crossed the Ural Mountains, with Mount Konjakofski to the south peeking through the clouds, the *Graf* began to panic the ignorant peasants below us. This kept up throughout Siberia and had been noticeable in the unpopulous regions of Eastern Russia.
>
> Many of the peasants, who have never seen a train, evidently

mistake the Zeppelin, with its thrumming motors and sylph-like speed and lines, for a celestial monster. We saw villagers run wildly into forests and houses and gather around churches, gazing to the sky in awe and terror.

Without difficulty, the *Zeppelin* flew out over the wastelands of Siberia, traveling for five thousand miles over uncharted, frozen vastnesses, virginal forests, meandering rivers, and monotonously patterned gray-green swamps and marshes. Endless desolation. Within the car, the temperature dropped and the crew and passengers bundled warmly against the penetrating cold.

"From Vologda, in the Urals," wrote Sir Hubert Wilkins, one of the passengers, "we passed fertile farms and villages and mountains in a sixty-mile wide area, all bathed in smokey haze. In the east beyond to the Yenissei River, over which we sailed at about 11:15 P.M. last night, eastern daylight time, it was practically a swamp, almost devoid of human life.

"There were some trails, a few tepee tents, shaggy people, shaggy horses and wolf-like dogs, a few birds. In the water we could see, occasionally, large fish near the surface."

As night fell over the hostile wastelands of Siberia, Hugo Eckener, in the control cabin, watched the barometer and looked out at increasing turbulence. In consultation with weather experts on board, he had determined that their course would be carrying the *Graf Zeppelin* near a low-pressure area with narrow isobars—rapid barometric pressure changes—and hence fast-moving winds. He did not fear the storm associated with the low, but rather was planning to alter his route to take full advantage of the prevailing counterclockwise rotation of the winds in the cyclonic depression. To effect this flight path, he flew a constant barometric pressure line, thus keeping his ship in an invisible aerial corridor of predictable winds and constant distance from the center core of the storm.

Within the airship there was irregular buffeting and occasional light squalls drumming rain pellets noisily along the taut skin of the monstrous ship.

Deep inside the oblong envelope of the dirigible the crew chiefs made continuous inspections of the balloonets and rigging. Beneath their feet they could feel the twisting of the beams as the mammoth airship groaned and creaked within the hollow cavernous interior. The men in the engine gondolas below could also feel the swaying of the giant craft.

On the afternoon of August 19, the *Zeppelin* swung over the naval base at Kasumi-ga-ura, Japan, where the ship was to land. Before landing, however, it was flown over Tokyo and Yokohama, cruising at only a few hundred feet above the rooftops to give as many people as possible a chance to see the airship.

The enthusiasm of the Japanese people, officially and unofficially, for the colossal airship was overwhelming. The captain, crew, and passengers were feted in an endless round of celebrations and overwhelming hospitality—business luncheons, theater parties, teas, and dinners—and the staff of flight officers were decorated and honored by the highest-ranking government officials. From the Imperial Palace, a spokesman for the Emperor, in honoring Commodore Eckener, announced in a wry prophecy: "No other nation need fear Japan will ever engage in a militaristic program of airship building."

The following morning was dark with storm clouds and flashes of lightning. Placing the passengers on half-hour notice, Hugo Eckener waited for favorable weather conditions. By two in the afternoon, the storm had passed. Within the hour, 450 sailors began walking the *Zeppelin* from the hangar. Once it was clear, the engines were started and the huge airship rose majestically over the cheering crowds. The mountainous Island Empire disappeared to the stern, as the *Graf Zeppelin* flew out over the Pacific Ocean.

At two-thirty the following morning, when they were 750 miles northeast of Japan, the voyagers encountered a formidable line of thunderheads. Eckener ordered the valving of hydrogen—the releasing of gas to permit the airship to descend to a more stable altitude. This was to avoid the necessity of valving the highly explosive gas when they were near the static discharge of lightning. The chief navigator took the elevator helm, and Eckener ordered the rudder hard to the right to veer the ship away from the worst of the approaching thunderheads. Within the giant bag, crewmen held tightly to the bracings along the catwalk as the rigid frame twisted in the turn. The airship "plunged into the inky black wall at the point Dr. Eckener thought was the weakest. We were caught in an uprushing current of tremendous force, and the *Graf* was carried up more than 300 feet in a few seconds. Then it plunged downward like a rock,'' von Wiegand related and continued on:

> Wittemann's skillful handling of the elevator wheel quickly had the ship on an even keel, at 900 feet above the turbulent Pacific, while the glare of lightning was our footlight in this great drama of aerial achievement.
>
> The *Graf* bucked like a bronco jumping stiff-legged, or trying to jump over a mountain. It all came quickly. Half of the passengers had no idea what was going on and two of them slept through it all.
>
> Commander Rosendahl and Lieutenant Richardson, with William B. Leeds and a few others, were hanging out of the windows watching the play of the elements, it being the first time that the big German airship ever encountered real lightning.
>
> Commander Eckener came from the bridge into the dining room and seemed to be feeling in good spirits as he announced: "We have broken through. The worst is over."

From the cloud and storm the *Zeppelin* entered Aleutian fogbanks and flew in and out of fog intermittently for several days.

At six-fifteen on the evening of August 25, with the lowering sun far astern, the *Graf Zeppelin* cast a long shadow over all who stared in wonder at the airship as it passed seven hundred feet above the Golden Gate. Airplanes flew out to greet the *Zeppelin,* and below, in the harbor, warships and private craft blew their horns in salute. After circling the business district of San Francisco, the dirigible turned southward for Los Angeles, where she was landed at 5:36 A.M. the next day.

Hugo Eckener allowed only the balance of the day for a brief rest and refueling, ordering the ship ready for takeoff by nightfall. Most of the scheduled celebrations had to be canceled, but at an early evening banquet Eckener was honored in a short ceremony attended by two thousand notables and other guests. The captain, his staff, and the passengers hurried directly from the banquet table to the *Zeppelin*'s moorings and the takeoff on the final leg of the epoch-making journey.

In the rush of the takeoff the dirigible nearly met with disaster.

The *Graf Zeppelin* in Los Angeles on its around-the-world flight.
**(National Air and Space Museum, The Smithsonian Institution)**

The night air had cooled during the two-hour banquet and caused the vessel to be slightly sluggish in its lift-off. The natural buoyancy of the craft, the release of ballast, and the upturned elevators, biting air as the five engines propelled the ship forward, all contributed to the ability of the airship to lift from the airfield. However, in the fading twilight no one noticed the high-tension wires running along one end of Mines Field, directly in the path of the ascending dirigible. They were seen only as the airship bore toward them, too late for action. There was only time for prayer as the passenger car cleared the lines by less than a foot and placidly continued its majestic climb northeastward.

Weariness from the long journey and the evening's celebrations had drained much of the earlier enthusiasm from the passengers, causing most of them to sink with relief into their small bunks. Their rest was soon disturbed, however, when the airship ran into strong and turbulent winds roaring across the vast openness of the American Southwest. The air was clear, but in the three-dimensional sea of frothing winds the silver dirigible rose in the currents to altitudes as high as six thousand feet and then sank to five hundred feet. Traveling like a roller coaster, the dirigible was solely at the mercy of the invisible air currents over the rugged land.

On August 28, the dirigible reached Chicago. The approach of the round-the-world *Zeppelin* had been well heralded. Its arrival was greeted with a blare of whistles and throngs of spectators crowding the streets and buildings to greet the historic vessel. Again, airplanes of all descriptions flew up to inspect and give welcome to the giant craft.

After a flyover of Chicago, the *Zeppelin* headed eastward, flying low for display over several other large cities.

The following day, the voyagers reached New York City and crossed the official finish line of their flight—the Statue of Liberty. The *Graf Zeppelin* had flown nineteen thousand miles in 21 days, 7 hours, and 34 minutes.

New York greeted the triumphant return of the captain, crew, and passengers with the honors only that great city can bestow.

"Tons of spouting water in the harbor, tons of falling ticker-tape—humanity packed upon humanity along the canyons of a world metropolis that all but halted to honor their coming," reported von Wiegand. "Dr. Eckener, the twinkle in his eyes undiminished along that long trail of welcome, bowed modestly, smiled modestly and made a new triumph of that glorious reception.

"He was led through the cheering thousands, into the colonial dignity of the City Hall, into the aldermanic chambers, garlanded and decorated in his honor, where Mayor Jimmy Walker, with newspaper publisher Paul Block and other officials, awaited him."

A record had been made. It was the longest flight in a lighter-than-air craft and the first aerial craft to carry passengers around the world. With a splendid record in the books and accolades coming from everywhere, including a personal welcome and plaudits from President Herbert Hoover in a special Washington ceremony, the dirigible as a vehicle for commercial aviation reached its finest hour. Plans were already in the making for a fleet of dirigibles carrying passengers and cargo to travel the airways across the Atlantic.

After the completion of its famous flight, the *Graf Zeppelin* (later joined by a larger sister ship, the *Hindenburg*) made over six hundred flights, 181 of which were intercontinental. For a five-year period the *Graf Zeppelin* was used for a regular passenger service between Germany and Brazil, the Friedrichshafen-Pernambuco Line, and the *Hindenburg* was put into service as a Frankfurt-to-New York transport. During these years, in England, France, and the United States, many military dirigibles were built, and they performed major patrol work.

The great whales of the sky grew larger and more complex. Their triumphs, however, were in the ever darkening shadow of tragedy, as the history of dirigibles became a trail of twisted wreckage—the U. S. Navy ships *Shenandoah, Akron,* and *Macon,* the British R-38 and R-101, the French *Dixmude.* In the end it was the incineration in 1937 of the *Hindenburg* at Lakehurst, New Jersey—probably caused by a spark of static electricity from the mooring post in the supercharged atmosphere of an approaching thunderstorm—that wrote a fiery finish to the dirigible dream. Dirigible builders, governments, and the public never again put trust in the giant airships.

A later generation of Montgolfiers have played an important role in scientific exploration, in the form of high-altitude balloons, and in national defense and naval convoy patrol, in the form of nonrigid airships, or blimps. But the significant long-distance records of lighter-than-air craft were made by dirigibles such as the *Graf Zeppelin.*

# CHAPTER 9

# Aviators Reach for Distant Shores

By the end of World War I the airplane had evolved into a promising means of transportation. Aviators and airplanes were in more than adequate supply and there was a great public interest in aerial exploits. An Aeronautical Exposition opened in New York in the spring of 1919, drawing huge crowds to view the vast assortment of aircraft on display at Madison Square Garden. The event was a symbol of the new era, as a newspaper writer aptly observed: "The domination of the air has been won, and securely won; and the whole direction of our life is likely to be changed in consequence."

Changes undoubtedly were going to take place and young aviators with their sights on distant horizons were ready to lead the way. The adventure and the glory of intercontinental air travel stirred their hearts and the attention of the public.

In England, two Australian brothers, Ross and Keith Smith, were readying a converted bomber for an attempt to fly from London to Australia. The Australian government had offered a prize of ten thousand pounds (46,000 dollars) to the first person accomplishing the feat within thirty days.

The airplane they selected for the eleven-thousand-mile flight was a "Vimy" bomber built by the Vickers Company with two Rolls-Royce Eagle VIII engines, producing 360 horsepower each. The bi-winged plane had a wingspan of sixty-seven feet, weighed thirteen thousand pounds, and cruised at eighty miles per hour with a thirteen-hour flying range. In spite of the vast size of

The two Australian brothers, Keith and Ross Smith.
*(The National Geographic Society)*

"The airplane they selected for the 11,000 mile flight to Australia was a Vickers Vimy bomber."

*(The National Geographic Society)*

the airplane, the pilot, copilot, and two mechanics flew in open tandem cockpits.

The Vickers Vimy, specially rigged, was in readiness in November, 1919, to carry the Smith brothers and their mechanics, W. H. Shiers and J. M. Bennett, to Australia. On November 12, blusterous and stormy weather turned fair and the adventurers were quickly aloft and flying southward. Their proposed route would carry them across France, Italy, Greece, then over the Mediterranean to Egypt, across the Holy Land to Baghdad, through Persia, India, Burma, Siam, into the Dutch East Indies, and finally, and hopefully, to their destination, the city of Darwin. (Others, too, had their eyes on the ten-thousand-pound prize money. Among them was a French contestant, M. Poulet, who left England in a small Caudron racing plane well ahead of the Smith brothers.)

There was the feeling of exhilaration among the four men, as they flew out over the English Channel with the wind in their faces and a great adventure ahead.

"The machine was flying stately and steady as a rock," recalled Ross Smith. "All the bracing wires were tuned to a nicety; the dope on the huge planes glinted and glistened in the sunlight; I was filled with admiration. The engines, which were throttled down to about three-quarters of their possible speed, had settled down to their task and were purring away in perfect unison and harmony."

Flying at four thousand feet, they reached the coast of France and immediately plunged into a cloud bank. Rime ice began to form on the plane and its occupants while snow swirled around them. Ross Smith applied power to climb through the dangerous clouds. They rose steadily in a wide, ascending spiral, until they broke through the top of the storm at nine thousand feet into the bright blue sky and brilliant sunlight, dazzling white on the cloud deck below. Keith Smith plotted their path and passed the information forward to his brother, who immediately swung the airplane onto its course. For three hours they held to a steady compass heading over the white, billowing cumulus, while Keith marked the chart in fifteen-minute increments, tracking their course over the hidden land below by dead reackoning.

The cold grew more intense. Their hands and feet lost all feeling as the icy wind penetrated their thick coveralls, and flying became clumsy as well as painful. Condensation from their breath salted their faces and face masks with a crystal-like white crust.

For over six hours the aviators battled the cold and held their course. Finally Keith motioned downward and pointed to a mark on the map where his calculations indicated they should be.

The almost limitless cloud sea stretched from horizon to horizon; the only break lay directly beneath them. The opening resembled a tremendous crater, with sides cut clear in a vertical shaft to the dark land below. Ross Smith throttled the craft back for a quick descent. Down through the opening spiraled the Vimy, bounding in the uneven currents as it descended. Down the gaping gateway, seven thousand feet deep, the airplane dropped. Beneath the clouds they found Lyons, precisely where Keith Smith had calculated it should be.

From Lyons, they crossed the Alps, flew down the Italian boot, over the Mediterranean to Crete and Libya, then westward to Egypt. Ross Smith noted: "We were not sorry to descry those landmarks of the ages, the Pyramids, and soon we could pick out the minarets and mosques of the Egyptian capital itself."

The landing at Cairo was easily made, completing a 680-mile, seven-and-one-half hour flight.

In the large crowd greeting the flyers were several wartime comrades. There was a brief celebration before they attended to their engines.

"It was quite like old times," remarked Ross, "to climb into a car, to spin through well known thoroughfares to Shepheard's Hotel to sink luxuriously into the arms of a great and familiar lounge chair, and to yearn over the events that had happened since last I occupied it."

While the Smith brothers were at Shepheard's a messenger brought a cable from General Borton, Ross's former commanding officer, congratulating them on their safe arrival in Egypt and wishing good luck for the next stage.

"While I was reading this kind remembrance from my old C.O.," Ross continued, "an Arab paperboy came crying his wares, and I bought a newssheet and read with amused interest the story of our doings during the last few days. I also read, with a shock of keen regret, of the accident that had befallen our gallant competitors, Lieutenants Douglas and Ross, who had both been killed practically at the starting post, just a few days after we left, through the crashing of their machine."

The next morning the Australia-bound flyers took off from Cairo's Leliopolis aerodrome and headed eastward across the barren wastelands. Unable to reach Baghdad during daylight because of a strong headwind, they made a forced landing on the old Ramadie battlefield forty miles short of their destination. Fifty soldiers from a nearby army encampment of the Tenth Indian Lancers suffered through a howling sandstorm as they held the giant airplane in the face of the wind. In Karachi, the gateway to the subcontinent of India, they were greeted with the heartening news that Poulet was at Delhi, only one day's flight ahead of them. This was a great surprise to the airmen, since they had fully expected the Frenchman to be well on his way to Singapore. The news added zest to the contest. Knowing that the Vimy was superior to Poulet's Caudron in both speed and range, they began to consider the race as good as won.

After a night at Karachi, the Smiths and their crew took off for Delhi, which lay 750 miles to the east. This was to be one of their longest legs, requiring a flight of nine hours.

That afternoon the Vimy encountered violent turbulence. A great rolling of the air created by strong convective currents boiling invisibly in the afternoon heat tossed the airplane about like a small vessel in a heavy sea. Ross Smith enjoyed the bronco ride as "welcome diversion" from the earlier flights of the past few days, in which boredom and sleepiness had been the enemy. Now he was in perpetual motion, maintaining level flight, keeping the machine straight, and fighting the air pockets and bumps into which they plunged and fell.

In the late afternoon the flyers reached the great Indian city, where they were greeted by an excited band of R.A.F. officials and friends. The flight thus far had set a record—a distance of 5,870 miles from London to Delhi in thirteen days. Their spirits, however, were dampened by the news that Poulet had left Delhi that morning and was still one day ahead.

From Delhi, after a good rest and a minor overhaul of their engines, they followed the course of the Ganges River to Allahabad, where they learned Poulet was on his way to Calcutta.

At the first ray of the next morning's sun, they were ready to fly to the same place. But trouble came from an unexpected quarter.

With its two Rolls-Royce Eagle VIII's roaring their harmony, the Vimy bounced across the field, ready for takeoff. From a nearby pasture, a thick-necked bull charged on the field and bellowed his own special prowess. As the airplane swung into the wind, the bull swung around to face it. He lowered his head and snorted as his front hooves tore the ground. Ross Smith raced the engines to frighten the animal. The bull jumped, afraid; but then thought better of running away and turned again to challenge the strange noisy bird. For a moment beast and machine were motionless, each awaiting a move by the other.

Smith held his engines at the idle for fear of causing the bull to make a disastrous charge. From the crowd a small boy rushed out to the prancing bovine. The bull, seeing an adversary more familiar in form, turned toward the boy and gave chase. The heroic toreador dove under a fence and the airmen seized their moment. Smith opened the throttle and the airplane leaped across the field and into the air. As the bomber rolled away the bull turned and pursued it until it winged over the fence and climbed out of sight.

From India the four Englishmen flew to Burma, still pursuing the elusive Poulet. As they circled the aerodrome at Akyab in southwest Burma, Keith Smith peered over the side and began gesturing wildly while Bennett and Shiers waved joyfully from their cockpit. All pointed down to the ground, where a small machine was parked near the center of the field. It was Poulet.

Their French competitor was the first to greet them on landing. He ran to the Vimy with a cheery smile and outstretched hand. The two machines, parked side by side, looked like an eagle and a sparrow. The Vimy towered above the tiny Caudron, which appeared to Ross Smith as altogether too frail for the hazards of flying that were still to come.

The next morning Poulet flew off first, followed several hours later by the Smith brothers. Flying a larger, faster machine, they arrived first at the next destination, Rangoon.

Because Poulet was unable to get his airplane ready in time for a double takeoff, the Smith brothers moved into the lead the following morning. Their flight was to Moulmein and then across a mountain range into the valley of the Irrawaddy River en route to Bangkok. The maps they carried, while very sketchy, showed the mountains to have peaks that reached seven thousand feet. Poulet was bid good-bye and was never heard from again as a serious contender.

Leaving Moulmein, the flyers headed southeast over country that rapidly became mountainous. But instead of encountering lofty summits, they approached a towering mass of cumulus clouds that reached to the stratosphere and extended on the horizon without visible break. The monsoon season was beginning and Ross concluded that one of the initial storms was probably ahead. Somewhere in the swirling clouds were the high peaks they would have to cross. The prospect was awesome. If this was the beginning of the monsoon, however, each day would bring a storm of even greater intensity and duration; so they plunged ahead.

The plane circled as the pilots consulted by gestures, shouts, and messages. Finally they agreed their safest course was to climb above the cloud mass, or at least to an altitude sufficient to clear the mountaintops. At nine thousand feet they emerged above the first layer, but eastward the clouds appeared to terrace up gradually, and in the distance there was still another great wall of cloud, towering several thousand feet higher.

Keith Smith took observations with the drift indicator and found to his dismay that they would be flying into a twenty-mile-an-hour head wind. There was no choice, however. Setting the compass bearing, he plunged into the cloudy mist and the dark unknown that lay beyond it.

At the bomber's ceiling of eleven thousand feet, they were still flying blind in the clouds. Ross Smith held to the compass course. Below the Vimy lay jagged mountain peaks buried by cloud. Ahead, around, and behind, the mist enfolded it in an impenetrable screen. If a sudden vertical current should topple the plane into a spin or if Ross should suddenly get vertigo, craggy mountains awaited in the squalls below.

The maps indicated that a flight of fifty miles should carry the bomber across the mountain range. After one hour, Ross and Keith decided that they were now above the valley, safely beyond the mountains.

Trusting their navigational abilities and the accuracy of their dead reckoning Ross shut off both engines and entered a power-off glide. He held up the nose of the machine to make their descent as slow as possible—forty miles an hour. The maneuver was like the captain of a sailing vessel plying uncharted shoal waters —expecting every moment to feel a crunch, but praying it never comes. Lower and lower the Vimy dropped—ten, nine, eight thousand feet. All eyes peered over the sides and strained to pierce the misty clouds.

As they approached the seven-thousand-foot level, the height of the mountain range, Ross flattened his glide. A small hole opened in the cloud, with something dark beneath. It was past in a flash, but Ross instantly pushed the throttle full open to level the plane even more. Was it the top of a mountain peak or the darkness of a valley far below? Deciding it was the lattter, Ross Smith once more shut off the engines and glided lower. When they had descended to four thousand feet without striking a mountainside, Ross concluded that the range had, indeed, been crossed; and the danger over.

A few minutes later, they burst into full view of a tree-carpeted glorious world just fifteen hundred feet below. They had traveled from night into day—from a nightmare into a bright awakening. Ross was soaked with perspiration as they completed their leg with a landing at Don Muang, the airfield of the Siamese Flying Corps, fifteen miles north northeast of Bangkok.

After a restful night for the pilots, and a night's work on the engines for the mechanics (who slept during flight in the aft cockpit on a few pillows amid the jumble of spare parts), the four men took off for Singora, halfway down the Malay peninsula. This portion of the journey was almost entirely through monsoon rain squalls, but by flying just off the coast they were able to avoid collision with mountains and hills and at the same time use known landmarks to maintain their course.

When the flyers reached Singora, the aerodrome was at least half underwater. There was, however, a narrow strip along the center which appeared more or less dry, but it required a cross-wind landing. Ross buzzed over the field to examine the strip, and to his great dismay observed that it was covered with the stumps of small trees.

Around and around the field they flew, but there was no other place to land. Down they went, with Ross flying just above a stall as he eased the bomber onto the narrow strip of stump-studded ground.

Touching down, he expected to feel the jolt of the undercarriage being wrenched off at any moment, or the machine going over on its nose.

Miraculously, however, the Vickers Vimy came to rest with only a damaged tail skid. When the aviators retraced their landing, they found several instances where the wheels had missed stumps a foot to eighteen inches high by a few inches.

That night, with the aid of three Englishmen who lived in this remote part of the Malay peninsula, materials were located for the ingenious mechanics to fashion a new tail-skid. At the same time, the monsoon rains reached Singora and men, plane, and airfield were buffeted by gale-force winds and soaked by a downpour. This left them with an agonizing decision the following morning: they had the choice of attempting a takeoff over the stump-strewn high ridge or through wheel-deep water. They elected the latter, finally struggling and splashing back into the air. Once aloft, they turned southward along the railway line and then followed the coast to Singapore.

At Singapore the only airfield was the racetrack, but a track smaller than those they had used in India. To effect a short-field landing, the adventurers devised a precarious flying maneuver.

Slow-flying the machine—that is, dragging the plane in a nose-high altitude at a flying speed just barely above a stall—Ross Smith brought it sluggishly over the end of the track and in a powered approach eased the bomber gradually onto the ground. In the rear cockpit, Bennett was leaning toward the tail poised to move quickly. As the wheels kissed the turf, Bennett, half-crawling and half-slithering, moved down the top of the fuselage to the rear empennage. The weight of his body forced the tail down and the sudden change of altitude with the elevator in the down position completed the landing stall. The Vimy stopped with a hundred feet from touchdown.

The takeoff was equally precarious, although performed without acrobatic finesse on Bennett's part. Once in the sky they swept wide above Singapore and headed for the open sea and Java, their destination. On the way they ran into characteristic doldrum weather—calm winds and isolated thunderstorm clouds from which rain poured down to the sea in thick, dark columns. Along the coast of Sumatra, the aviators encountered a light head wind and very bumpy flying conditions. One convective current dropped the airplane with extraordinary force, lifting their stomachs into their diaphragms and causing the wings almost to flap.

"That's the equator," announced Keith Smith, who by dead reckoning had calculated that the big bump had dropped them across the line into the Southern Hemisphere.

Cruising above mangrove-fringed bays and tranquil islets surrounded by turquoise waters, the Vickers Vimy winged on to Batavia—now Djakarta—where Ross Smith put down at the Dutch Flying School's Kaledjat airfield. The next day they flew the length of Java to land at Surabaja, where the bi-winged giant touched gracefully onto the grassy aerodrome and then cut deeply into mud that squished softly beneath a thin later of grass.

The takeoff from Surabaja took two days and was accomplished only with the aid of a long double row of bamboo mats placed like a railroad track in front of the airplane. During the first attempt at takeoff, the mats had blown dangerously into the air and against the plane. Ross Smith cut the engines and the mats were replaced, this time carefully pegged into the soft turf. The second attempt was successful and the Vimy was airborne. The flyers learned later that most of the mats had been brought in by natives from the roofs of their huts for this spectacular purpose.

Across the jungles and along the coast of Bali and Lombok, flying at two thousand feet, they held a straight compass course to Bima, Atambua, and then over the Indian Ocean on to the final leg of their journey.

"It was just 2.6 P.M. when as our diary prosaically notes, we 'observed Australia,'" wrote Ross Smith, "At three o'clock we not only observed it, but rested firmly upon it, for having circled over Darwin and come low enough to observe the crowds and the landing-place, we settled on Terra Australia on December 10th, twenty-seven days and twenty hours after taking off from Hounslow."

The four men received an official welcome from the administrator of the Northern Territory and the mayor of Darwin, and then they were escorted from the field by two thousand cheering Australians.

Later, in Melbourne, Ross Smith noted: "Not the least pleasant incident upon our arrival finally in Melbourne was the paying over of the 10,000-pound prize money by the Prime Minister, the Right Hon. W. M. Hughes, on behalf of the Commonwealth Government. As all participated equally in the perils and labors of the enterprise, the prize was divided into four equal shares."

All of the world had anxiously followed the bulletins and press reports on the progress of the aviators, and their successful flight was a record universally hailed as a landmark for modern aviation.

In sixteen years to the month, a man had carried the development of the airplane from a flight of a few hundred feet in a precarious machine to a journey halfway around the world. A spectacular record had been made, but it was not an official F.A.I. record. Not all of the great flights of history have made it into the official F.A.I. book. Sometimes, as in this case, official F.A.I. timers were not available at the destination point. The Smith brothers hardly noticed the omission, however. They had won the coveted prize and they were later elevated to knighthood by George V, the King of England.

# CHAPTER 10

# The Airplane
# Circles the World

Inspired by the Smith brothers' successful flight from England to Australia, serious aviators were now setting their sights upon the ultimate in long-distance flight—the circumnavigation of the world.

Ross and Keith Smith were a logical team for this more difficult attempt, and in the early months of 1922 the brothers were completing plans for the flight, which, coincidentally, would celebrate the four-hundredth anniversary of the circumnavigation of the world by one of Magellan's ships.

For the world trip, the Smith brothers again looked to their reliable Vickers Vimy. This time the bomber was converted into an amphibian to accommodate the aviators on transoceanic flights and for use in those remote areas that had neither landing fields nor racetracks.

During one of the initial test flights Keith Smith was at the controls of the modified bomber with J. M. Bennett flying as mechanic. The flight characteristics of the plane had been materially changed by the addition of pontoons, and at fifteen hundred feet it unexpectedly stalled and fell wing over into a spin. Smith was not able to effect a recovery and the plane crashed, killing both men.

A second group of British flyers took up the challenge. For their attempt to circumnavigate the world they selected a *De Havilland 9* three-place biplane. Capt. Norman Macmillan was the pilot; his teammates were Capt. Geoffrey Malins and Maj. W. T. Blake, the organizer of the mission. They planned to use three separate airplanes, shipping the two additional ones to various points along the route as replacement ships. For the Pacific leg of the journey they would use a Fairey III floatplane.

When all was in readiness, Macmillan set off along the route already proven by the Smiths: down through Europe, across the Mediterranean Sea, then eastward across the desert. But misfortune beset the Englishmen almost from the beginning. In the desert sun their engines boiled and their fuel evaporated. White ants ate away the inside of their propellers, requiring them to await replacements. In India they ran headlong into drenching monsoons, and Major Blake was grounded with an attack of appendicitis. Macmillan and Malins continued the flight. In Calcutta the jungle dampness and the torrential rains warped the plywood pontoons on the Fairey III and the hastily patched floats barely got the machine out of the water.

The bad luck continued. Over the Bay of Bengal, an engine failed and the plane dropped, sputtering into the churning sea. For six harrowing days, Macmillan and Malins stayed with their slowly disintegrating craft. Rain squalls nearly drowned them and the burning tropical sun seared their skins and blistered their lips. Finally, the harbor master of Chittagong, their destination from Calcutta, set out in a steam launch along Macmillan's anticipated course and made a fortunate rescue.

Shrugging off the narrow escape, Captains Macmillan and Malins returned to England to seek new sponsors for another attempt at aerial circumnavigation. They were not successful.

In the spring of 1924, five nations prepared to launch aviators for the honor of being the first to fly around the world.

Capt. Stuart MacLaren left Calshot in a Vickers Vulture on March 15, 1924, in company with Flying Officer W. N. Plenderlerth and Sergeant R. Andrews in an attempt to win the blue ribbon for Great Britain. Initially, MacLaren's route roughly followed the one successfully flown by the Smith brothers. However, a forced landing near the shores of Avatcha Island in the Bering Sea, a broken airplane, and a wait for replacement parts grounded them until seasonal bad weather barred further flight.

To snatch the glory for his country, Major Pedro Zanni, an Argentinian aviator, with his mechanic Felipe Beltrane, left Amsterdam, Holland, in a German Fokker on July 22, 1924.

By August 19 they reached Hanoi, Indochina, but they then wrecked their aircraft on takeoff and were obliged to return home by boat.

A Portuguese airman, Cabral-Sacadura, who had already achieved fame by flying the South Atlantic, made plans to retrace the route of Magellan. He could not secure the necessary financial backing for this adventure, however. Two of his countrymen, Major Brito Paes and Major Sarmento Beires, had better luck and were able to enter the race for Portugal. They took off from Lisbon on April 2, 1924, and reached the Portuguese possession of Macao, where they cracked up their plane and ended Portugal's chances for the national honor.

In France, Capt. Peltier D'Oisy and his mechanic, Sergeant Besin, acquired a Breguet and on April 24, 1924, took off from Paris. Flying eastward, they reached Shanghai, where the airplane was destroyed as D'Oisy attempted a landing on a golf course. D'Oisy, also, returned home by boat.

Later that year an Italian pilot, Lt. Antonio Locatelli, made an effort to reap the glory for Italy with a high-performance Dornier WAL, an airplane in which he had originally intended to fly across the pole with Roald Amundsen. Locatelli began on a westward course. However, engine trouble forced him into the water off the coast of Labrador, requiring a sea rescue by an American warship.

Meanwhile, in America, the United States Army Air Service decided it would also attempt to send an airplane around the globe. After studying earlier failures, the Air Service carefully prepared the men, the machines, and—even more important—the logistics for the venture. Army officers were sent in advance around the world to map out a route and make plans for the depots and supplies needed for the journey. Four special airplanes were ordered from aircraft builder Donald Douglas. The amphibian biplanes, with fifty-foot wingspans, were powered by single four-hundred-horsepower Liberty engines.

In April, 1924, the U. S. Army Air Service was ready to field its team for the global record. Eight young men—four pilots and four mechanics—and their "World Cruisers" were in Seattle awaiting takeoff on a flight that would carry them around the world, farther than man had ever flown before.

Christening one of the Douglas amphibians at Seattle, Washington.
**(U.S. Air Force)**

The Air Service had selected a route that was markedly different from the routes of its competitors, but the American effort alone was to be successful. The flight was planned in a westerly direction instead of along the generally eastward course used by the others. The Air Service chose the westward route to enable its flyers to cross Alaska before it was completely fogbound, beat the typhoon season in Japan and China, outrace the monsoons of India and Burma, and make the final leg across the North Atlantic before the arctic winter gripped the northern seas in ice and fog. The Air Service effort was well organized with specially designed and constructed aircraft, carefully selected aviators and mechanics, and, finally, carefully considered plans and procedures.

On April 6, national attention was again focused upon Seattle, where for the third straight morning a great crowd huddled on the shore of Lake Washington to witness the start of the first flight around the world.

On the two previous mornings these same spectators had set their alarms early and made the trip to the lake, only to return home in disappointment. On the first day, heavy fog had made any attempt to take off an obvious impossibility. On the second day the commander of the expedition, Major Frederick L. Martin, flying the lead craft, the *Seattle,* had broken a propeller on takeoff and in his haste to replace it had dropped a wrench through the pontoons, causing a day's delay.

On the night of the fifth, President Coolidge had sent a *bon voyage* message: "More than 400 years ago men first circumnavigated the world. Two years were required, in which many hardships were encountered. Now men travel around the earth by land and water in twenty-eight days. You are going to demonstrate the practicability of making such a voyage by air. Before another 400 years this may be the safest and most comfortable way. Your countrymen will watch your progress with hope and record your success with pride."

Those who stood on the shores of Lake Washington that morning were soon rewarded by the hoarse sputter of Liberty 12 engines roaring across the open lake as the four planes, one after another, raced over the water, their pontoons etching parallels on the lake's smooth surface. The planes broke away, first the *Seattle,* then the *Chicago,* then the *New Orleans.* The fourth plane, the *Boston,* lumbered heavily and would not rise. Lieutenant Wade, the *Boston*'s pilot, discovered that the control wires to the elevator had not been properly adjusted and no matter how hard he pushed his wheel forward the elevator would not lift the empennage high enough to tilt the seaplane into the takeoff "step" position. A hurried adjustment corrected the defect, and the *Boston* roared from the lake, circled in a climbing turn, and headed westward to follow the other three ships.

Many of those who watched from the chilly shores of the lake had grave doubts that the flimsy craft could make so long a journey. Gen. Mason M. Patrick, Chief of the Air Service, commented: "In future years, when these planes are viewed in the National Museum, people will no doubt wonder, contrasting them with the air liners then in use, that men could be found who were bold enough to undertake so hazardous a voyage in such small and fragile craft, although they were the best planes of their type which could have been produced anywhere at the time when they were constructed."

In the flagship *Seattle,* Major Frederick L. Martin was accompanied by Sgt. Alva L. Harvey, who was a pilot as well as mechanic.

The second plane, the *Chicago,* was piloted by First Lt. Lowell H. Smith, the most experienced of all the expedition aviators with seventeen hundred flying hours. He had placed second in the Transcontinental Reliability and Endurance Contest flight from New York to San Francisco in 1919. And in 1923, Lieutenant Smith had conceived and carried out the refueling of an airplane in midair, although the first time he tried it was almost his last. The friend assisting him had accidently knocked open the valve as he grabbed for the dangling nozzle and gasoline, at the rate of fifty gallons per minute, had poured into the cockpit. If any of it had touched the red-hot exhaust manifold, the refueling would have ended in a huge orange puff. For a young man, his flying experience was vast and much needed on this expedition.

Smith's mechanic was First Lt. Leslie P. Arnold, who was also an experienced pilot as well as mechanic.

First Lt. Leigh Wade, the *Boston*'s pilot, had served with the American Expeditionary Forces of World War I as a test pilot, instructor, and finally as the commanding officer of the 120th Aero Squadron. His mechanic was Sgt. Henry H. Ogden, who, like the other noncommissioned officers on the flight, was commissioned as a second lieutenant at the completion of the world flight.

First Lt. Erik H. Nelson, a Swedish-born American, was the oldest of the voyagers and the most experienced cross-country flyer. He had served as the engineering officer on a Gulf-to-Pacific flight in 1919 and had flown from New York to Nome and returned, and from San Antonio to Puerto Rico the year before. He piloted the fourth plane, the *New Orleans,* and his mechanic was Second Lt. John Harding, Jr., who had served as a mechanic during the "Round the Rim" flight of the United States by Col. R. S. Hartz and Lt. E. E. Harmon in 1919.

These men had been carefully chosen from hundreds of volunteers for the round-the-world flight. After their selection they were sent to Langley Field, Virginia, for six weeks of intensive briefing. Their cram sessions at Langley ranged from meteorology to marine law, with lectures on the rudiments of surgery and medicine. From there they went to Santa Monica, California, to watch the World Cruisers being built so that they would be completely familiar with every detail of the planes' construction. This was time wisely spent and served them well in the months that followed.

The first day's flight was to take the planes along the western coast of Canada, the Queen Charlotte Sound and Hecate Strait to Prince Rupert on the coast of British Columbia. Soon after the flyers crossed the border into Canada, they entered a thick fogbank hanging sleepily over the coastal waters. As fog grew thicker the planes eased down to just above the water in order to maintain their course. Suddenly an excursion boat loomed ahead. The World Cruisers veered sharply to bypass it. "If we were surprised—and believe me, we were—I wonder what folks on that steamer thought when they saw a fleet of giant [*sic*] planes come swooping toward them out of the fog," commented Lt. Arnold.

The fog changed to a driving rain, which in turn gave way to sleet and finally a blinding snowstorm as they struggled the 650 miles to Prince Rupert.

After several days at Prince Rupert, they took off at nine-twenty on the morning of April 10, heading for Sitka, nestled among coastal mountains in the panhandle of Alaska. It was raining when the airmen flew low over the water to the island of Kuiu. Major Martin had decided to fly over the island rather than travel an extra seventy-five miles down the Sumner Strait to avoid Kuiu. Their route would carry them over a mile of rugged terrain where a forced landing for a pontoon-equipped plane would be disastrous.

Just as they approached Kuiu, the airmen once again plunged into a roll of low clouds that forced them down to treetop level. They were flying single file in a narrow passage with Lieutenant Smith in the lead. As he brought the *Chicago* around, the *Boston* was caught up in its prop wash. Lieutenant Wade described the incident: " . . . a wash will make a heavily loaded seaplane gyrate wildly and in your wildest imagination you will be unable to conjure up a picture of what it is like and of what a shiver it sends down your spine. It shakes you and throws your ship about and puts you through a series of crazy maneuvers that will turn your hair gray if anything will. We were only twenty-five feet off the ground at the time, so we couldn't dive down out of it without smashing up on the rocky coast of Kuiu Island. We managed to get out of it by swinging to one side, but it was a close thing.''

The weather had cleared by the time they landed at Sitka early that afternoon, but the next morning they awoke to a howling gale blowing in from the Pacific.

While waiting for the winds to abate, the aviators did some sightseeing. They were browsing through a photographer's shop when an Eskimo, his weathered face a mask of infinite patience, came in and stood quietly by the door for a full five minutes. At last the proprietor of the shop asked him if there was anything he wanted. ''Yes,'' he said quietly. ''I wanted to let these men know that one of their airboats is adrift.''

The eight men raced to the shore. Working waist-deep in the freezing water and with the aid of a Forestry Service boat, they battled windy seas for six hours until they had secured the errant World Cruiser.

By morning the gale had subsided and weather reports, radioed in especially for them, indicated that they could expect fair weather for the next leg. But the round-the-world travelers had been airborne less than an hour when they ran into low cloud layers. A few minutes later the air chilled and once more they were in the middle of a raging snowstorm. They let down to beach level where they zoomed through the swirling snow, just above the white line of the breakers.

''Sometimes we flew so low that our pontoons almost dragged on the water,'' Lieutenant Nelson recalled. ''Occasionally, we passed over wrecked boats, half buried in the sand or over piles of logs washed up by the sea, and I kept wondering if we should hit them.

''Most of the time I flew standing up in the cockpit braced against the back of the seat with my feet on the rudder bar so that I could look out the front of the plane as well as out over the side. Neither Jack nor I dared to sit down because if we did, we wouldn't see the beach. Every few minutes I had to change goggles because the snow driving against my face melted, trickled down behind them and blurred the lenses.''

Because of the weather, Martin decided to overfly Cordova and land at Seward, where the four planes remained until the snowstorm abated. On April 15 they were airborne again, headed for Chignik, near the base of the Aleutian island chain, when a three-inch hole in the crankcase of the *Seattle* forced Major Martin to make an emergency landing. Word of the mishap was relayed to General Patrick, who ordered the three planes at Chignik to proceed to Dutch Harbor, a major supply base on their route, and await the *Seattle*. He also dispatched the Coast Guard cutter *Algonquin* with a new engine for the stricken World Cruiser.

It was not until the twenty-fifth of April that the *Seattle* took to the air again. The flight to Chignik was accomplished in another raging snowstorm, with Martin suffering from a severe cold caught wading in the frigid water to break ice from the airplane's pontoons.

At Chignik, Major Martin waited with growing impatience for the storm to let up. He learned that the British attempt at a round-the-world flight under the command of Capt. Stuart MacLaren in a Vickers Vulture had moved down through India in its eastward journey, and on the twenty-fourth of April the French competitors, Capt. Peltier D'Oisy and Sergeant Besin, had left Paris in a swift Breguet.

On the thirtieth of April, the snowstorm showed no signs of slackening, but the winds had lessened considerably and the snow was sifting down in fat, lazy flakes. It was not ideal flying weather, but Martin decided to chance it to Dutch Harbor. An overland shortcut had been suggested by the superintendent of the salmon cannery at Chignik. He spoke of a pass through the mountains but added a warning that near the end of the pass it would appear that a turn to the right would carry the pilot out to sea; it was a false lead, he cautioned, and should be ignored. Instead, the airmen should continue on the route that looked the worse. The other planes had already flown out by this same route, and Martin decided that he, too, would try the shortcut.

As he followed the mountain pass across the island, Major Martin was forced lower and lower by the sinking ceiling of the swirling snow. An opening appeared and he turned right to fly out of the pass. In the snow he did not see that this was the false lead. In a few minutes Martin was flying by instruments, hopelessly lost in the storm and headed toward a certain crash. During a momentary break in the blizzard he thought he saw water off to the west and he winged over toward the safety of the sea. Again the blinding storm closed in and there was no further sign of the ocean. Was that Bristol Bay or the Pacific Ocean they had seen? If it were Bristol Bay the westward course would carry them safely beyond the islands, where they could hold a westerly course and then turn south to Dutch Harbor. If it were the Pacific, the westerly bearing would carry them directly back into the mountainous islands of the Aleutian chain. Martin was certain that the mountains were behind him, but he decided to try for the safety of altitude anyway.

Fully loaded with fuel, the World Cruiser rose heavily. As he squinted ahead, his heart suddenly skipped a beat and an icy fear gripped him: through the clouds he had caught a momentary glimpse of the ground below. He had taken the false lead through the pass and the *Seattle* was still in the mountains.

Almost at the same instant Sergeant Harvey yelled a warning, but his voice was lost under the roar of the Liberty 12. Dark patches of rock, blown clean of snow in fierce arctic gales, suddenly filled the landscape before them. Martin acted swiftly, kicked hard rudder, slammed on full throttle, and pulled the stick back into his stomach. The Douglas answered his command, but the action had come too late. The *Seattle,* cushioned somewhat by her pontoons, crunched into the sloping side of the mountain, sliding and crashing forward for over a hundred feet and finally coming to a stop in a tangle of wreckage. The plane was demolished, but miraculously neither of the men was injured. Even so, they could not count themselves the luckiest men on the face of the earth. They were over one hundred miles southwest of Chignik, in one of the most desolate spots on the Alaskan peninsula, and lost in the middle of a blizzard. The airmen sat in the wreckage and waited for the storm to subside. But when the snow stopped a blanket of fog settled over them, holding them prisoner in the wrecked plane until the morning of May 2. Then the weather cleared enough for them to make their way down the mountain to a lake and a vacant trapper's cabin. They remained at the cabin until the ninth of May, when they began a slow, painful trek around the lake toward Port Moller. En route, however, they met several Eskimos who agreed to ferry them across the lake to the cannery at Port Moller and civilization.

The disappearance of the *Seattle* had not held up the world flight. Accidents were lamentable, but they were a calculated risk that all flyers accepted. On the morning of May 2, Lieutenant

Smith was named the new commander of the expedition and ordered by General Patrick to continue the flight. "PLANES TWO, THREE AND FOUR TO PROCEED TO JAPAN AT EARLIEST POSSIBLE MOMENT," read the telegram.

The three remaining ships took off on May 3 for an island-hopping leg along the curving chain of the Aleutians. After reaching the end of the chain at Attu, the flyers had to wait for a letup in the storms and blanketing fog before starting their longest overwater flight, 878 miles to Paramushiru in the Kurile Islands. It would be a record flight over the Pacific.

The six Americans flew to the Komandorski Islands and then turned southwestward through heavy fogs and blowing snow. After stopovers at Paramushiru, Hitokappu, and Minato, they finally flew back into spring sunshine and landed at Lake Kasumi-ga-ura near Tokyo.

Major Martin and Sergeant Harvey on arrival at Port Moller.
**(U.S. Air Force)**

Tokyo was a major stop for the Americans. Here the engines were overhauled, pontoons changed, and general repairs completed while the government and the Japanese people provided hospitality in abundance.

Les Arnold described their arrival: "As we approached the pier at the Japanese Naval Air Base, the people waved thousands of American and Japanese flags and shouted 'Banzai.'

"There were thousands of frail-looking little Japanese women in their fancy kimonos and sashes, with their hair piled up on their heads so neatly. For variety and color we had never seen anything like it. And their smiles—ah, we knew we were going to like Japan!"

Parties, official luncheons, teas, dinners, and banquets had been planned by the Japanese, enough festivities for two weeks, but the Army had to ask their hosts to cancel some of the celebrations. The visit could only be a short one if the circumnavigation was to be completed on schedule.

While the Americans were in Tokyo, word reached them that Major MacLaren had crashed in Akyab. The Englishman was unharmed, but the crash of his plane put him temporarily out of the round-the-world race. To help the unfortunate MacLaren the American flyers and the American liaison group in Japan arranged for a U. S. Navy vessel to transport a British replacement airplane, already crated and waiting in Hong Kong, to the stranded aviator. This gesture of sportsmanship gained the gratitude of the English people; and later, when the American flyers arrived in London, the First Lord of the Admiralty offered Lieutenant Smith the protection of a patrol of British navy ships when he crossed the Atlantic.

On June 4, the world flyers were approaching Shanghai. "As we flew across the mouth of the river and drew near Shanghai," wrote Lieutenant Nelson of the *New Orleans*, "we were amazed at the number of craft below us. The river teemed with tens of thousands of junks, sampans, and steamers. But we found when we came down that the harbor-master had held up all traffic in the river for hours. Just in one bunch there were over two hundred and fifty boats loaded with fish and these hardly represented a hundredth part of all the bedlam of boats. Not knowing just how much space we should require, the harbor-master had cleared several miles of water-front in order to save us from the fate of D'Oisy, the French world flier, who had crashed on the outskirts of Shanghai a few days before.''

As the aviators proceeded southward through Asia, the crush of people and harbors teeming with water traffic were a recurring problem. On June 9, their takeoff from Amoy was delayed by thousands of curious spectators whose boats crowded around the three planes, some sailing dangerously near. The airmen were ever on guard against accidentally crushed pontoons or broken wings. Lieutenant Harding recalled the moment: '' . . . when we were called at daybreak, we saw hundreds and hundreds of little Chinese boats crowded around the planes. More kept coming from shore until we could scarcely see the water. We hurried out, got up on the pontoons, and for an hour struggled to keep them from drifting into us and damaging the planes. The launch from the *Preble* tried to protect us but the officer in charge got disgusted and decided the only way to drive them off would be to sink a few. Something had to be done to prevent the planes from being crushed by those thousands of boats. So he backed off a few feet, and then shot his boat full speed ahead. Some of the sampans capsized, throwing the occupants over into other craft or into the water. It wasn't long until he had cleared a space. From then on the boatmen kept at a respectful distance.''

They had to bypass a roaring waterspout twisting out of a thunderhead over the sea, but the airmen reached Haiphong harbor in Indochina without incident. That night at a reception they were told that a radio broadcast had carried the news that the Portuguese aviators who were attempting to circle the earth in the opposite direction had reached Rangoon, Burma.

"This news," said Harding, "of the progress of the Portuguese was like a tonic to us. Excusing ourselves from the reception, we hurried back to the destroyer, got a good night's sleep and were up at dawn the next morning, June 11th, hoping to reach Saigon, or at least halfway down the coast of French Indo-China that day."

Their hopes were not to be realized, however. En route the block cracked in the engine of the *Chicago*. Thick black oil breached from the engine; the oil pressure fell to zero. Smith and Arnold had no choice but to make a forced landing in an isolated lagoon. Oil and water poured into the slipstream from the cracked block and the superheated engine clanked as a broken rod punched holes through the crankcase. The possibility of fire was imminent. When the plane touched onto the smooth lagoon, Arnold leaped over the side and scrambled along the pontoons as the plane skimmed through the water. Holding the bracing, he stood ready with a fire extinguisher to quench any blaze. The World Cruiser eased to a stop without a fire, however.

The thick foliage that surrounded the lagoon made the Americans' isolation seem complete, but they knew that their companions in the *Boston* and *New Orleans* had watched their descent and would bring them help from Tourane, where spare engines were aboard a destroyer—one of the vast fleet of U.S. Navy support vessels stationed around the world for this flight.

Smith and Arnold tied their airplane to a clump of bamboo reed and settled themselves for a long wait. Their tranquillity was soon disturbed when the jungle growth parted to reveal a number of curious natives. In moments the lagoon was alive with native dugouts. The Asians approached the aviators, offering food, drink, and friendship.

Meanwhile, Lieutenants Wade and Nelson made their landings at Tourane and immediately contacted the waiting destroyer. The next problem was to find the downed flyers in the Indochinese jungle by land. Leaving Sergeant Ogden and Lieutenant Harding to care for the airplanes, Wade went to the nearest communications facility to make arrangements for transporting the spare engine to Hue, while Nelson, with the help of a Standard Oil agent, worked out an overland route to the stranded *Chicago.*

Using aerial maps and enlisting the aid of French officials, Nelson and the oil-company agent secured a car and headed toward the city of Hue. When roads stopped, they traveled by sampan. By midnight a local village leader had rowed them to the lagoon where Smith and Arnold were being entertained by a band of happy Indochinese.

At dawn arrangements were made for three war sampans to tow the World Cruiser twenty-five water miles to Hue. Each sampan was powered by ten native friends pulling heavy oars and commanded by a patriarch beating a synchronized tom-tom beat.

Meanwhile, the spare engine arrived at Tourane. It was immediately loaded into a truck for overland travel to Hue. Sergeant Ogden rode with the Liberty 12 and later recalled the truck ride through the deep jungle night: "The driver of that lorry cared little for his own life and less for mine. We left Tourane after sunset and it was so dark I couldn't tell what sort of country we were going through or what pace we were making, but it must have been fully thirty miles an hour. Traveling at that rate in a truck over a jungle road is enough to shake your toenails to your throat."

Ogden told of climbing to the top of a mountain from which the driver let the truck and the precious engine coast down, reaching speeds of almost sixty miles an hour on the winding jungle road. "Sometimes we'd skid around a corner," related Ogden, "on one and a half wheels." The truck careened around a steep turn and "suddenly the bumping ceased and I felt as though I were riding in an airplane again. Sure enough, we were flying, and a moment later we flew into some trees. Mr. Annamite, the driver, had buzzed right off the road into the jungle." Thirty minutes later they were again propelling along, and after two more mishaps, in which the engine miraculously escaped damage, they arrived at the plane.

Without wasting a moment, the men removed the old engine and installed the new one. Barely seventy-one hours had elapsed since the forced landing when all three World Cruisers were again airborne and heading for Saigon, Bangkok, Tavoy, and finally, Rangoon.

In Rangoon, the aviators faced a new and unexpected problem when Smith was stricken with dysentery. His illness might have eliminated him from the flight had not delay occurred from another quarter.

During the first night in Rangoon, while the flyers were getting a full night's sleep, sailors from an American destroyer were entrusted with the protection of the World Cruisers. The planes were bobbing lightly at moorings when the dark hull and tower sail of a heavy Burmese barge loomed suddenly close. The first sailor to see the approaching vessel shouted an alarm. Other sailors in a nearby longboat responded by quickly rowing between the onrushing Burmese boat and the closest airplane, the *New*

*Orleans*. As the two boats crunched together, one sailor leaped from the longboat to the Burmese vessel, rushed to the stern, shoved the startled helmsman from his post, where he had been drowsing, and slammed the helm all the way over. The sailboat obeyed the helm, and the heavily laden vessel yawed away from the airplane, damaging the bottom left wing of the World Cruiser as it did. Only the swift action by the alert Navy men had saved the *New Orleans*.

The repair of the *New Orleans* closely paralleled the recovery of Lieutenant Smith, and by June 25 both were ready for takeoff.

One of the problems that perpetually plagued the airmen was taking off with a full fuel load from a smooth water surface. Surface tension on smooth water is a strong adhesive force; until the plane could be put on the "step" and the adhesion of the pontoons to the water broken, the airplane could not break away. One solution was to take off in the wake of a ship, which they did at Rangoon. Lieutenant Arnold described that takeoff:

"With not a breath of air stirring and the Irrawaddy smooth as glass, we left the land of teak and whacking white cheroots. The *Boston* and *New Orleans* got onto their pontoon steps by following the waves left in the wake of an ocean steamer and then Wade flew down in front of us and let his pontoons ripple the surface for the *Chicago*."

From Rangoon the Americans cut across the delta to the little seaport city of Akyab. On the same day the British round-the-world flyer Major MacLaren took off from Akyab for Rangoon in the airplane that the U.S. Navy had delivered to him.

In Calcutta, the airmen removed the World Cruisers' pontoons and replaced them with wheels for the overland flight to England. While the pontoons were being removed, Linton Wells, an Associated Press reporter in Calcutta, learned that the change from pontoons to wheels meant a large savings in weight and decided that he would try to hitch a ride as a stowaway. Unnoticed in the crowds of people milling around the airplanes, he quietly slid into one of the baggage compartments and stretched himself out for a ride across India.

Wells was discovered at Allahabad, but he was allowed to continue on to Karachi, where a message from General Patrick awaited the airmen. In response to a cable from Lieutenant Smith,

General Patrick had ordered the stowaway to find a more conventional mode of travel.

When it was still an hour out of Karachi, Erik Nelson's *New Orleans* developed engine trouble. Amid puffs of white smoke, oil splashed out over the side of the ship and parts started to fly out of the engine. A piston began to disintegrate and the exhaust springs were blown out of the stacks. In a few minutes two more cylinders fell apart in the heat and pressure and an exhaust valve broke, smashing the connecting rod and throwing it into the bottom of the crankcase. While this decomposition was occurring, the Liberty-12 continued to run.

Hot oil and pieces of twisted metal erupted from the airplane as if from a volcano. Finally the engine stuttered, coughed, and died. Lieutenant Nelson put the *New Orleans* into a dive. The Liberty 12 sprang to life, coughing, clanging, and spewing broken pieces of metal, but it kept going until the oil-splattered machine and men touched the ground safely at Karachi.

Karachi was a major depot for the flight and new Liberty 12s were installed in all three airplanes. As usual, the aviators stayed with their craft, working on them until sunset before beginning an evening of social activity. Invitations from governmental and military officials were divided among the airmen so that a number of groups could honor the world flyers. Lieutenant Arnold's host was Major General Cook, the commanding general of the Army in eastern India. He recalled:

> We worked on the planes until dark. I was so smeared from head to foot with oil and grease that when General Cook's Rolls-Royce, complete with chauffeur and footman, took me to his big white mansion I felt like the ragged urchin in the story books who dreams that he is a prince.
>
> As I whirled up the driveway through an avenue of palms I could see a crowd of men and women in spotless white sitting on the lawn. I was in my one and only suit of grimy overalls, so as soon as the car stopped I ran up the steps in order not to be seen. But with my face black from smoke and dirt and my overalls coated with grease, the General insisted that I must come right out to meet the assembled company. They were so charming, treating me as though I were a Knight of the Garter or a Commander of the Bath instead of a mere unwashed lieutenant, that I soon felt quite at ease.

The overhaul took several days, and the mixture of long hours of mechanical work and evenings of duty social engagements made them all glad to be finished and ready to push on. They flew out of Karachi without incident and winged across Persia, where brown rocks and deep canyons marked the desolation of the land. In late afternoon, after hours of bleakness, the minarets of Baghdad began to appear in the western sky. Below was the Tigris, on which river steamers struggled around the sandbanks.

From Baghdad the airmen hopped to Aleppo and Constantinople. After that the flying grew easier and the welcomes at each port of call more elaborate. Bucharest, Belgrade, Budapest, Strasbourg—then Paris.

"Fifty miles from the city we caught our first glimpse of the familiar Eiffel Tower," recalled Leigh Wade, "and farther to the right the white dome of the Church of the Sacre Coeur on Montmartre. When we arrived over Paris, the boulevards were packed with people. It was the afternoon of July 14th, Bastille Day, and thousands of people were cheering and waving flags when at five-fifteen we taxied up to the hangars at Le Bourget."

Paris was a holiday, a rest from the journey past and a respite before the crossing of the North Atlantic. Gen. John Joseph Pershing personally entertained the lieutenants and all of Paris honored and feted the American heroes.

When they left for London, they were escorted on the entire journey by enthusiastic pilots in aircraft of many descriptions. Two airplanes containing American tourists flew alongside and continually waved to the world flyers.

From London the aviators flew north to Brough. Arrangements had been made with the Blackburn Aviation Company at Brough to replace the pontoons for the final open-water crossing.

It took several days to prepare the planes for the Atlantic leg of the journey, and it was July 30 before they took off into a low cloud bank, winging northward to the top of the British Isles and the city of Kirkwall on the edge of the North Atlantic. At Kirkwall the airmen found winter conditions again.

The three planes left Kirkwall for Iceland on Saturday, August 2. Ten minutes after takeoff they flew into a thick fog that forced them to descend to a mere five feet above the water in order to maintain visibility. Then they ran into a heavy rain squall and climbed to twenty-five hundred feet where they found clear weather above the stratus deck. Below, down near the water, there had been three airplanes, but breaking out on top there were only two, the *Chicago* and *Boston*. There was no sign of the *New Orleans*.

"For twenty minutes we circled around wondering whether Erik and Jack had flown on or whether they had met with an accident and fallen into the water," reported Arnold. "Lowell finally decided that the safest thing to do would be to turn back and report at Kirkwall, so that the destroyers could start search. If Erik and Jack were actually lost, and if we flew on to Iceland, the boats might hear nothing of the accident for six or eight hours, until we reached our destination. If on the other hand, they had passed safely through the fog, then a report would be sent back."

While flying within the dense layer of fog, Nelson and Harding had run into trouble. It was impossible to keep formation in the chilling condensation and Lieutenant Nelson had lost sight of the *Chicago* and the *Boston*. Unable to see beyond the nose of his plane, he had eased the *New Orleans* skyward in a shallow climb.

After attaining some altitude, the *New Orleans* suddenly tossed and bounced, as it crossed the invisible prop wash of one of its sister planes. The engine labored and the airspeed jerked and dropped as the airplane began to mush awkwardly in the swirling fog. The plane stalled, snapped over, and fell into a tailspin.

Nelson could feel the pull of centrifugal force as the plane spun, but the thick mantle of fog obscured the horizon. Without a point of reference to help him fly, he was strictly on instruments, needle, ball, and airspeed as the *New Orleans* spun crazily toward the icy waters below.

Lieutenant Nelson kicked hard rudder in the opposite direction of the turn indicator. The gyrations abruptly stopped. He snapped the yoke forward. The airplane lurched from the stall and dove forward, once again a flying machine. Feeling the biting grip of the lift of the wings, he knew they were out of the spin. The airspeed started to build and the altimeter was unwinding. He pulled back on the wheel and the *New Orleans* roared from its dive. "As we pulled level," said Nelson, "we shot into a clear spot and from then on we were lucky enough to be able to fly under the fog until we were entirely out of it."

Lieutenants Nelson and Harding flew on to Iceland without further incident and were surprised upon arrival not to see their compatriots. It wasn't long, however, before Nelson learned that the others had returned to England to start a search for the *New Orleans.*

Now anxious to catch up with the *New Orleans,* Smith and Wade left Kirkwall for a second time en route to Iceland. Aided by a stiff tail wind, the two planes in a loose formation were making well over one hundred miles per hour when trouble struck the *Boston.* Leigh Wade, now a major-general, retired to his comfortable home on a quiet, tree-shaded street in Washington, D.C., described that moment:

> All of a sudden, I noticed the oil pressure going down. In a few seconds it dropped to zero. So there was nothing to do but land at once. Our altitude at that moment was approximately five hundred feet, so I had no difficulty in turning and landing into the wind.
>
> When we reached the water I discovered how deceitful the sea is when you are above it. At five hundred feet it had looked fairly smooth. But when we landed, we found it so rough that the left pontoon nearly wrapped itself around the lower wing, and snapped two of the vertical wires.

Lowell Smith, who had watched the *Boston* dropping away to the sea, circled until he was certain Wade and Ogden had made a safe landing. Waved away from attempting a sea rescue in the rolling gray ocean, Smith headed toward the nearest destroyer, where he dropped a message telling of the forced landing, and waited until he heard three whistle blasts confirming that it had been received.

In the downed *Boston* Lieutenant Wade and Sergeant Ogden prepared themselves for a long wait for a rescue ship. The heavy sea rolling against the wind dangerously tossed the fragile airplane. A fishing trawler, the *Rugby-Ramsey,* finally spied them adrift in the sea and drew abeam of the airmen, who were standing in the cockpit waving flags.

"Do you want any help?" the *Rugby-Ramsey's* skipper shouted.

"Well, I should say we do!" replied Wade.

"What kind of help?" asked the old fisherman.

"Throw us a towline," said Wade.

Soon they were in tow, but towing in the heavy seas and fierce wind began to tear up the airplane.

When the destroyers from the deployed naval force arrived, the line was transferred to one of them and a hoist was rigged to lift the *Boston* from the sea. Wade and Ogden scrambled aboard the destroyer and the plane was readied for removal from the ocean. "The signal was given," reminisced General Wade, "and I can recall the feeling of joy that swept over me as I saw our beloved plane rising off the water. Then the crash came. The tackle was wrenched loose from the main mast, and the plane fell."

Further efforts to retrieve the damaged plane were soon halted by the increasing force of the wind. Finally, the *Boston* capsized and sank in the sea.

Meanwhile, the *Chicago* and *New Orleans* made the short run from Hornafjörthur to Reykjavik, arriving just as the destroyer *Richmond* steamed through the breakwater with Leigh Wade and Henry Ogden on board.

After thirteen days in the capital of Iceland, during which the airmen enjoyed the enthusiastic hospitality of its 25,000 inhabitants, the weather improved enough for the *Chicago* and the *New Orleans* to take off for Greenland. The improvement was only temporary, however.

Near Greenland they "plunged into fog and rain and wind," as Smith recalled, "and the farther we flew the denser grew the fog and the greater became the velocity of the wind. This is an unusual combination, but as luck would have it, we encountered both.

"We were forced to fly close to the water on account of the fog. But even then it was so thick that we flashed over the *Raleigh* without seeing her. Seventy-five miles out from Greenland we struck the first floes. As we neared the coast, the ice increased until we were flying over a seeming endless expanse of fantastic bergs of every size and shape."

As the ice increased, so did the steaming fog.

"Three times we came so suddenly upon huge icebergs that there was no time left to do any deciding," Smith continued.

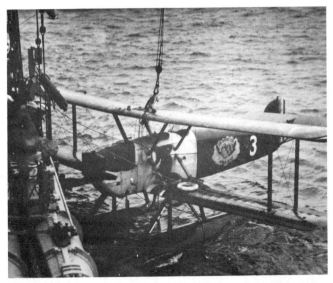

The attempt to lift the cruiser *Boston* to the deck of the U.S.S. *Richmond*.

The *New Orleans* beached for repairs at Reykjavik, Iceland.

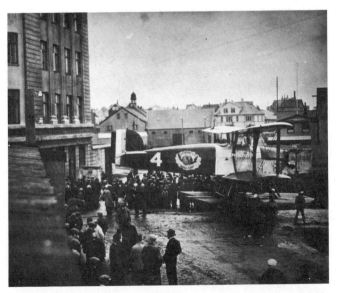

"We simply jerked the wheel back for a quick climb and were lucky enough to zoom over the top of it into the still denser fog above. Here we were completely lost and unable to see beyond the 'prop' and wingtips. Blindly we would grope and feel our way downward, hoping against hope that the little space we should eventually descend into just above the surface of the water would be clear of ice for a great enough distance to enable us to glance around, size up the situation, and get set for dodging the next one."

With their attempt to climb on top frustrated by a heavy fuel load and the ceiling limits of the aircraft, the flyers were forced to plunge on through the fog while they tried to hold to a compass course. They remained fogbound for an hour, dodging the icebergs that fairly leaped at them from the mist as they winged past.

"Suddenly," Smith recalled, "instead of the white, ghostlike shadows of the icebergs we had been passing, a dark patch loomed up in front of us. That was encouraging because we knew it must be land, and we knew that at last we had reached the mainland of Greenland."

The *Chicago* and the *New Orleans* left Greenland on August 31 for a Labrador landing in the midafternoon at Icy Trickle. Their next stop was Hawkes Harbour, Newfoundland, and on September 3 they flew to Pictou, Nova Scotia. As the *Chicago* and the *New Orleans* circled over the harbor at Pictou, the flyers saw below them a new World Cruiser, the *Boston II,* sent to Pictou by General Patrick so that Leigh Wade and Henry Ogden could rejoin their companions for the completion of the round-the-world flight.

Smith recalled: "Every whistle in Pictou was tooting its shrillest and the shore was lined with cheering Canadians when we taxied to our moorings. Here we were to get our first taste of the reception that was to follow us now all the way back to Seattle."

And thus it was as the world flyers continued on to Boston and down the East Coast of the United States to meet President Coolidge. From Washington they turned westward in what was literally a triumphal tour of the country. The six aviators were cheered and hailed by Americans at every stop: Dayton, Chicago, Omaha, St. Joseph, Muskogee, Dallas, Sweetwater, El Paso, Tucson, San Diego, and finally Seattle. To insure that no one aviator would be credited with the first circumnavigation of the globe by air, they purposefully flew wingtip to wingtip, side by side, across Seattle's Sand Point Field for a planned photo finish on September 28, 175 days from their start.

The round-the-world flight, more than any other aerial feat, illustrated the commercial potential of aviation. National honors were bestowed upon the six successful airmen. In San Diego, an admiral made the remark that perhaps best summarized the single honor most valuable to the flyers: "Other men will fly around the earth, but never again will anybody fly around it for the first time!"

President Calvin Coolidge and Secretary of War Weeks (right) greet Lieutenant Smith in Washington, D.C.

**(U.S. Air Force)**

# CHAPTER 11

# Over the North Pole by Air

At the geographic top of the earth, at a point existing unmarked in the midst of a horizon-to-horizon mass of jagged ice, lies the North Pole. From this spot, which can be located only by instruments, stretches the earth cap of the Arctic Ocean, frozen into an ice pack and jumbled in a bizarre disorder of jagged peaks, ice floes, and uneven ridges.

The possible existence of an arctic region was first suggested in the sixth century in passages of the celebrated legend, the *Navigation of Saint Brendan*. Supposedly, the protagonist sighted floating crystal castles—icebergs—during his journeys into the northern seas. It was not, however, until the twentieth century, in 1909, that Robert Peary first reached the North Pole, and man began to unlock the great mysteries of that frozen region. Finally it fell to the airplane to provide the practical vehicle for meaningful explorations into the vast, unknown polar ice.

While some of the aerial adventurers of the 1920's set their sights on conquests of the oceans and continents, a few looked to the greater challenge of the unyielding Arctic and the North Pole. One of these men was Roald Amundsen, the Norwegian explorer who in company with four others had first reached the South Pole on December 14, 1911, after a ninety-nine-day trek by dogsled and skis.

Having conquered the South Pole, Amundsen was determined to explore the still mysterious regions of the North. He was one of the first to consider the possibility of using aircraft for polar

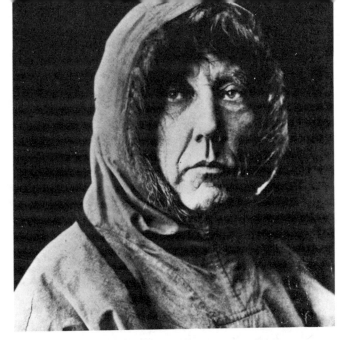

Roald Amundsen, the Norwegian explorer.
*(National Air and Space Museum, The Smithsonian Institution)*

exploration. "I had now become obsessed completely with the vision of a new method of attacking the arctic problem, a method which, I felt sure, would revolutionize the whole practice of arctic exploration ... aircraft for use in the arctic," Amundsen wrote.

In 1922 he made preparations for an aerial assault upon the North Pole, but a collapsed ski defeated his plans and delayed his attempt. The explorer then decided that ski-planes were not the practical answer when the possibility of a forced landing was very real. The Arctic Ocean was a frozen surface contorted by the crushing pressures of wind and ocean currents pressing ice into ridges and hummocks, which sometimes rose as high as sixty feet. Amundsen knew that leads, or channels of open water, would appear in the ice floes for short periods of time; and he concluded that seaplanes would provide a more practical mode of transportation. Leads could always be found, while the ice itself was seldom flat enough for a safe ski landing. His plans for a seaplane exploration of the pole met with financial setbacks, however. It was not until 1925, when he met the wealthy aviator Lincoln Ellsworth, who also yearned to participate in polar explorations, that Amundsen was able to begin his assault upon the North Pole in earnest.

In the summer of 1925, the two men made exploratory arctic flights in two Dornier WAL multi-engined seaplanes. The main purpose of the flights was to penetrate as far as possible into the unexplored arctic regions—an area where reasoned speculation indicated the possible presence of yet unknown arctic landmasses. Robert Peary in 1908 reported having seen a shoreline on the horizon northwest of Ellesmere Island. He named what he thought was a landmass Crocker Land, and it appeared on maps until later explorations revealed that only the ice packs of the polar sea capped the planet. There was also an area denoted as Keenan Land, supposedly a mountainous region far to the north of Alaska. Later observations revealed this to have been but a mirage. However, in 1925, these reports added zest to the allure of the unknown area.

At 5:00 P.M. on May 21, 1925, Amundsen and Ellsworth took off from Kings Bay, Spitsbergen, in their twin Dorniers and headed north. Flying in the seaplane N-25 with Amundsen were two other men, Hjalmar Riiser-Larsen, who in World War II would become commander of the Norwegian Air Force, and a German mechanic, Hans Feucht. Ellsworth piloted the second plane, the N-24, in company with Leif Dietrichson and Oskar Omdahl. The two planes had flown to within 140 miles of the North Pole when they lost their course in a fog. The problem was compounded when an engine on Amundsen's plane failed while he was circling a lead, forcing the N-25 to make an emergency landing. Ellsworth, who soon lost sight of the N-25 in the fog, put his own plane down in a nearby stretch of open water in order to aid his companions. Once in the water the Ellsworth plane began to ship water. Only quick action by its crew, who pulled the aircraft onto an ice floe, kept it from sinking into nine thousand feet of Arctic Ocean.

With both planes down it was imperative that the crews join forces. Slowly the shifting ice floes brought the two groups to within one half mile of each other. Abandoning their leaking airplane, Ellsworth, Dietrichson, and Omdahl painfully climbed hummocks and crossed crevasses to join with the old arctic warrior Amundsen. They carried fuel and supplies from the damaged plane to the N-25, which was repaired and hauled from the water onto the ice. While some of the men remained with the N-25, others explored the areas nearby in search of a flat stretch of smooth ice suitable for takeoff. At length one was found. The plane was stripped to make room for the weight of six men; and finally, after twenty-five days on the ice pack, the six arctic explorers crowded silently into the plane and Riiser-Larsen prepared to take off.

Slowly at first and then with increasing rapidity the seaplane slid across the virtually frictionless ice. Just as it reached the end of the run, the wings bit into the cold arctic air and the adventurers became precariously and miraculously airborne.

It was eight hours before the heavily laden N-25 arrived at North East Land, Spitsbergen, where the airmen landed safely in spite of a damaged rudder. Once on the water they hailed a passing sailing ship to tow them once again to Kings Bay.

Later that same summer, an American group, the MacMillan-Byrd expedition, crisscrossed Ellesmere Island in open-cockpit Loening Amphibians. It was too late for an aerial assault upon the Pole since late summer invariably brought bad weather and fog, but during the half-dozen days that were fit for flying, the Americans mapped hitherto uncharted regions of this area of the Arctic. MacMillan finally terminated the flights and returned his expedition to the United States, with the observation that the airplane was a useless vehicle above the Arctic Circle and that the Eskimo sled dog was still "king of the Arctic." Commander Richard Byrd, who did not share this pessimistic view, spent the winter preparing for a flight to the North Pole in the spring of 1926.

Two other groups also entered the race. Umberto Nobile, Roald Amundsen, and Lincoln Ellsworth had teamed together in an Italian-Norwegian-American venture to cross the pole in the dirigible *Norge*. Capt. George Hubert Wilkins, backed by the Detroit Aviation Society, the North American Newspaper Alliance, and the *Detroit News* planned to fly from Point Barrow across the North Pole to Spitsbergen. His pilot was Lt. Carl Ben Eielson, an ace Alaskan bush pilot; the commander of the Army Air Corps First Pursuit Squadron, Major Thomas G. Lanphier, on leave for the expedition, was copilot. The news syndicate sent a young reporter, Palmer Hutchison, with them to write firsthand accounts of the flight. The party was equipped with a Fokker trimotor christened the *Detroiter*, and a single-engine Fokker, the *Alaskan*. The primary purpose of the Detroit expedition was not only to reach the North Pole by air but also to discover and hopefully be the first to explore the uncharted arctic landmasses.

The plan of the Detroit expedition was to establish a base at Point Barrow from which the men would fly into the Arctic, mapping the area as they went. However, tragedy and bad weather doomed the expedition to failure. While preparations were under way, the news reporter, Hutchison, accidently stepped backward into one of the spinning propellers of the *Detroiter* and was instantly decapitated. Shortly thereafter the landing gear and engine mounts were torn loose from the trimotor during a landing, and a few days later the *Alaskan* suffered a similar crash.

Umberto Nobile and his mascot dog, Titina.

**(Library of Congress)**

Nobile, Amundsen and Lincoln Ellsworth planned to cross the Pole in the dirigible *Norge*.

*(Library of Congress)*

After the *Detroiter* had been repaired, Wilkins and Eielson made one notable flight. On March 31, 1926, they flew out of Fairbanks, heading northward over the Brooks Range. Their journey through the narrow passes, squeezed between the lofty and rugged unmapped mountains, was in itself an adventure. From Point Barrow the flyers continued northward over the unmapped arctic ice floes. They penetrated 140 miles north beyond Point Barrow, viewing over six thousand square miles of unexplored territory, significantly reporting that they had sighted no island, no mountains, no land.

Meanwhile, plans were finally completed for the team of Amundsen and Ellsworth to travel to Spitsbergen, where they would meet the Italian dirigible designer and pilot Umberto Nobile, who was leaving Rome in his dirigible. From Spitsbergen the trio planned to fly across the North Pole to Alaska, something Nobile had wanted to do for some time. In his own words:

It was May, 1925, while the world was still anxiously awaiting news of the Amundsen-Ellsworth Airplane Expedition, which had come to grief on the Polar ice, that I began to consider the problem of using other aerial means for polar explorations.

Heavier-than-air apparatus did not appeal to me. Polar ice is too uneven, and during the good season, too often hidden by fog to permit landing with any considerable degree of safety. Moreover, even if a successful landing is managed, the resumption of flight is problematical, owing to the continuous movements in the formation of ice, caused by winds and tides.

On the other hand, with a dirigible, there is the possibility of slowing down and even coming to a full stop in the air without being compelled to land, whether for the purpose of taking observations or repairing damages. As to the discharge of men and materials, the landing maneuver presents some difficulties, but it is free from excessive danger when the necessary preparations have been made, and provided, of course, that atmospheric conditions are not utterly unfavorable.

For these reasons I conceived the idea of preparing and effecting an Italian Polar expedition with a dirigible, and by June, 1925, my plan had already taken shape in its main lines. We would start from Spitsbergen in order to explore all that Polar zone within a radius of 600 to 900 land miles. I did not contemplate a mere run to the Pole, but a campaign of exploration, taking advantage of favorable weather conditions prevailing from May to September. We would, in this manner, have effected a fanlike series of explorations from our island base.

While this Italian project was ripening, Captain Roald Amundsen asked to meet me. In our interview he explained his idea to use a dirigible to cross the Arctic from Spitsbergen to Alaska. His idea was conceived independently of mine, but after mine.

Agreement was soon reached and the *Norge* was specially prepared for the flight. Mooring masts were prefabricated in Italy and forwarded for erection at Kings Bay and Vadso in northern Norway, and a special dirigible hangar was built by the Aero Club of Norway at Spitsbergen to house the 348-foot dirigible. Amundsen and Ellsworth went to Spitsbergen to prepare for the arrival of the *Norge* and awaited the airship. On April 10, 1926, Nobile departed from Rome in the *Norge* and wrote of that moment:

> None could foresee with any degree of certainty when we would return; so we took leave of our loved ones as if we should never see them again.
>
> At 9:30 A.M. I gave the signal for the departure. I was so occupied with the ship that I could not even lean out of the cabin to wave good-bye to my dearest ones who were on the field; but I was carrying in my heart the image of the pale visage of my little daughter, and there still resounded in my ears the last words whispered to me by my wife.

> The motors started, and our flag, unfurling below the commander's cabin, flew to the breeze in all its glory in the dazzling sun of a Roman spring.

Far to the north the S.S. *Chantier* was churning through the North Atlantic, having sailed from New York on April 6 carrying Commander Richard E. Byrd, aviation-machinist Floyd Bennett, and a company of forty-six men. Byrd had two airplanes—a tri-motored Fokker monoplane christened the *Josephine Ford,* mounting Wright Whirlwind two-hundred-horsepower air-cooled radial engines, and a spare Curtiss "Oriole" with a single Curtiss C-6 engine. Both planes were equipped with skis, a gear disliked by Amundsen but regarded by Byrd as essential for a flight to the North Pole.

The Byrd expedition was backed by a group of wealthy sportsmen that included Edsel B. Ford, John D. Rockefeller, Jr., and Vincent Astor. The Standard Oil Company supplied the gasoline for the planes and the Vacuum Oil Company supplied the oil.

When the *Chantier* steamed into Kings Bay harbor on April 29, the *Norge* was still en route. Byrd and his men were quick to deny a race, but all the elements were present. Kings Bay, the only unloading dock along that icy arctic shore, was occupied by a Norwegian gunboat, the *Heimdal,* a support vessel for the anticipated dirigible flight to the Pole. Byrd sought permission for the *Chantier* to tie up long enough to unload the important *Josephine Ford,* but the captain of the *Heimdal* refused to vacate his favored position—at least not before the *Norge* arrived.

Undismayed, Commander Byrd directed the *Chantier* to an anchorage as close to the long, gently sloping, snow-crusted beach as the ship's captain dared to sail. He then directed the construction of a makeshift pontoon raft overlaying the four lifeboats. His plan was to drift the airplane to the shore. Braving the biting cold and their own fatigue, the Americans worked through the sunlit arctic night to float the odd sea vessel to the beach. Wind and tide drifted heavy chunks of ice into the precarious jerry-built raft, but the plan was successful.

Byrd later wrote in *The New York Times* of this incident:

> First the fuselage was taken out and secured to the raft. Much

of the time this was being done it snowed and the ice got thicker in the bay. Then the great sixty-three-foot wing was carefully hoisted to the deck. Had this wing fallen, the expedition would have ended right there.

Now we had the fuselage aboard the raft and had conquered our first enemy, the ice jam, but just as we were hoisting the wing from the hold, a fresh breeze blew up which made it impossible to lower the wing overside and bolt it to the fuselage.

Bennett and myself consulted as to the possibility of taking the fuselage ashore first and putting it safely out of the way of the ice jamming and grinding around the *Chantier* and our raft moored alongside. But that would mean assembling the plane on shore. To lift the great wing into position we should have had to build a scaffolding, and even then we feared some accident might happen. We decided to defer mounting the wing until the wind died down.

In the morning the wind had gone down, but the ice was packed in between us and the shore in a dense mass. There was a slight swell from the tide so that the ice remained in broken pieces.

Carefully the wing was lowered on to the fuselage and the men, awkward in their heavy bundled clothes, struggled to bolt the wing into its mounts. In a half an hour their work was complete.

Byrd described the final effort to dock his plane:

When everything was ready, the *Hobby,* which was standing by to assist if necessary, cut a circle around the *Chantier,* loosening the ice nearest the ship. Captain Holm of the *Hobby* joined Isaksen in the small boat that preceded the raft, and between them they performed a herculean task. With boathooks and picks they hacked and shoved at the tide drifted ice until they made an opening wide enough for the raft to nose in.

After that, a dozen of us, with oars and poles, struggled to keep the ice from crushing our frail convoy as we advanced toward the shore.

Isaksen and Holm leaped about from cake to cake like lumberjacks in a log jam, while our three enterprising motion-picture operators, who had their cameras at every vantage point, ground out film and encouraged us with admiring shouts.

A hundred yards from the *Chantier,* our course took us

between two icebergs which, while not large in comparison with those seen in Greenland, were many times larger than our whole raft and plane put together, and could have crushed us like nuts in a nutcracker.

Along the icy shore the one hundred inhabitants of Kings Bay had gathered to witness the strange procession. Most had predicted the failure of the unsteady operation because they "knew the ice" and that only "greenhorn American venturers would dare to push a raft across the icy bay."

Finally the raft touched the shore and was moored to two pillars of ice hewn from the land for just that purpose. Next Byrd and his men rigged a block and tackle and slid the *Josephine Ford* on planks cut from the ice up the beach to the safety of the snow. "The crowd gave a spontaneous cry of surprise," wrote Byrd, and "from that moment, the Kings Bay people were our firm friends and we were overwhelmed with offers of their services." Even Amundsen and Ellsworth, awaiting the arrival of the Italian ship, gave advice and contributed survival equipment to Byrd and Bennett.

Now the Americans faced the task of getting the engines running and tuned, the skis fixed to the craft, and a runway selected and smoothed.

They erected a temporary shack for the plane at the top of the hill near the empty, roofless dirigible hangar. First the engines were readied, then the skis were installed. But the heavy plane split the skis, and they had to be replaced with a reinforced set. Meanwhile, other men undertook the tedious task of trampling down the snow and knocking out the ridges and bumps over a distance of a thousand feet down the slope.

During the *Josephine Ford*'s first trial runs the engines performed perfectly. The skis continued to plague the adventurers, however. By working literally around the clock, the American crew was able to bring the expedition up to a state of final readiness by May 9, six days ahead of schedule and before the arrival of the *Norge*.

As Byrd described the final efforts:

The next afternoon we were ready for the big take-off. I

had decided to head straight Poleward and return via Cape Jesup, as I felt we would want better designed skis to put down a base at Cape Jesup with a heavy load as we had originally planned. We would not get our base down but would see a thousand miles of unexplored polar area. So we decided to put off until the next trip exploration of my advanced bases. I have learned a lot, I think, about skis that I did not know before. We loaded the plane for a minimum of twenty-three hours flying. The total weight of the plane and equipment was 10,000 pounds.

Finally the engines roared and we were under way. My whole attention was riveted on those skis. Would they stand the strain? Would we crash and break up the plane as well as ourselves? The snow was hard, but I saw the skis digging in dangerously. Our speed did not pick up, but still was almost that of a racing automobile. What a long run those few seconds seemed! Finally we reached the end of the smooth ice, and with the motors cut dashed into the deeper, softer and more rolling snow. There was a series of terrific bumps that nearly upset us several times. Finally we came to rest in a deep drift.

Bennett looked at me, his face as white as snow.

"She wouldn't do it, Commander," he said.

Bennett and myself have been through a great many rough experiences together and I never saw him show more perturbation.

I climbed down to the ground and examined the skis and landing gear. It was O.K. It had stood the terrific strain.

By that time our men had reached us, breathless. I never saw such a disappointed lot of men. They had given every ounce of their energy to get us into the air. Their hearts were entirely wrapped up in the success of the expedition. Some of them could hardly stand up. ...

I got the men together then and told them we would take some of the gasoline and equipment from the plane and try again the same night for the Pole and the unexplored regions. It was almost astounding how that cheered them up. Their enthusiasm came back, and their strength with it, for I am sure they were all worn out.

With superhuman effort the plane was dug from the snowbank, carefully taxied up the hill, and turned for a second run. While some of the men off-loaded gasoline and selected items of equipment to lighten the load, others, with Commander Byrd, walked over every foot of the icy runway, smoothing, filling, and preparing for a second run.

Byrd wrote:

> Finally, at 12:30 Greenwich the next morning, we were all set to go, the motors were warming up, the snow immediately in front of the skis was iced, and the runway, named by the men 'Byrd Boulevard,' had the finishing touches put on. I had planned for Lieutenant Noville to hold the tail of the plane with a line while we put the motors on full power; then let the tail go and start the plane with a rush.
>
> Again the motors roared and the plane began straining on the line holding the tail. Noville cut loose and the *Josephine Ford* rushed down the slippery ice. Again I watched the skis. It occurred to me at that critical moment that man is a curious animal. Here were Bennett and myself putting our best physical and mental efforts into getting a big load of gasoline into the air so we could fly into the unknown and into danger.
>
> Soon we gathered going speed. The great wings began to take more and more of the weight of the plane and we knew we were going to get off.
>
> At last, with a zoom, we got off for the Pole and the unexplored regions that had been my coveted goal for years.

Slowly the airplane rose to the north. The sky was clear, visibility was unlimited, and the sun hung low on the horizon in a position to afford Byrd excellent sun shots for his polar navigation. They quickly reached Cape Mitre, twenty miles from Kings Bay, and approached it at an altitude of one thousand feet in their ponderous climb to two thousand feet. Twenty-six miles from Cape Mitre they passed Haakon Peninsula, marked by a jagged two-thousand-foot mountain peak. Taking fixed bearing from this point, the flyers were able to line up the airplane with "true north" and correct their compass for variation. In five or six minutes they crossed over Danes Island, the final point of land before the Arctic Ocean.

As Byrd noted: "To my great surprise, I saw the edge of the great polar ice-pack only a few miles ahead. I had expected it to begin fifty or a hundred miles further north. Then, when we reached the edge of the ice-pack, I got another surprise. There were a very few small, broken pieces of ice at the edge of the solid pack. That probably was because it was early May and before the edge of the pack could be broken up by the heat.''

Commander Byrd made a last bearing check with the mountain on Haakon Peninsula and the western edge of Amsterdam Island. He compared the reading with a sun shot he made from the trapdoor that opened in the top of the airplane just aft of the wings. Byrd made the shot standing on a box with his head and shoulders outside in the windstream, which at their flying speed was almost a polar blizzard. His nose and part of the rest of his face were quickly frozen, causing him to rub and slap his face to restore circulation. The navigational fix from the sun shot confirmed his plane's position, and he felt reassured.

Byrd next opened a lower trapdoor to read the drift indicator in order to determine crosswind and course over the ice, and during the reading his fingers froze.

Byrd described these moments:

> I found myself extremely busy. On the average I calculated the drift and speed once every three or four minutes and when I found any change in the drift made the corrections for the course on the sun compass and then checked Bennett on his new course. I had on the plane a magnetic compass as large as that used by some big sea-going ships and it was far more reliable that a smaller one would have been. If the weather was rough we would be able to steer with it, though not a perfectly straight course as can be done when the weather is calm. With the sun compass I could tell when Bennett was off his course.
>
> I was astonished at the accuracy of his steering. Luck was with us. There was not a bump in the air, no upward and downward currents that tilt the plane and throw the compass spinning. The sun was bright and we had a wonderful view of the formidable ice pack. It was covered everywhere with snow and crisscrossed with pressure ridges like a crazy quilt. The constant movement of the polar ice pack causes ridges and opens leads of water, but we saw very few such leads that had not recently been frozen over with the fresh snowless ice looking greenish against the white snow around them.
>
> Some of these frozen leads, probably older than the others,

had a layer of snow over them and looked as flat as a table, but I knew them for dangerous sirens. They gave the appearance of affording an excellent landing but they were very probably too thin to hold the plane, which in landing, would crash through to destruction.

We were flying now at 2,000 feet and the temperature was eight degrees above zero or twenty-four degrees below freezing. No wonder none of the ice was melting into pools of water. I looked hard for some sign of life, but there was none, not a polar bear track, not a seal nor a bird.

Conversation between Byrd and Bennett was impossible because of the deafening pounding of the engines. Whenever it was necessary to communicate, notes were passed between them and occasionally Byrd would relieve Bennett at the controls. As their steady progress carried them nearer and nearer to their goal, excitement began to mount. Suddenly a black streak appeared on the starboard engine, an oil leak. The line grew thicker as more oil flowed backward along the nacelle and into the slipstream. As the oil leaked from the engine the vital fluid was blown against the wire and onto the tail surfaces. Long, black fingers of frozen oil extended from the bracings and the trailing edges of the elevator. Byrd and Bennett determined to continue to use the engine even if the oil pressure dropped, and to reach the North Pole even if the engine failed altogether. They were now only ninety miles from their goal. Holding the starboard engine at cruising power, they maintained their course.

Byrd recalled those tense moments:

> As I navigated I cast frequent glances on the oil running from the motor and lodging on one of the wires and tail surfaces. When would it stop? It fascinated me. The motor was still turning up full revolutions and power, and we are making knots over the ground with an increasingly lighter load as the gasoline was burned up.
>
> At the end of the hour I took my calculations and found that we were at the Pole! We reached it at 9:04 Greenwich time, just about the hour we hoped to get there.
>
> Bennett and I shook hands simply, and I went back into the cabin, stood at attention and saluted for Admiral Peary. The Navy had reached the Pole again, the blessed old Navy.

I did not drop an American flag. Peary had done that. The ice and snow were similar to that which Peary had described, but the ice was not the same as in the Polar Sea. There it is in constant motion. It was slightly rougher here than it had been when I first described it, but criss-crossed in the same way.

We flew several miles farther, circled and then took some still and motion pictures. As we flew there at the top of the world, circumnavigating it in a few minutes of flight, I regretted that we had not found land, and that our leaky oil tank would prevent our returning by way of Cape Morris Jesup.

Having attained the coveted goal, the aviators now turned their attention to the return journey. Oil was still pouring from the starboard engine.

Reported Byrd: "Much writing went backward and forward. Bennett wanted to try to find a landing place and land to repair the motor, but I vetoed that, for landing in uncertain places has ended a number of otherwise successful aviation expeditions.

"For some hours yet we would be over regions from which it would be impossible to return afoot. We decided to fly with that motor until the oil pressure should drop, indicating that the oil was gone."

By keeping careful navigation logs en route to the Pole, Byrd had noted systematic variations in the magnetic compass, and concluded correctly that he could utilize the inverse recession in computing compass headings for their course back from the Pole to Kings Bay on the edge of the Arctic Ocean.

As Byrd recalled their departure from the Pole: "The wind began to freshen and change direction after we left the Pole and in an hour we were making more than a hundred miles an hour. The elements were surely smiling on us that day, two insignificant specks of mortality flying there over that great, vast area in a small plane, speechless and deaf from the motors—just a dot in the center of 10,000 square miles of visible desolation."

Anxiously watching the leaking engine and the course line, the two men spelled each other at the wheel as they continued southward. Oil continued to pour from the engine, but the machine itself showed no sign of faltering. At length they reached a point from which they had calculated that they could easily have reached

Kings Bay on two engines, and they relaxed their vigil. But the leaking engine did not fail.

The hours now dragged, and the aviators anxiously scanned the horizons for a sign of landfall.

And then: "About 2:30, Greenwich, I started forward to ask Bennett if he could make out any land ahead, but just as I did he nodded his head, indicating there was something of interest to see. I hastened to the pilot's seat with my field glasses and sure enough, there was land at least 100 miles away. We had found the visibility in the Arctic remarkable in clear weather."

An hour later the *Josephine Ford* was approaching Kings Bay.

Russell D. Owen, staff correspondent of *The New York Times,* reported that final moment of triumph:

> The return came dramatically and suddenly at the end of an anxious day, for no signals had been identified by the American wireless operators after 4 o'clock in the morning, and anxiety was prevalent that something had happened.
>
> All the *Norge*'s crew and the others of the expedition were at dinner save two or three scanning the hills before going in.

After flying over the North Pole the *Josephine Ford* approaches to land at Kings Bay. Amundsen is in the foreground.
**(National Air and Space Museum, The Smithsonian Institution)**

All was quiet on the *Chantier* and none of her crew was ashore. In the *Norge*'s mess hall Captain Amundsen, Mr. Ellsworth and the others were ranged about the big tables finishing their soup, when the cry came "Byrd is coming!"

Sure enough, high over the hills on the other side of the bay a tiny speck showed the returning wings of the Fokker, darker blue against the pale blue sky. The hum of the motors was faintly heard—the sturdy motors which bore Commander Byrd and Pilot Bennett safely under the midnight sun, over the frozen sea whirring smoothly and tirelessly.

The plane swooped low over the field in a salute of victory, pulled up sharply, and then arched wide for the approach and landing. As the weary aviators climbed from their craft, men swarmed around them cheering and shouting. Finally the two heroes were carried across the field on the shoulders of their fellow Americans. Among the first to greet them were Amundsen and Ellsworth, sincere and enthusiastic in their congratulations.

"Then," reported Owen, "Byrd and Bennett turned and walked down the hill, led by Amundsen and Ellsworth. They got into a little boat which put out to the ship as the crew of the *Heimdal* lining the rail gave cheers and their band played 'The Star-Spangled Banner.' "

The cheering over, all attention now turned to the *Norge*. When he was asked if he would still attempt a dirigible flight to the Pole, Amundsen replied:

Amundsen congratulates Richard Byrd and Floyd Bennett upon their return from the North Pole.
**(National Air and Space Museum, The Smithsonian Institution)**

Charles A. Lindbergh congratulates Byrd upon his return to the United States from his successful Polar expedition.

**(National Archives)**

Commander Byrd's flight was a splendid deed, daringly carried out. All of us here were most happy to see him and Bennett return, enabling us to congratulate them on their well accomplished task.

He is the first to reach the North Pole through the air, having now, in a worthy manner, carried the American flag through the air to where Admiral Peary took it afoot across the polar ice.

No feeling of disappointment is mingled with my joy at Byrd's flight, owing to their start before us. Our plan is not changed. Already, early this Spring we cooperated with mutually beneficial results.

Byrd's object was to reach the Pole. Ours is to fly to Alaska via the Pole. I only hope we succeed as well as Byrd has.

Two days later the semirigid dirigible was ready for its flight. The rubberized bag was braced by a steel keel, joining latticed steel ribs, and filled with cells containing 550,000 cubic feet of the highly explosive hydrogen. The crew rode beneath the balloon in a forward control cabin stripped of its usual appointments to accommodate sixteen men. The dirigible was powered by three Maybach engines mounted in gondolas.

The balloon men had with them a sun compass, bubble sextant, drift indicator, and Commander Byrd's charts showing the compass variations of the polar regions. The charts had been presented to Amundsen by Byrd at a dinner the adventurers had shared the previous night aboard the *Heimdal*.

The *Norge*'s journey northward proceeded without serious mishap, although the formation of ice inside a gasoline line caused a temporary stoppage of one engine. As Nobile described the journey for *National Geographic Magazine:*

> For a while we caught occasional glimpses of white fishes here and there in the free water; then traces of polar bears on the ice; but when the latitude 84° N. was reached every trace of life utterly disappeared. The desolate Polar desert stretched to the horizon.
>
> At 11:15 P.M. we reached latitude 88°30′, only a degree and a half from the Pole. The fog is still very dense. Twenty minutes later, however, it begins to disperse and we can see the frozen sea below. High clouds hide the sun from time to time. Observations taken at 11:45 P.M. give: altitude, 2,500 feet; temperature, 12 degrees above zero.
>
> We are getting nearer and nearer the Pole. The moment so anxiously awaited is almost at hand. That minute for which I dreamed and labored months and months is imminent. I feel impatient, rather restless. An immense joy which I am hardly able to restrain is swelling my heart. I call Alessandrini and direct him to open the casket, to unfold our flag, and to fasten it to the spear which had been prepared with so much love by the Italians at King's Bay. Alessandrini joyfully sets himself to his task.
>
> We are drawing nearer and nearer. According to our calculations, we will be at the Pole in a few minutes. Impatiently I call to Alessandrini to hurry. Finally the flag is ready.
>
> At exactly 1:30 A.M., May 12, the sun's altitude shows that we have reached 90 degrees.

We are there at last!

I bring the *Norge* down to less than 700 feet and order the motors slowed down.

Amundsen is the first to throw his flag, the Norwegian; then Ellsworth releases the Stars and Stripes. Then it is my turn. I unfurl the Italian ensign from the window.

Soon all three flags stood in a soldier's row atop the North Pole. After taking pictures the airmen headed southward from the top of the world toward Alaska and regions never before seen by man.

Shortly after the *Norge* left the Pole, all communications between the dirigible and the listening posts on the shores of the Arctic Ocean trailed off into whistles and static. The *Norge* was moving beyond radio range and communications were further muffled in the radio interference of the Northern Lights and the layers of ice that coated the dirigible's antenna. An anxious world waited and listened. At Kings Bay, Byrd ordered the *Josephine Ford* made ready for a possible search mission. His airplane, he knew, was the only vehicle on station equipped to search the mid-Arctic Ocean reaches for the explorers if they had been forced onto the ice. But Amundsen had earlier warned that there would come a time of radio blockage, so those at Kings Bay waited.

Aboard the *Norge* new difficulties developed. The grizzly arctic explorer Amundsen clashed openly with Nobile, accusing the Italian of failing to act with calm and good judgment in minor crises. Nobile likewise grew short with the old man, declaring him to be an irascible grouch occupying his hours with unwelcome and erratic behavior. During the squabble, an ice fog began slowly to coat the ship, particularly the metal-skinned gondolas, with a dangerous, hard, white layer of ice. Some of the ice formed on the propellers only to crack loose in the fury of the spinning blades and fly with bulletlike force into the side of the hull, punching holes in the outer shell and threatening the hydrogen-bearing inner cells.

The worried crew raised the elevators to lift position and advanced the engines to full power in an attempt to climb above the fog, but the dirigible could not generate the necessary lift in the heavy chill of the frozen sky.

Frederick Ramm of *The New York Times* was aboard the ship to report the historic crossing and recalled:

> Ice formed on the engine gondolas and rigging and dropped off in pieces and was then caught by the propellers and shot through the ship, together with the pieces of ice formed on the propellers themselves.
>
> These were very exciting hours, the crew being engaged continuously in patching holes in the fabric covering the keel and all the air balloons. The gas bags fortunately had been strengthened to meet this eventuality, but we could not know if our precautions had been sufficient.
>
> Therefore, watching the ice pack beneath us was no longer platonic but was mingled with the thought, "how could we walk on it?"

At length the northern tip of Alaska was sighted. Approaching Point Barrow, the polar explorers attempted to establish radio communication, but without success. Turning the airship westward, they sailed slowly into the Bering Strait for the added safety factor of flying over water. When they had passed through the strait and into the Bering Sea, they turned eastward on a course toward Nome. They were running in ice fog and bucking a head wind which had reduced their ground speed to thirty miles per hour. They were lost. As Ramm reported: "Then we observed that the course was giving us first open water and then ice, even toward the south. Such drift ice is better to come down on than open water. We changed our course accordingly by turning northward, where the ice was better.

"We made slow progress with 40 degrees of drift, at times more than we had all last night. We called wireless stations in an effort to get our bearings, but in vain. At last we crossed land and saw an Eskimo hut. We tried to go down and ask our position, but heavy squalls and bumps in the air prevented this."

Turning in circles, the ship crept above the heavy fog, took a sun position, and dropped slowly through the mist to locate land. Twisting and turning in hyperbolic curves, the dirigible-balloon battled violent winds and blinding clouds for two days as it attempted to reach Nome, where a mooring mast and a crew awaited.

Within the crowded cabin the crew, painfully chilled, hungry, and at a point of almost total exhaustion, struggled through their duties. And Nobile and Amundsen were in constant argument.

Finally the *Norge* reached a frozen bay bounded by giant snowy banks and a small cluster of houses. This was Grantley Harbor at Teller, Alaska, where a few white men and fifty-five Eskimos made their home.

Umberto Nobile later wrote of this moment:

> We were drawing near the coast. The open sea ended and the ice began. Running along a dismal, grayish shore, bordered by dreary hills, we crossed a frozen creek. A few black spots [shacks] appeared, and, to complete the picture of desolation, an abandoned three-masted steamer lay on her side in the middle of the ice.
>
> Wisting was at the steering wheel, with Captain Amundsen standing at his side. We tried to proceed over a frozen lagoon separated from the sea by a narrow strip of land, but it was soon seen that with such a wind it would be impossible to pass through the hills along the river. We veered to the right. Yonder, a few miles away, we could discern some houses. I tried to get there, running all three motors at 1,200 revolutions, but notwithstanding these desperate efforts, we were advancing at a snail's pace.
>
> The weather grew rapidly worse; the sky was black. While crossing the coast near a hill, the ship pitched on the bow and tilted at an angle of thirty degrees. Apparently Nome was still far away.
>
> With the crew completely exhausted, to continue our run in the face of such a tempest seemed to me the acme of madness. Cecioni and our motor mechanics had been working for four days at a stretch. It was nothing short of a miracle that they could still stand on their feet.
>
> It was a dramatic moment. A delay of half an hour in coming to a decision might spell disaster, the tragical end to our achievement. I deemed it imperative to land immediately, before the tempest should force the ship out of control.

The *Norge* descended cautiously. As the battered vessel eased to the ground an anchor was dropped and Sgt. Ettore Anduino, assistant mechanic, bravely slid down the rope in the teeth of the chilling wind. With the aid of the handful of villagers who had come running to witness the arrival of the strange vehicle, the ship was pulled to a landing. Nobile immediately ordered the venting of the hydrogen; and the giant dirigible sighed to a collapse on the frozen bay, leaving only a skeleton of metal to be disassembled for return shipment to Italy.

The adventurers had flown 2,700 miles in 70 hours, 40 minutes, traveling over the North Pole and charting previously unmapped regions as they went. They, too, reported that they had seen no islands, no mountains, no land in the endless Arctic Ocean.

News of the *Norge*'s safe landing was flashed to a waiting and anxious world. Once rested, fed, and warm again, several of the crewmen volunteered to travel with Amundsen on any further arctic adventures he might command. To this the old lion replied: "When I was a young man I made up my mind to visit the globe's two Poles and pass through the Northwest and Northeastern Passages. Now that these things are done, a new generation may continue."

But he was to have one final journey to the Arctic.

The race by air to the Pole was over, but to George H. Wilkins and Carl B. Eielson of the Detroit arctic expedition the allure and the challenge of the Arctic had not been diminished by the Byrd and *Norge* triumphs. Determined to make up for their earlier failure, the two men were back at the rim of the Arctic Ocean the following year. They made several exploratory flights in their Lockheed "Vega" monoplane, not enough to establish any records, but enough to bring them back to the Arctic again in the spring of 1928. This time they planned to reverse the direction of the *Norge* and to fly from Point Barrow to Spitsbergen, not over the North Pole but over the polar seas north of Canada.

With the aid of friendly Eskimos, the two men dug a runway fourteen feet wide and five thousand feet long as a ski run for their fuel-laden Lockheed. On April 15 the airmen made good their takeoff and set their course for Spitsbergen. The flight over the ice pack was without incident. But as they approached Norway, they flew into ice fog that forced them up to six thousand feet. Near Svalbard, where the clouds reached higher, the airmen began to follow routes through valleys, not penetrating the clouds themselves in instrument flight for fear of the mountains which

The Lockheed Vega airplane of Wilkins and Eielson being towed by dog team to the takeoff position at Point Barrow.
**(National Air and Space Museum, The Smithsonian Institution)**

lay hidden in the cloud cover. Because it was impossible to see the ground, they could not get a positive fix on their location. Captain Wilkins told the rest of the story in *The New York Times*:

> Suddenly two sharp peaks, almost needle-pointed, appeared beneath us. Down we spun through a break in the clouds for a closer view. The air was turbulent above the heavy clouds and between and beneath them it was boisterous. Our almost empty plane was tossed like a cork on a stormy ocean. Close to the ice-strewn water the wind was furious. Salt spray whipped from the sea filled the air. Over the land the snow drifted high and thick. To judge distances was impossible. A smooth patch of snow covered land flashed by for a moment, then dead ahead a mountain loomed. With a quick swerve it was avoided by a narrow margin. We swung broadside to the wind and crabbed low over the water. Soon it appeared that what we had missed was an island. The glimpse was too fleeting to identify it.
>
> As we were running short of gas, the safest procedure was to find the smooth spot we had noticed and try to land. The wind was so strong that we stopped within 30 feet after the skis touched the snow.

For five days the storm raged, piling five-foot drifts over their landing strip. The two men remained inside the airplane cabin, subsisting on a few biscuits and chocolate bars and smoking what few cigarettes remained between them. When the storm abated they shoveled their way from the machine and hurried to clear a crude runway while the good weather lasted. After six hours of digging they started their engine, and using only a minimum warmup to conserve gasoline, Eielson opened the throttle for takeoff. The plane would not budge: the skis were frozen to the ice.

Wilkins recounted:

When I got out and pushed the tail, she started fine, but to climb back in as she moved was difficult. The first time I hung on to the step and tried to climb in, but soon fell off. Eielson, unable to see behind from the pilot's seat, thought I was in and took off. When he turned he saw me forlorn on the ice. He circled and landed, slinging out a rope ladder provided for such emergency.

I decided to hang on at all costs. We started again. As the machine gathered speed I climbed to the tail and struggled desperately to gain the cockpit. I grasped the rope with my teeth to help hang on. Eielson, feeling the weight on the tail, thought I was safe and took off, but just before he left the ground I slithered from the shiny fuselage, was struck by the tail of the machine, and flung to the snow. When the snow was freed from my eyes and mouth I found that I had escaped with no more harm than loosened teeth.

Eielson in the air soon discovered I was still on the ice, so he circled and landed again. We decided on one more try. We had been running the engine for an hour, using half our precious gasoline. The next time I stuck one foot in the cockpit and pushed with my other foot on some driftwood found on the land. As soon as the machine moved I tumbled into the cockpit regardless of bruises, and off we climbed in the air. Since the sky had cleared, we had been too busy trying to get away to think of our exact location, but soon after we circled a headland, having climbed to 3,000 feet, we could see in the distance the wireless mast at Green Harbor ice bay after having been stormbound for five days on Dead Man's Island.

During that same spring, Umberto Nobile, now a general, returned to the Arctic in a new dirigible, the *Italia*, but without

Roald Amundsen, who as a result of their continued public and private arguments was now his enemy. It was Nobile's purpose to prove that he, in his own ship, without Norwegians or Americans, could make a successful polar flight, for the glory of Italy and General Umberto Nobile.

By easy stages the *Italia* reached Kings Bay from Milan. Two flights in early May established Nobile and the *Italia* as *bona fide* polar explorers. The first was not spectacular, but the second was seventy hours long and covered a distance of 2,375 miles, providing superb photographs of previously uncharted arctic regions from Franz Josef Land to Severnaya Land and back.

On May 23, Nobile turned the *Italia* toward the North Pole. One day later her wireless reported that she had attained her goal. The next day, May 25, the *Italia* reported all well and that she was returning home. The optimistic message was premature, for within the hour a violent storm broke and radio communication ended.

For a week there was no word from General Nobile or his ship. When hope had been all but abandoned, faint dots and dashes of the international SOS were heard. Then the anxiously awaited message came. Ice had formed on the large gas bag, making the *Italia* unmanageable and causing it to crash into the polar ice 220 miles from her base. General Nobile and ten of his crew had been thrown out, one man was killed, and the forward gondola had been wrecked. The gasbag became a balloon in the wind, a cork in the sea. Completely out of control and still carrying six men aboard, the *Italia* drifted off to the east. Nobile insisted later that he saw a burst of flame and smoke, but nothing was ever heard or seen again of either the *Italia* or of the men who vanished with the dirigible.

Meanwhile, in response to desperate pleas for help, relief expeditions converged on Spitsbergen by dog team, icebreaker, and air. Five nations joined in the search. Amundsen forgot his quarrel with Nobile and agreed to accompany René Guilbaud and four other men in the French seaplane *Latham 47* in a search-and-rescue attempt.

Tragedy doubled upon itself. After one brief radio communication from the Amundsen party, they too disappeared for eternity into the grinding polar sea. Search efforts to find Amundsen now overlapped those seeking Nobile.

A tent dyed red was set up. The majority of the remaining crew stayed with Nobile to wait and hope for rescue. The other men set out to cross the arctic pack on foot. On June 20 an Italian, Major Umberto Maddalena, searching in a large Savoia seaplane, sighted the red tent and located those who had remained with General Nobile. The men were on a floe and had drifted to within thirty miles of the northern tip of Spitsbergen. Because the ice around the stranded adventurers was breaking up, a landing by either a ski or seaplane appeared impossible. Maddalena did not attempt one; instead he dropped supplies and radioed the location of the stranded men.

Four days later, Lt. Einar-Paal Lundborg, a Swedish pilot, landed his tiny ski-mounted Fokker monoplane near the *Italia* survivors. Eager for the honor of rescuing Nobile, he convinced the general that he should be the first off the ice, an offer Nobile accepted and one he would regret for the rest of his days.

Lundborg returned Nobile to civilization; but when he went back for the others, he crashed on landing and joined the ranks of the shipwrecked. Thirteen days later Lundborg was rescued by a friend and fellow aviator; the remaining men were picked up by the Russian icebreaker *Krassin,* which had been able to cut through the melting floes. Miraculously, this same ship also found the survivors among the men who had attempted to walk.

At one time or another twenty-four planes were busy with the search, and like Lieutenant Lundborg some of the rescuers had to be rescued. The entire episode was one of disunity, folly, tragedy, and finally pathos.

Charges and countercharges flashed among the survivors. A full board of inquiry called by Generalissimo Benito Mussolini found Nobile responsible for the disaster. He resigned his commission. The public at large could never forgive him, the captain of the ship, for allowing himself to be rescued from the ice before he had seen to the safety of his men. Thus damned, Nobile faded from the scene, a plaintive and broken man.

It should be noted that not all of the polar adventurers belong to an older generation. In 1950, a quiet forty-year-old commercial-airline pilot, Capt. Charles Blair, made up his mind that he would challenge the arctic ice pack, alone, in an Air Force surplus North American P-51 "Mustang." Blair spent the winter converting

Capt. Charles Blair in *Excalibur III*.
**(National Air and Space Museum, The Smithsonian Institution)**

the World War II fighter. He installed enough spare fuel tanks
to carry it across an ocean and fitted the craft with a 1,700-
horsepower Rolls-Royce Merlin engine. The plane, christened
the *Excalibur III*, was decorated with an American flag near
the cockpit and a red-and-white barber-pole insignia on its tail.
Blair was ready for the North Pole.

For a shakedown flight Blair sought the jet stream and rode
that invisible tunnel of zooming air from Idlewild International
Airport to London, England, in 7 hours, 48 minutes. A world
record in itself, and he had yet to begin his real flight.

He planned to take off from Bardufoss, Norway, and fly a direct route across the North Pole to Fairbanks, Alaska. To handle both a navigator's and pilot's tasks in the single-place craft, he "prepackaged" his navigation, a blueprint for future polar explorers. Captain Blair prepared a flight log, plotting his course in advance for a precise calendar day, May 29, and for a takeoff exactly at 1500 Greenwich mean time. This allowed him to calculate in advance the exact angle of the sun at a specific time and place along his route. Making the sun a route marker, he could take fixes with a sun compass and the angle measurer mounted in the cockpit. These instruments, along with a bubble sextant. were his navigational equipment, plus the radio direction finder which would be useful near his destination.

The *Excalibur III* was ready for takeoff from Bardufoss, a small field beside an icy-gray fjord bordered by spectacular mountains, at 1430 hours on May 29, 1951. Everything was carefully checked, and the handsome crew-cut aviator, wearing a baggy tweed suit, climbed into his fighter. None of the trappings of the arctic explorer were to be seen: no heavy parka, no animal furs, no skis, not even a pickax. Blair *had* to fly across the pole; surely he was not equipped to walk back.

At precisely 1500 hours Blair snapped his toes forward on the rudder to release his brakes, and the heavily loaded *Excalibur III* lumbered down the runway. The field had only one direction—down the gorge—and a tail wind added to the problem, but the magnificent Rolls-Royce engine lifted man, machine, and 865 gallons of gasoline into the air and northward for the pole.

As the plane crossed Spitsbergen, the northernmost tip of land, Blair was able to get a radio fix and double-check his prepackaged navigation system. He was on course and on time.

The *Excalibur III* climbed easily to its cruising altitude of 22,000 feet, where Blair carefully adjused his oxygen mask.

Below stretched the great polar ice cap, broken by leads and gray-blue hummocks of aging ice. This was the same Arctic Ocean that ended the Amundsen-Ellsworth expedition and brought the *Italia* to its tragic finale. A forced landing, however, would be impossible for Captain Blair in his converted fighter with its 145-miles-per-hour landing speed. When Blair's preplanned log indicated that he was fast approaching the magical latitude 90 degrees north, he raised his sextant and looked at the sun. Charlie Blair was at the North Pole.

A sense of conquest and of awe swept over him—a swell of triumph, and a feeling of humility as he contemplated the smallness of man in the vastness of the arctic waste. In his pocket he had a letter addressed to Santa Claus from his young son; and he mailed it out of his window, dipping his wing to watch as the letter fluttered downward until it was no longer visible.

The sun moved slowly from the side of the airplane to a point at its front, causing a blinding glare from the ice below. Blair held his course over the islands and arctic ice north of Canada until, at a moment predetermined in his log, he reached up and snapped a small toggle. His radio direction compass jumped alive, and through the headset came the faint radio signal: dit, dah, dah, dit—dah, dit dit dit—dit, dah—PBA, PBA, the code letters for Point Barrow. The needle of the instrument pointed straight up, his destination was dead ahead. Ten hours, 27 minutes from takeoff, the *Excalibur III* flashed over the end of the runway, then banked in a tight 360-degree turn to the left, rolling out in a fighter approach to touch down on the airstrip at Fairbanks. Charlie Blair had, as he later told a friend, "gotten the North Pole out of my system!" The flight, however, captured few headlines. Regardless of the flying skill and personal daring required of Charlie Blair to pilot his small fighter airplane across the Arctic, the North Pole had already been conquered. Only those challenges that could take man yet higher or faster could again arouse the public to acclaim an aviation feat.

CHAPTER 12

# A Long Flight
# Across the Pacific

The adolescence of aviation occurred during those sensational years between the World Wars. World War I brought the airplane out of its infancy and gave wings to countless young men who restlessly sought the adventures to be found in aeronautics. The Armistice disengaged an army of ready airmen and released them to a society that as yet had no commercial uses for their skills. One former Army pilot summarized the situation by observing that "the greatest hazard in aviation today is starving to death."

Men and machines electrified the public with one spectacular aerial exploit after another as they traveled higher, faster, and farther.

U. S. Army flyers circled the earth, Lindbergh crossed the Atlantic, Byrd reached the North Pole, and, predictably, aviators were eyeing the challenges of the open waters of the mid-Pacific for aerial conquest. To fire an interest in westward flights, James D. Dole, the "Pineapple King," offered 35,000 dollars to the first and second aviators who flew nonstop from North America to Honolulu. The distance was not as great as that which had been flown by Lindbergh; but the navigational skills required were more exacting, because an error of only a few degrees could carry a plane past the cluster of the Hawaiian Islands and out of reach of land. The "Dole Derby" became a mad scramble as planes and pilots set out to capture the prizes. On August 17, 1927, Art Goebel and Bill Davis in the *Woolaroc* made the first successful flight, followed two hours later by Martin Jensen and Paul Schluter in the *Aloha*. Others were not so lucky, and

210

accounts of planes unreported and presumed lost in the Pacific were a tragic reminder that there was still much to be learned in the development of long-distance aircraft.

Amid the excitement of the Dole Derby, two Australians arrived in the United States with a government grant to locate a proper airplane, outfit it, and fly from America across the Pacific to Australia. The two men, Capt. Charles E. Kingsford-Smith and Charles T. P. Ulm, both former World War I flyers, declined the opportunity to participate in the Dole Derby as they made elaborate plans for a more ambitious Pacific flight.

In spite of their grant, Kingsford-Smith and Ulm faced formidable financial problems. They purchased a slightly damaged Fokker tri-motor from the arctic explorer Capt. George H. Wilkins, who had failed in the aerial assault upon the North Pole in 1926. They used the balance of their funds to equip the plane with three Wright Whirlwind engines, which they believed to be the most reliable.

Handicapped by a mounting lack of funds and a change of heart by the newly elected Australian government, the two men came close to abandoning their endeavor. They were ready to accept their government's cancelation of their flight orders, sell their airplane, and catch a boat for home when they met a millionaire shipbuilder, G. Allan Hancock. He liked the eager Aussies and believed they had the skills necessary to complete their ambitious enterprise.

Hancock told the flyers: "It's crazy as hell, but I'll pay for all the fuel you'll need for the trip, cover your out-of-pocket expenses as far as hotels, clothes and anything else that needs paying for on the trip is concerned, and I'll give you sufficient cash to pay for anything you need immediately. You can pay me back some day. Right now just get at it."

When two Americans, Harry W. Lyon, a navigator, and James Warner, a radio operator, joined the flight, the trans-Pacific crew was complete.

Kingsford-Smith and Ulm christened their ship the *Southern Cross* after the majestic constellation of the Southern Hemisphere. By dawn, May 31, 1928, the *Southern Cross* was ready for takeoff from Oakland, California.

A gray blanket of mist lay across San Francisco Bay as the

four men climbed into the cockpit and signaled to crank up the three engines. A slight offshore breeze stirred across the airstrip. Kingsford-Smith recalled:

> We knew that beyond Wheeler Field, Honolulu, we were to face a great sweep of ocean, over which the steady drone of an airplane motor had never been heard. We fully appraised the chances against us on the long unflown 3,100 mile airline to Suva, with its Island landing places, were not such as would add to the peace of mind of any pilot. Yet there, beyond Hawaii, lay the charm—the intriguing thrill of the flight for us. Out over that 3,000 miles we were to face with what might be termed "virgin air" in tropic conditions that we fully realized would test both the skill and the equipment of the expedition to the utmost. There was mystery beyond the green pinnacle of Mauna Kea and the crater of Mauna Loa, the kind of mystery that called Magellan far south in the trackless wastes of the same ocean.
>
> At the takeoff, each of the three motors reached 1,800 revolutions, giving us a takeoff speed of 76 knots. We climbed 1,000 feet in seven minutes at 80 knots, and then turned to fly over the city.

Through the day the three engines hummed in loud but comforting harmony. The small cockpit was cramped and the engine's roar was deafening to the airmen. Their only means of communication among themselves was by scribbled notes. Boredom, more than the elements, was their greatest enemy. As Kingsford-Smith later noted:

> Refreshing sleep was not possible with the continuous roar at our ears. Yet the monotony grew and grew with the passage of the hours, and the lack of incident.
>
> It was then that we passed pencilled messages to and fro that were not always concerned with the navigation of the plane. Personal chaff of a forcible kind went back and forth. Some of these notes none of us had the hardihood to keep. The good-humored banter embellished at times by colourful adjectives would not have looked as amusing in cold unsympathetic print. At the time, however, they were as manna from heaven during that long period of monotony the first day out.

Soon the bright sun dropped into the sea, splashing a brilliant sunset on the horizon ahead. Night brought a gentle breeze, a calm sea, and a lustrous full moon. "We just sat there with that painful smarting of eyes that have had no rest intensified by the bite in the air," remarked Kingsford-Smith. "A numbness crept into our frames, and we had to whip up our brains to make them work at all."

Later the monotony was broken by a cloud deck that stretched ahead, horizon to horizon. The *Southern Cross* climbed to six thousand feet, where it skimmed the top of the clouds as the moonlight cast the shadow of their airplane on the cloud-layer billows below.

Then slowly, almost painfully, the faint light of dawn began to push back the darkness. With full daylight, they descended to 1,250 feet and leveled under a thin cloud layer drifting before a mild breeze. They had been flying for twenty-four hours, and their redrimmed eyes searched ahead for a glimpse of land. Overly anxious, they would nudge each other, pointing to suspected land-falls that turned out to be cloud formations. Although falsely encouraged by the clouds and their weary, mirage-inclined minds they still had presence of mind to hold to their predetermined course.

Ulm described the actual landfall: "It was 10:52 A.M. when it happened. Kingsford-Smith was at the controls. We were look-ing for solids in the cloud drifts, and were being deceived time and again. We were now continually jabbing each other in the ribs and pointing down to a possible solid. But the possible solids proved negative; till far away on the port bow a brown bulge suddenly emerged—a dome-like island that rose from a vast ocean of vapour."

"It was Mauna Kea—the snow-capped extinct volcano. At last we had our guide to the Islands. We had been 26 hours in the air."

The *Southern Cross* flew on to Oahu and passed over Honolulu. Kingsford-Smith brought the plane in for a smooth landing at Wheeler Field, where the trans-Pacific flyers were greeted by a wildly excited crowd of well-wishers.

Escorted to the Royal Hawaiian Hotel, the airmen fell into deep and welcome sleep. While they slept, men of the United States Military Command, directed by one of the round-the-world flyers, Capt. Lowell Smith, worked on their airplane to have it in readiness for the next and most dangerous leg of their flight—to Suva in the Fiji Islands.

The following afternoon a lightly loaded *Southern Cross* flew to a beach at Barking Sands on the island of Kauai, where there was a runway long enough to permit a heavyweight takeoff.

In the early dawn of June 3 the *Southern Cross* lifted from the beach after a 3,400-foot run. The airmen climbed to three hundred feet, leveled off to conserve fuel for the unknowns ahead, and held an outbound course on a radio-beacon leg which would guide them for at least the first seven hundred miles out of the Islands. "Ahead of us every mile was to be aerial exploration," wrote Kingsford-Smith. "We were indeed on the borders of a new air world. Out over the sea there was the thrill and charm of uncertainty."

At eleven-forty, beyond the range of the radio beacon, the *Southern Cross* plunged into dark rainsqualls.

"The rainstorms surged in round us," recalled Kingsford-Smith. "We were 600 feet up, and as we had been flying for only six and a half hours, our petrol load was still tremendous. To fly low in such atrocious conditions, heavily overloaded, was an experience that did not at all add any to the peace of mind."

In and out of storms rolled the airplane, as the aviators clung to the lower altitude to conserve the precious fuel. Noon came, and they still battered through storms.

Ulm remembered: "The cloud curtains thickened; the rain lashed us with greater fury, and again we were in that dim opaque world flying blind. The windshields began to leak, and water started to trickle in on us. Then our real personal discomfort commenced. Water splashed into the cockpit and soaked our feet and legs. In less than half an hour we were very damp and a little disgruntled."

Throughout the day the *Southern Cross* bore into the rainstorms. Kingsford-Smith and Ulm alternated at the controls, one hour on, one hour off. In the afternoon a clogged fuel line caused one engine to sputter and threaten to quit. While the men were checking their engine instruments, the fuel-line stoppage cleared itself and the engine purred again.

As daylight began to fade, the aviators increased engine power and began a gradual climb to altitude for night flying. As the storm continued without letup, there was added safety in altitude. When darkness fell Kingsford-Smith and Ulm flew by instruments in the eerie lights of the flight panel. They kept climbing. At eight thousand feet they burst through the top and according to Kingsford-Smith "looked down into a world of tumbled vapour, ranging away in ragged fringes on every side. Above us, as we emerged from the murk, glittered the Southern Cross, the constellation whose name we were proud to bear on our ship. It winked out a genial welcome to us after the stress of the battle far below. It glimmered on the port bow like a shower of diamonds in a vault of the deepest blue."

Climbing and dodging storms had cost the airmen a precious hour. Shortly before midnight, they reaffirmed their course by a star fix on the Southern Cross and flew over the equator. Soon the dashlights failed and the pilots were reduced to using a flashlight to illuminate the instrument panel.

"From 1 o'clock to 4 o'clock on that tropic morning," wrote Kingsford-Smith, "were hours of monotony. Our eyes were again beginning to feel dragged and worn from lack of sleep. We were slowly drying out in the waves of heat from the engines after our earlier ducking by the leak of the wind-shield."

The monotony, however, was of short duration. By six o'clock they were once again riding the bucking currents of a tropical storm while lightning slashed around them. Changing course, the aviators swept wide around the storm, occasionally circling away from their track. Dawn came, but the storm did not abate.

The day wore on, and finally the tempest faded astern. The flyers were able to get a fix on their position, but now the tropical heat became oppressive, forcing them to strip out of their heavy flying suits.

Winging over the Pacific, turning and circling as they wound their way around new thunderstorms, they had to make a landfall on a dot of an island. They were approaching the most critical moment of their journey.

The weather began to clear. Cotton puffs of clouds accented the tropical sun that blazed down upon the azure waters, as Harry Lyon hurried with the sextant to take a sun shot and relocate their position. He found that they were slightly east of course, but the Fiji Islands were somewhere just ahead.

Ulm wrote:

We had been 32 hours in the air, and we felt that it was high time that we sighted land. Before us stretched a mirror of turquoise, broken only by the white crests kicked up by the southeast trade wind. It had now swung almost dead against the ship. With our great spread of wing we often got a savage jolt as the wing tip picked up a puff of contrary wind, and we fell or rose on the invisible hillock of air that was formed.

For three hours we glided steadily across the tropical sea of deep blue flashing in the glare of a sun like burnished copper.

Then came the next memorable moment of the flight.

Our eyes were strained for the first glimpse of the dot that was Fiji. It seemed as if the dot would never show up. So much had we been told of the long shot that we were making for a dot on the map, that we began to think in terms of "dots."

But at 1:10 P.M. Fiji burst into view, not as a dot, but as a small brown dome. Still 70 miles away, it was minute enough to be a silent traffic cop set in the ocean!

By three-forty-five the aviators had winged through the islands and swung in a wide sweep over Suva, with twelve hours of fuel remaining in their tanks. Kingsford-Smith was at the controls as they let down toward Albert Park, the green and grassy area which was to serve as their landing site. Prior to this moment there had never been an airplane in the Fiji Islands.

Ulm recalled:

Below us the white roofs glinted among great banks of trees and shrubs. Every house seemed to stand in the centre of a grove of trees and on a hill the official residence of the Governor stood out against the deep bronze-green background of bush.

For us it was at once a moment of triumph and anxiety. Strange as it may seem, an airman's most tense hour is the last hour he is in the air.

The landing ground at Albert Park Sports Oval was barely 400 yards long. We had asked the local authorities to have the telegraph wires at the northwestern corner of the ground removed. Three large trees had also been cut down to give us as clear a space as possible in which to land. Our old Flying Corps friends, Major Clive Joske and Captain Samuel Ellis, had put in place bold distinguishing marks long before we arrived.

There is no question that his was the most difficult landing we had to make since we owned the Fokker. After thirty hours in the air we were not altogether as bright as when we stepped into the cockpit at Barking Sands. The savage battering of the rain squalls, too, had added to our fatigue. An awkward problem for us was a sudden drop of ten or twelve feet from the road to the surface of the field itself. Kingsford-Smith had the controls, and he brought the machine on over the road at 65 miles an hour.

For a few seconds we had that nasty feeling that a crash was certain. The machine touched the ground halfway up the field. At the end of the field was a sharp rise clothed in trees and thick undergrowth. As we rushed on towards this rise, however, our hearts rose again. There was room there to swing to the left. Smith ground-looped the plane, and we finished our run without imposing any strain whatever on the machine.

As the engines coughed to a stop, great throngs of people who had been waiting under the trees surrounding the park rushed toward the plane. There was a tumultuous welcome for the weary and temporarily deafened airmen. Sensibly, however, their hosts quickly ushered the flyers across the road to the Grand Pacific Hotel and needed sleep.

Two days later the *Southern Cross* was on its final leg to Australia. Out of Fiji the airmen ran into storms more fierce than any encountered thus far. Sheets of lightning flashed across their paths as they battled the weather hour after hour. The *Southern Cross* was a small cork bobbing in vicious convective currents of air, buffeted by strong winds, and lashed by pouring rains.

By morning the *Southern Cross* had passed through the thunderheads, and the great continent of Australia stretched before the joyful eyes of the four aviators. At Brisbane 65,000 people jammed Eagle Farm Airport to hail the conquering heroes.

At 9:50 A.M. Ulm stated in his flight log: "In an hour or so we will have satisfied our ambition to be the first ones to cross the Pacific by air." It was ten-fifty when the *Southern Cross* touched gently onto the field.

An Australian newspaper reporter who watched the historic landing wrote: "It is a long time since Brisbane has been so stirred by any event. The northern capital takes life in a casual sort of way for the most part, and no flight has so gripped the imagination of the people as the present one. It was the idea, the vision in the public mind of the sudden swoop of the *Southern Cross* out of the blue grey vault over the boundless Pacific that set Brisbane pulses beating faster."

A cheering crowd carried the four airmen to a waiting motorcade and a victory parade through the jubilant city. The entire populace of Brisbane turned out to salute the weary aviators who had established a new world record.

In 1934, Charles Ulm set out once more from California to retrace the route of the *Southern Cross*. For the return he selected a twin-engined British Airspeed Envoy, and George Littlejohn and J. Leon Skilling flew with him. Ulm's announced purpose was to chart a course for commercial airplanes, but he never reached Hawaii. Radio messages indicated that the Airspeed Envoy was in trouble, and "Come and get us. On the water now" was the last communication from the stricken aircraft. A naval search ensued, but the three airmen had vanished in the boundless Pacific.

The following year, Kingsford-Smith and Tom Pethyridge left England in an attempt to break the seventy-one hour flight record from England to Australia. Winging low over the Bay of Bengal, Kingsford-Smith at the controls fell asleep for a single, fateful moment; a wing kissed a slapping wave, and the *Lady Southern Cross* and its aviators perished in the churning sea.

Kingsford-Smith is still honored by the proud Australians. In 1966, Ward McNally said of the trail-blazing flyer: "Those of us old enough to remember him as he was when he flew the *Southern Cross* out of the mists of the Pacific, to climb red-eyed and grinning from her cabin, need no reminding. To us he is forever linked to aviation; his name immortal."

# CHAPTER 13

# Faster and Faster
# Around the World

As men traveled farther in airplanes, the lure of circumnavigating the world faster was a recurring summons to adventure. The U. S. Army pilots had first shown the way by circling the globe in 175 days. In 1928, John Henry Mears and his private pilot, C. B. D. Collyer, traveled by plane and steamship to gird the earth in a record time of 23 days, 15 hours, and 21 minutes. As noted in Chapter 8, the mammoth dirigible *Graf Zeppelin* shattered both records in 1929. This spectacular success was a challenge to aviators everywhere who believed that heavier-than-air flight was the destiny of future air travel.

The following year Wiley Post, a test pilot, parachute jumper, and daredevil wing-walker from Oklahoma, set his sights on shattering the *Zeppelin*'s round-the-world record. Securing the sponsorship of his boss, F. C. Hall, an oil-rich Oklahoman, Wiley Post made plans for the flight. He enlisted the aid of Harold Gatty, an Australian navigator, and the two men carefully mapped their route, making advance arrangements for fuel and supplies. Post's specially equipped Lockheed Vega, a high-winged monoplane powered by a single Pratt & Whitney engine, was christened the *Winnie Mae* in honor of Winnie Mae Fain, the airminded daughter of their benefactor, F. C. Hall.

When all was in readiness, the adventurers went to Washington and marched into the Department of Immigration and Naturalization passport office to explain their special visa needs. Post's unilluminating explanation: "We want to take the record away from the balloons,'' only served to confuse an already bewildered clerk, but visas were finally obtained.

On June 23, 1931, Post and Gatty arrived at Roosevelt Field, on Long Island, New York, just before dawn for their scheduled takeoff. The probing headlamps of autos and the floodlights on the hangars illuminated a drenching rain that poured sheets of water across the airport apron. A handful of spectators stood huddled under umbrellas. There was no actual daybreak that morning, but rather a faint lightening of the gray darkness of the rain-filled sky. A reporter described the scene: ''Post stuck a swarthy hand out the window of the automobile and observed that the rain was slacking. 'All right, Harold, let's go,' he said as he tumbled out of the car and walked toward the *Winnie Mae*, calling to a small group of drenched spectators: 'Somebody want to crank me up?'

''The light of photographers' flares and the stabbing finger of a revolving beacon picked out the *Winnie Mae* for a moment at the head of the runway. Then a roar from the supercharged Wasp motor, a streak down the field, and the ship's navigating lights were blinking a 'goodbye' from the North at 4:56 A.M.''

Within seven hours the aviators had reached their first destination, Harbour Grace, Newfoundland, a distance of 1,153 miles. From this field they headed out across the Atlantic, boosted by a thirty-mile-per-hour tail wind. They held their course by compass heading and calculated drift, intending to make landfall by

Post's specially equipped Lockheed Vega.

**(National Archives)**

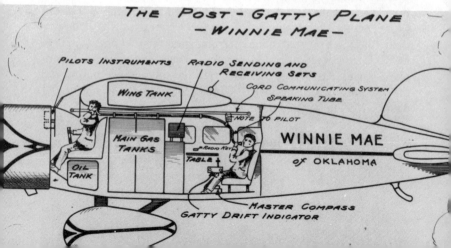

dead reckoning. Gatty's special navigational skills, which he had learned at the Australian Naval Academy, were useless in the heavily overcast skies. Heaven and sea blurred into an indistinguishable gray and often were completely black. Sixteen hours from Newfoundland they saw daylight again.

"I don't think we can honestly say we were lost," Post said later, "but we just didn't know where we were [sic]." Daylight also brought a sighting of land. Rolling into a steep diving turn, Post winged down through a hole in the cloud deck below. Beneath this cloud layer, in the early morning haze, they saw an airport. Upon landing they asked, "Is this England, Scotland or Wales?"

"England," came the reply, and indeed they had reached the Sealand airdrome near Chester, England.

After a brief two-hour refueling stop, the two men roared off the English soil to Berlin; but numbed with fatigue, they erroneously landed at Hanover. Informed of their error, they took off again for their original destination, only to realize they hadn't refueled. Without enough fuel to reach Berlin, they were forced to return to Hanover. Chagrined, the flyers noted that their second

Post and Gatty.

**(National Archives)**

landing elicited somewhat less enthusiasm from the sprinkling of spectators at the airport.

A tremendous ovation greeted them, however, when they arrived that evening at Berlin's Tempelhof airdrome. A massive throng of spectators shouted and cheered the spectacular flight and intrepid flyers.

At a hotel near the airport, Post and Gatty had their first meal since leaving America, followed by hot baths and a good night's sleep.

Wiley Post wrote that evening: "A lot of people wonder what a pilot thinks about while winging over empty water. I suppose they would be surprised to know that one really does not think about much of anything. There are three instruments that have to be kept just where they ought to be, and that pretty well displaces other thoughts." Post referred to the altimeter, airspeed indicator, and compass, his basic instruments for the circumnavigation of the world.

At seven o'clock the next morning, the aviators were well rested and ready for their next destination, Moscow.

"The distance was 925 miles, according to our charts," wrote Post. "We left early in the morning and pretty soon crossed the border into Poland. There we had absolutely the dirtiest flying of our whole experience on this or any other flight. The ceiling simply closed down on us and forced us right down on the tree tops. We had to fight wind and rain as well as fog. Landmarks slipped by so fast that we had trouble checking the course, anything like celestial observation was impossible. The drift indicator held out, though, and from it we hit our mark on the nose through dead reckoning."

In Moscow they were greeted by the *Ossaciakhim,* the Soviet Society for Aviation and Chemical Defense, who insisted on feting the aviators with a spectacular party and a nine-course dinner at the Grand Hotel. Because of the elongated festivities, the two men were not in the best condition when they left the next morning to follow the Trans-Siberian Railway over the Ural Mountains to Novosibirsk. Moreover, the Russian mechanics who refueled the plane had confused the measurement of liters for gallons and overloaded the machine. It took Post and Gatty nearly four hours to siphon off the dangerous overload.

Eleven hours after leaving Moscow, the weary and slightly hungover Americans landed safely at Novosibirsk, where they slept for eight hours before flying on to their next destination, Irkutsk. There they refueled and immediately left for Blagoveshchensk, to the eastern side of the desolate Yablonovy Range.

At Blagoveshchensk the round-the-world flyers ran into their first real trouble, the enemy of all the early long-distance aviators —mud. As Wiley Post eased the heavy plane down on the porous field, he felt the wings cease their weight-bearing functions. The wheels disappeared in the sticky mire. Within seconds the *Winnie Mae* was locked in mud.

The accommodating Russians brought in several teams of husky, thick-legged plow horses in a vain attempt to pull the plane free. Finally a detachment of soldiers were ordered to the field, and with the added power of an American-built tractor, they freed the mud-bound craft. The operation took fourteen exhausting hours. Although their Russian hosts suggested a much-needed sleep for the aviators, Post and Gatty firmly declined. Soon they were airborne and on their way to Khabarovsk, their last stop in the Soviet Union and also their jumping-off spot for crossing the North Pacific.

At Khabarovsk, Post took the necessary time to give the *Winnie Mae* a careful inspection. He tuned and adjusted the engine, and with everything ready, the two men enjoyed a good twelve hours of sleep.

Post and Gatty headed northeast to the Kamchatka Peninsula, the Bering Sea, and Alaska.

Post recounted, "Down the Amur River to the mouth we flew, incidentally scaring away all the fishermen, who apparently were not used to planes. Passing over the northern tip of Sakhalin Island and on across the Sea of Okhotsk at its northern part, we then skirted along the western side of the Kamchatka Peninsula.

"There was a lot of bad flying which had to be done blind. All that night we sailed along 7,000 feet above this lonely part of the world. We only had about two hours of real darkness, but the daylight with its rain and fog was just as bad as darkness."

Their first landing on American soil was made at Solomon Beach thirty-six miles from Nome. After a two-hour rest they winged their way along the winding course of the Yukon River to Fairbanks and from there around the snow-capped peaks of the Wrangell Mountains, southward to Canada and the great wheat plains of British Columbia.

The flight of Post and Gatty had been a banner newspaper story throughout the world, so when the aviators landed at Edmonton, Canada, they were greeted by an enthusiastic throng of well-wishers. On hand were radio-network microphones to carry their voices live to listeners in the United States. When pressed for a statement, Wiley Post announced in a tired, but matter-of-fact voice, "We expect to be in New York tomorrow night."

In Edmonton local pilots seriously doubted that the two Americans would be able to live up to so brash a prediction. New York was a long way from Edmonton and, more significantly, a steady rain was falling. The airfield at Edmonton was becoming soggier by the minute; by dawn the field would be more lake than land. Post was not unmindful of the mud, and with special permission from the local officials he made his takeoff from a concrete highway adjoining the field. Traffic was being held at each end of a two-mile stretch when the *Winnie Mae* rose from the Canadian highway the next morning. In the late afternoon the *Winnie Mae* landed at Cleveland and after refueling took off on the last leg of the round-the-world journey.

Ten thousand New Yorkers were gathering at Roosevelt Field to await the arrival of the record makers.

A newsman wrote of the event: "The swift-flying "Winnie Mae" came out of the West as the sinking sun turned the cloud-fleeced sky into a brilliant pink back drop. A white flash in the sky, the plane tore past low flying biplanes, monoplanes and flying boats in the air, banked steeply and circled the field twice. Its wheels touched the ground at 8:47 P.M. The crowd broke through the police cordon, and carefully laid plans for an orderly reception went awry. Police clubs flew as the crowd claimed the smiling fliers."

Harold Gatty later described the final moments of that flight:

> That last hour before we got to New York just dragged along.
> We never knew before that the Jersey marshes were so wide.
> Presently, though, the ground haze that covers New York City

came up over the nose, and it was the most welcome sight you can imagine.

After coming over midtown New York and admitting to ourselves that the New York skyline was the most impressive sight we had found in the whole world, we dived in the direction of Roosevelt Field and were making pretty close to 200 miles on the airspeed indicator when we reached 500 feet and the field hove into sight. We didn't know which of the two fields we were supposed to land on, but judged from the crowd grouped at the corner of field No. 2 that that was our finish line. We made two circles and found that the wind was blowing directly over the hangars toward us. We came in a little high because we were both tired and didn't want to take any chances.

As we came over the runway, 150 feet high, Post dropped his left wing and kicked the right rudder, cocking the plane into a fast, deep side slip. He straightened out and touched his wheels just as our chronometer told us we still had eight hours and nine minutes to go before we had used up nine days on our flight.

A new record had been made: 8 days, 15 hours, and 51 minutes, and all America cheered the two heroes. Will Rogers later said of Post and Gatty: "We want to thank both our foreign neighbors, Australia and Oklahoma, for loaning the U. S. these two fine boys."

The achievement of Wiley Post and Harold Gatty stood for only two years. The magic of the airplane continued to stir the nation and encouraged pilots to greater and faster feats. The next summer James Mattern, a flyer from Fort Worth, Texas, who was long on skill but short on luck, set out with his friend Bennett Griffin to topple the Post-Gatty record in a round-the-world dash. Mattern picked up some advice from his friends Wiley Post and Harold Gatty, plus extra fuel tanks from the *Winnie Mae*. With Griffin he spent long hours making careful and detailed plans for their record attempt.

When they were ready, they called John P. V. Heinmuller, the chief timer for the National Aeronautic Association, to make it official.

John Heinmuller reported:

On July 4, 1932, they were ready, and at 10 o'clock that night they called me to Floyd Bennett Field for the take off.

They had seen the Weather Bureau, checked over reports from areas along the proposed route, and found all indications as favorable as they could have expected.

When I reached the Administration Building at the field they were just finishing a shower and were ready to take care of last minute details for the take off early the next morning.

They got away at 5:01 A.M. under ideal conditions, lifting the big monoplane after less than thirty seconds along the 4,000 foot runway. It was a Lockheed Vega powered by a super-charged Wasp radial engine, made by Pratt and Whitney. The plane was painted blue, with the wings white and red. The usual side door had been sealed and an upper hatch cut in the top of the fuselage to give access to a rear pilot seat that could be used if desired. The plane had a very complete outfit of instruments, including blind-flying aids and ice indicators.

In a few days the specially cut upper hatch would play a major role in the failure of this record attempt.

The flyers' northeast course carried them to Harbour Grace, Newfoundland, in slightly more than ten hours. After a quick refueling stop they flew nonstop across the Atlantic to Tempelhof in Berlin, a distance of 2,900 miles, in 10 hours, 50 minutes, a new record in itself. Already the two aviators were well ahead of the Post-Gatty record flight. The sweet promise of success gave them added impetus to press on. Forsaking a night's rest in Germany, they left Berlin at 4:00 P.M. and headed for Moscow. They did not make it.

Over Russia the Vega drifted off course. Four hundred miles southeast of the Russian capital, not far from Minsk, the upper hatch snapped open and the airstream ripped it loose. Spinning like a freewheeling saw blade, the hatch sliced backward into the vertical stabilizer, cutting off the top of the upright fin. The damaged airplane spiraled downward. Desperately Mattern looked for an emergency landing site. As luck would seemingly have it, he spotted a smooth green field and headed the Lockheed toward it. The "green field," however, did not represent Lady Luck; it was a peat bog—smooth, level, and treacherously soft. As the wheels touched the surface they sank, causing the plane to nose over onto its back and wrecking the aircraft. Mattern and Bennett were not injured, but their round-the-world journey had ended less than a fourth of the way.

The following summer, both James Mattern, back home with his airplane repaired, and Wiley Post, with a modified *Winnie Mae,* announced separate plans for solo round-the-world flights. Post had equipped the *Winnie Mae* with a Pratt & Whitney engine of greater horsepower and with several other modifications, including a controllable-pitch propeller to permit greater cruise control. In addition, he had added the newest of aircraft gadgetry: a Sperry gyroscopic autopilot, a remarkable system of air-driven gyros initiating electrical messages to hydraulic actuators that operated the trim-tab controls, permitting prolonged flight without the guiding hand of a human pilot.

Mattern dismissed the idea of an autopilot, and as a result his airplane was ready first. On June 5, 1933, he was at Floyd Bennett Field ready for takeoff.

He got away without incident, flying the now-familiar Great Circle route northeastward to the Atlantic. Over the ocean he penetrated a warm front and soon found himself in a horizontal cloud layer with gradually lowering temperatures. Clear ice accumulated on the leading edge of his wings, changing the shape of the airfoil and lessening the lift. Slowly the Lockheed Vega sank toward the ocean swells.

Mattern swung north to escape the stratus clouds, and to his relief great chunks of ice began to crack and snap loose in the slipstream. He held his course and made landfall along a rocky coast he calculated to be Scotland. He followed the coast southward, planning to land in England. This was a mistake, because he was farther north than he had reckoned. The coast he had spotted was not Scotland, but Norway. His fuel ran low and he was finally forced to make a landing on a rock-strewn beach in the Oslo Fjord.

It took a team of horses to pull him off the rocky beach to a more suitable takeoff strip. After the Vega had been fueled from tins of gasoline, Mattern headed toward Moscow. From there he continued steadily across the vast expanses of the Soviet Union. By the time he reached Khabarovsk in Siberia, he was already ahead of the Post-Gatty record flight of two years earlier. But now his bad luck came back to plague him again. Storms blew out of Manchuria and he was forced to remain grounded until he was so far behind in lapsed time that he had no chance to beat the Post-Gatty record. Still, he was on the world's first solo circumnavigation, and on June 15 he was able to leave Khabarovsk and head northeastward toward Nome.

Those who waited in Nome for his arrival waited in vain. Good fortune was not riding with Mattern over the craggy and desolate tundra that day. He later recalled:

> The 1,000 miles over the Okhotsk Sea went fast, and upon reaching the coast I found myself on the course, with navigation easy.
>
> The Wasp motor was singing her faithful song beautifully. It was only a short time until I came to the mountains and bad weather—awful weather. I flew into the clouds and pulled up to 8,000 feet altitude. There I collected ice and had to descend. I was flying blind many times, below the altitude of the hills, so I changed my course 30 degrees to the left so I would get over into the Anadyr River valley.
>
> I was thirteen hours and about 1,800 miles out of Khabarovsk when my oil ran dry.
>
> I had fixed another oil tank on the rear of the ship, which had thirty-five gallons in it. This I couldn't get to the main tank, as it wouldn't flow, due to extremely cold temperature. The fog closed down on the valley, and I flew down over the river. I couldn't get into Anadyr, and I couldn't fly blind to Nome, as it would have been suicide to try to fly over the Bering Sea.
>
> I would have given anything for only ten gallons of oil. It would have meant the success of my venture.
>
> I flew on two hours when I decided I had to crash the best equipment in the world. It was like shooting your best horse with nothing the matter with him.

Beneath Mattern was that desolate wasteland of northeastern Russia that lies just below the Arctic Circle. With infinite skill he brought the plane lower and lower over the tundra with the throttle wide open. The Lockheed was flying at top speed when the wheels touched the ground. They struck the tundra with full force, ripping the landing gear from the fuselage. Quickly, Mattern chopped the throttle and flicked his magnetos closed. The comforting thunder of the 550-horsepower engine was abruptly replaced by the infinite stillness of the empty land and the soft whisper of the fading slipstream. The airplane settled onto the turf, twisting and tearing as it slid and bounced along the jagged ground. Mattern's ankle was broken in the crash.

Crawling from his craft, he gathered his supplies, a few biscuits, and several chocolate bars. Aided by a makeshift crutch, he limped off in the direction of the Anadyr River. Unless he reached the river, he realized he had no chance of being rescued. He spent two days dragging himself through the cold wilderness before he reached the river, where he built a crude lean-to. Rescue finally came in the form of two boatloads of Eskimos paddling down the river, but before they arrived, "Bad Luck" Mattern had received severe burns on his body. His flying suit had been soaked in a fall into the icy river, and he lit a fire to dry it, forgetting that his underwear had been drenched in gasoline from the crash. As he struck up the fire his underwear ignited in a spontaneous puff, causing Mattern, injured ankle and all, to plunge once again into the frigid waters.

While Mattern awaited rescue on the icy banks of the Anadyr River and the world wondered what had happened to the missing aviator, Wiley Post was rushing preparations for his own attempt at a solo flight around the world. On July 7 a radio message was received in Moscow and immediately flashed around the world: "Safe at Anadyr, Chukotka, Siberia. Jimmy Mattern."

Eight days later Post and the *Winnie Mae* were at Floyd Bennett Field, ready for flight. John Heinmuller was the timekeeper on hand again to officially record the event. As Heinmuller recalled:

> An hour before he took off from Floyd Bennett Field, on July 15, a cable came in from Paris warning that bad weather was developing over Europe and that a real storm was gathering speed and force in southern Europe and moving northward toward Russia.
>
> I translated the message for Wiley and we discussed the potentialities. He shrewdly figured out that with the *Winnie Mae* averaging a speed of around 180 miles an hour he would be in Berlin within about 24 hours and thus escape the bad weather. At least he felt certain that he would not encounter it in its worst aspects until he was at the German capital.
>
> The accuracy of his calculations was evidenced by the fact that he made a record run to Berlin, setting the plane down less than 26 hours later. The importance of such accuracy of

timing in aerial navigation was strikingly illustrated by a double
tragedy on the same day.

While Post was preparing to take off, on the night of the
14th, two Lithuanian flyers, Stefan Darius and Stanley Girenas,
were waiting at Floyd Bennett Field for permission from the
Department of State to make a flight direct to Lithuania. They
were impatient and were determined to leave, spurred on by
the fact that Post was blazing the trail ahead.

I reasoned with them, explaining that their *Bellanca,* flying
at only 100 or 123 miles, at the best, would certainly be caught
in the bad weather long before they could get to their objective.

Despite all efforts to restrain them they took off, leaving
a few hours behind Post. A crash amid the full fury of the
storm took both courageous lives on the following day in
Pomerania, Germany.

Meanwhile, Post had reached Berlin, where his eager hosts
offered him beer and food. He declined, accepting only ice water
and a wet cloth to wash his face. "I don't want to eat. I don't
want to shave. I don't want to bathe. I want to clear out of

Post in Berlin on his way to a world record solo flight.
**(National Archives)**

here. I flew here on tomato juice and chewing gum, and that's enough for me," declared the tired and impatient aviator.

As soon as the *Winnie Mae* was refueled, Post raced eastward, hoping to beat approaching thunderheads and to fly nonstop all the way to Novosibirsk. But ominous black clouds moved in rapidly from the south; dancing lightning between the billowing thunderheads warned him of the deadly convective currents they carried. Putting down in Königsberg in East Prussia (now Kaliningrad, Russia), he snatched some much-needed sleep while waiting ten hours for the front to pass.

When the storm finally eased and the rain became gentle and steady, Post was off, going slightly south of his course to fly out of and around the still-present thunderheads. Winging eastward, challenging his own record across the vast Russian countryside, he stopped at Moscow, Novosibirsk, and Khabarovsk. As Post later described his second epoch flight:

> There were hours when I was forced to fly absolutely blind or above the clouds. It was called a solo flight, but I never could have made the record without the efficient little co-pilot—the Sperry Pilot for automatic flying. Without it the strain of flying through the worst weather I ever saw would have been far too great.
>
> Most of the first hop from New York to Berlin was flown in clouds and rain. Between Khabarovsk, Siberia, and the Alaskan coast the automatic pilot did all the work and took me through a continuous blind-stretch for seven hours.

Post even dozed during part of the flight, trusting his fate to the gyro-autopilot. As a safety measure he tied a wrench to the back of his hand; if he dropped into a deep sleep and his hand fell, the wrench would crash to the deck and awaken him.

At one point in his flight across Siberia, Post was aided by weather reports radioed out of Anadyr for his benefit by his friend, the rescued but stranded James Mattern.

On the twentieth of July, Wiley Post had reached Flat, Alaska, 275 miles west of Anchorage, where he put down in a fog, bending his propeller in the process. A new propeller was quickly flown to him and he was again on his way. After a fuel stop at Edmonton, Canada, he headed directly for New York, where he touched down at Floyd Bennett Field on July 22, 7 days, 18 hours, and 49 minutes after takeoff, setting a new world record—and solo at that.

Acclaimed a hero by a proud nation, Wiley Post spent the two years following his spectacular flight pursuing altitude records and making occasional easy-paced pleasure hops. Then on August 15, 1935, he was, for one irretrievable moment, careless in an unforgiving aircraft. He was flying with his friend, America's beloved cowboy humorist, Will Rogers, on a recreational tour of Alaska and Siberia. Their plane was a hybrid craft: a Lockheed Orion fuselage mated with Explorer wings, mounted on a set of pontoons picked up in Seattle. Post attempted a hurried takeoff from a narrow lagoon near Point Barrow on the Arctic Ocean, but a few feet above the water, the airplane's engine sputtered and the plane stalled at a point too low for recovery. The poorly balanced aircraft snapped over in the stall and fell, inverted, into the icy waters, carrying Will Rogers and Wiley Post to their deaths.

As men of aviation's golden era rushed to encompass the planet in less and less time, some writers began to point out that none of the flights had been true circumnavigations. This was because the flights were around the upper perimeters of the earth and thus shorter in distance than a true circle of the globe along the equator line or along a meridian passing through both poles. An around-the-poles flight was not inviting; moreover, aerial equipment was not sufficiently developed for such a journey. Circumnavigation at the equator meant flying across the sullen stretches of the South Pacific, where islands were scarce. The struggles of Kingsford-Smith and Ulm in that region had not been forgotten. There was little interest in such a flight until the lady eagle Amelia Earhart decided that she would circle the globe just that way— flying an eastward course as nearly in line with the equator as possible.

Miss Earhart's aircraft was a low-winged, twin-engine Lockheed "Electra," and she was accompanied by Fred J. Noonan, who had pioneered trans-Pacific routes for Pan American Airways. The United States Navy provided valuable assistance to Miss Earhart as she planned her journey.

Taking off from Miami, Florida, the Earhart-Noonan team

"Amelia Earhart with her husband George Palmer Putnam as she planned her circumnavigation of the globe."

*(National Archives)*

dropped south along the South American coast, then swung eastward along the equator across the South Atlantic, across Africa, then northward to cross the Arabian deserts, India, Burma, then south again to the equator line in New Guinea.

On July 2, 1937, Amelia Earhart and Fred Noonan departed on an eastward course from Lae in New Guinea. Neither the pilots nor their plane were ever seen again. The last message received from the aviatrix was picked up by the Coast Guard cutter *Itasca* on station near Howland Island, her next destination. The message, climaxing a series of increasingly more urgent radio transmissions, was: "We are on the line of position 155-337 [a sun line]. We are running north and south."

After this transmission there was only silence and a mystery that has stirred inquiries by hundreds of diverse investigators.

One persistent supposition is that Amelia Earhart perished not in the pursuit of an aviation record but in a flight to "allow" her "accidentally" to fly into the Marshall Islands, an island chain anchored on the northeast corner of tropical Micronesia. Controlled by Japan under a mandate from the League of Nations, the Marshall Islands were not to be used for military installations. But Japan was rattling the chains of war, and there was good reason for the United States to try to learn what the Japanese were doing on their island outposts. There are many who believe Amelia Earhart and Fred Noonan found the answer to that question, but lost their lives in the learning.

Officially, the aviators were listed as presumed lost at sea, having failed to complete their circumnavigation of the equator.

As the third decade of the twentieth century drew to a close, Howard Hughes, in an earth-circling flight, toppled all earlier records and significantly advanced the development of intercontinental air travel. Hughes, a multimillionaire from an oil tool-manufacturing family, had taken more than a sportsman's interest in aviation, treating aeronautics as the science it was and not as a sport for the rich.

In his capacity as the aeronautics director for the 1939 New York World's Fair, Hughes established a powerful radio station on the fairgrounds and made it the headquarters for his flight around the world. He organized a global system of radio relay stations, and cooperating with the United States weather bureau and naval ships, he set up a weather observation system which

"Howard Hughes significantly advanced the development of intercontinental air travel."

**(National Archives)**

could feed reports into his radio headquarters at Flushing Meadow.

Hughes planned his flight with great care. On July 10, 1938, he flew out of Floyd Bennett Field in a twin-engine Lockheed "Super Electra," equipped with the most modern flight instruments and radio gadgetry known to air science. In just 3 days, 19 hours, 17 minutes, Hughes and his crew of four men stepped from the same plane, having circled the globe in record-breaking hops from Paris to Moscow to Omsk to Yakutsk to Fairbanks to Minneapolis and back to New York.

This record stood unbroken when the world plunged into World War II and aeronautics was largely confined to the field of battle. After the war there was one last adventurous fling at a round-the-world record flight, before aeronautical circumnavigation was left to the more serious purposes and greater capabilities of the U. S. Air Force and the armada of equipment available only to the nation's military air arm.

This civilian effort, cheered by a postwar world that still remembered the exciting record flights of the 1920's and 1930's, was

Hughes inspects the tail of his airplane just before takeoff from New York City.

**(National Archives)**

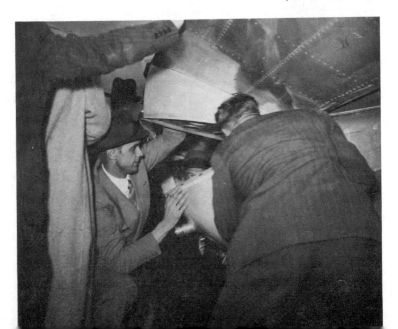

made by the crew of the *Reynolds Bombshell*. The *Bombshell* was a converted surplus Army Air Force twin-engine Douglas A-26 attack bomber. The plane was purchased from the War Assets Administration by Milton J. Reynolds, a Chicago pen manufacturer, who had it stripped of its armor and fitted with extra fuel tanks. Reynolds admitted that his round-the-world flight, which would utilize an airplane already proven in combat, instrumentation developed during the war, and routes flown many times by others before him, would make little if any contribution to the aeronautical sciences. "But," said Reynolds, "some people collect stamps, some buttons. I want to break the round-the-world record."

Reynolds decided to make the flight in March. He employed William Odom to pilot the venture and T. Carroll Sallee to fly as the flight engineer. Reynolds, an aviation buff and holder of a private pilot's license, flew as navigator and passenger. He was obliged to lose thirty pounds in order to squeeze into the navigator's seat, in which he rode facing the rear, thus achieving among other things a record for being the first to fly around the world backward.

By April the *Reynolds Bombshell* was ready to go. Minor mechanical difficulties delayed the takeoff, but finally at 5:11 P.M. on April 12, 1947, the plane roared from La Guardia Field in New York, heading along the familiar Great Circle route across the North Atlantic. The Douglas attack bomber was much faster than the prewar plane used by Howard Hughes and had little difficulty beating his record time. Odom, an airline pilot and former Army pilot with six thousand hours of flight experience, remained at the controls throughout the entire trip and was dubbed by one news commentator as truly "one of the iron men of the cockpit."

An enthusiastic crowd was on hand at La Guardia Field some 78 hours, 55 minutes, and 12 seconds later to greet the returning trio. They had set a new world's record over a route of twenty thousand miles, flying four thousand miles farther than Howard Hughes had nine years before. The additional mileage was made necessary by the refusal of the Soviet Union to permit the men to fly over their country, "on the grounds that the Soviets could not assume responsibility for the crew's safety at a time when its specialists were preoccupied with reconstruction."

According to Odom, the toughest leg of the trip was the 2,200 miles from Calcutta to Shanghai over the hump of the lower Himalayas, which they crossed at 24,000 feet. Said Odom: "An Indian weather bureau man gave me a forecast of winds aloft over China. I knew there was no communication there and I asked him where he got it. He pulled a five-year-old aeronautical almanac out of his desk.

" 'There, Sahib,' he said, and pointed to the prevailing winds for April. But we got through. I raised Shanghai and got a bearing about 200 miles out, and we were right on course."

A *New York Times* reporter described the great finale: "As the plane sped across Pennsylvania and New Jersey, La Guardia Field authorities 'cleared the air,' sending scheduled airliners into a holding pattern to give the fast plane ample room to maneuver in its approach to the runway.

"The plane made one of the tight turns typical of its performance as a wartime attack bomber and set wheels down on the runway a few seconds later. A crowd of nearly 2,000 persons swarmed on the field."

The record flight generated some criticism, as might be expected: "There are some people in aviation today," wrote Frederick Graham for an Atlantic City newspaper, "who feel that a flight, however spectacular, that contributes nothing to the advancement of aviation can justify itself only as a stunt. These people feel that aviation has grown to a point where the spectacular stunt is no longer needed to get attention. They also point out that a serious accident on such a flight can do aviation more harm than completion of the flight can do good."

However, the general reaction was favorable, and on April 17, 1947, President Harry S. Truman received the airmen at the White House and extended the nation's congratulations to the three men. One editorial writer hailed the event: "The round-the-world flight of Milton Reynolds and his crew in the *Bombshell* is one more graphic demonstration of how fast our planet is shrinking." But Reynolds, who had spent roughly three days riding backward in the cramped confines of the Douglas bomber, had a different view. He told newsmen, "These people who say what a small world it is haven't gone around it lately."

Four months later, on August 7, 1947, William P. Odom, in the same *Reynolds Bombshell,* made the same flight, this time solo, and broke the earlier record, making the circumnavigation in 73 hours, 5 minutes. His biggest enemy during the flight was exhaustion. During the final legs, fatigue almost conquered the iron man of the cockpit; but Odom was, as Reynolds had earlier described him, "not only the best pilot in the world, but the luckiest."

"The good Lord was taking care of me for a while last night," recalled Odom of his solo flight, "because I just collapsed with fatigue out over the wildest mountains of Canada."

Flying a southeasterly course at 21,000 feet without an autopilot, Odom had dozed off, and he remained asleep while the plane flew itself for an hour and forty minutes on the balance of trim tabs alone. Suddenly he awakended with a start.

> First thing I saw was that compass. It said we were going due north. When I fell asleep we were flying 107 degrees —southeast.
>
> Then I saw my height was 16,000 feet, but it had been 21,000. The clock said 6 P.M., Chicago time, but I remembered I'd looked at it just before settling back in my seat and it had said 4:20 P.M. So I turned back to 107 degrees and began climbing again.
>
> I even turned on the cockpit lights, which blinded me for outside vision, and dug out a couple of charts. When I had snapped them off I looked up and I was headed straight for a huge cloud. No, I thought that's not a cloud. I turned to go around it and then saw it was a huge, treacherous, waiting ledge of ice. It looked like a glacier. It was the top of a mountain, 19,000 feet above the ground, the second highest on the continent.
>
> It made me sick at my stomach. There I'd been milling around, circling around down at 16,000 feet for who knows how long and that thing was there to be hit. I knew the Army had had a few investments on its slopes. I just pulled back on the wheel and spiraled right up into the stars, up into the clear on top of the clouds and mountains before I straightened out for home.
>
> You know, I'd been tortured by engulfing sleep up to then. But that business scared me so much I've not been sleepy since.

This solo record flight was generally greeted with the same national enthusiasm as the earlier spring flight, but one veteran of aviation observed: "I surely hope we're not in for another wave of spectacular flights such as we had in the Twenties and early Thirties. With all those surplus planes around to be bought for a few cents on the dollar we may have more attempted 'record' flights than most people think.''

However, more record attempts did not materialize. The *Bombshell* flights were not the beginning of a new postwar round of circumnavigation, but rather the last of their kind. Thereafter, the record round-the-world flights were strictly military business.

On February 26, 1949, a heavily laden B-50A Superfortress, *Lucky Lady II*, bearing a crew of thirteen men under the command of Capt. James Gallagher, roared down the long concrete runway at Carswell Air Force Base in Fort Worth, Texas. The long, silver, cigar-shaped, four-engine giant increased its speed slowly. As it approached unstick speed, its nose wheel began to bounce, the long thin wings achieved lift, and the heavy Strategic Air Command bomber was airborne and headed northeast around the world. At selected points along the route KB-29 tankers climbed out on schedule to rendevouz with the lonely bomber. This was a training mission to determine the capabilities of the B-50, the feasibility of relying upon air-to-air refueling, and the efficiency of the Air Force communications system. The mission was a military one and went as planned: in ninety-four hours the *Lucky Lady II* had completely circled the globe nonstop on a 23,452-mile route. A new record had been set, although it should be noted that the slower speed of the B-50 prevented it from beating the record times of earlier round-the-world flights. The B-50's ground speed averaged only 239 m.p.h. at altitudes between one thousand and twenty thousand feet.

When asked the significance of the record flight, Lt. Gen. Curtis E. LeMay, commander-in-chief of the Strategic Air Command, said that it meant that the United States could drop an atomic bomb, taking off from this country, flying nonstop to ''any place in the world that required the atomic bomb.''

In 1957, three Air Force bombers broke all existing records when they circled the globe nonstop in 45 hours, 19 minutes. This was Operation Power Flite, deploying five multi-engined jet B-52 Stratofortresses from Castle Air Force Base in California, under the command of Major Gen. Archie J. Old, Jr., commander of the Fifteenth Air Force, a part of the Strategic Air Command.

The giant jets began their journey on January 16, 1957, and two days later three of them, as planned, touched down again at Castle Air Force Base. The flight carried the B-52s from California to Newfoundland to Casablanca, then to Dhahran, Ceylon, Manila, and Guam, and finally back to California.

The flight was described by Gordon Williams in the February, 1957, issue of *Boeing Magazine*:

> The takeoff on that clear morning of January 16 saw five B-52's leave the runway of Castle Air Force Base near Merced, California, and head northeast. They crossed Labrador, where one landed. Then on across the Atlantic, where by prearrangement another B-52 slid out of formation and landed in England.
>
> The three *Runners* (the code names of the successful craft were Runner one-one, three-three and four-four) droned on over the sandy wastes of North Africa, Saudi Arabia, down the Persian Gulf and past Ceylon. They made a mock bombing attack off the Malay Peninsula and cut up over Manila. Then they flew across the Pacific to the California coast.
>
> Refuelings from the double-deck Boeing KC-97's were made as scheduled and as practiced thousands of times. Often rendezvous points were in the midst of storm areas, and some were at night. All three B-52's took their loads of JP-4 fuel and roared on.
>
> Crewmen managed a few winks of sleep. Even though most of the men from the 93rd said they "just weren't interested in food," they managed to swallow bite-sized pieces of pre-cooked hot steak and canned chicken. They drank ice cold milk, fruit juice and soups, and munched on cake and candy bars.
>
> There was plenty of work for each nine-man crew. Crew chiefs monitored engines and the array of dials, switches and lights which told them how each item of equipment was functioning. Navigators checked and rechecked positions, plotted refueling points and kept airplane commanders up to date on courses and average speeds. Tail gunners dozed, read, ate and watched the world unfold behind them between vapor trails from their own engines.
>
> Only planes sighted during the entire flight were the welcome KC-97's, waiting and ready at each rendezvous point. Otherwise, no planes; just sky, clouds and glimpses of ocean, desert, jungles, mountains and more sky.

The B-52s on the record flight were refueled while in flight by Boeing KC-97 tanker airplanes.

**(U.S. Air Force)**

The trip was a familiar one to Lt. Col. James Morris. He had been a co-pilot on the Boeing B-50 *Lucky Lady II*, which in 1949 had become the first airplane in history to be flown in circumnavigation of the earth nonstop. Time on that flight had been 94 hours, with an average speed of 239 m.p.h. This, his second time around (as an aircraft commander of one of the B-52s), was "a lot easier."

With the B-52 record flight closing out the records in this general category, for all intents and purposes, the F.A.I. came to the rescue with a decree that private planes and business jets could establish round-the-world records within their various weight classes. And the records book was soon filling with a variety of global flights.

Then on April 12, 1961, the yellow flames of igniting liquid oxygen and kerosene rocket fuel sent the Russian cosmonaut

Yuri  A. Gagarin once around the earth at 17,500 m.p.h. The globe was spanned in one hour and 48 minutes. If this was the grand finale of the round-the-world record flights, it was both an ending and a beginning—the first of those remarkable journeys that would carry men farther and farther into the realm of the science fictions of the French novelist Jules Verne, who in 1865 published *From the Earth to the Moon* and in 1870 *Around the Moon,* depicting with amazing accuracy modern space travel.

On February 20, 1962, Lt. Col. John H. Glenn, Jr. in his Mercury capsule, *Friendship 7,* was launched into earth orbit at 17,500 m.p.h.

*(NASA)*

# CHAPTER 14

# *Man Goes to the Moon*

In 1919, while many aerial devotees pursued the development of the machines of winged flight and others chased the dirigible dream of lighter-than-air locomotion, few gave serious attention to the experiments of the Clark University scholar Robert H. Goddard. In that year the quiet college professor published a scientifically sophisticated treatise on rocketry: *A Method of Reaching Extreme Altitudes*. He proposed in his paper that a sufficiently powerful multi-stage rocket could actually reach the moon.

A second generation of myopic newsmen, in a sense related to the gentlemen of the press who ignored the Wright brothers and dispatched Professor Langley to his tomb in ridicule and scorn, found amusement in scoffing at the visions of Goddard. His treatise elicited an editorial in the January 13, 1920, edition of *The New York Times,* captioned "A Severe Strain of Credulity." The editorial made fun of the professor and his dissertation.

> It is when one considers the multiple charge rocket as a traveler to the moon that one begins to doubt, and looks again, to see if the ... Professor is working under the auspices of the Smithsonian Institution.
>
> That Professor Goddard with his "chair" in Clark College and the countenancing of the Smithsonian Institution does not know the relation of action to reaction, and of the need to have something better than a vacuum against which to react—to say that would be absurd. Of course, he only seems to lack the knowledge ladled out daily in high schools.

Goddard responded to the public rebuke by becoming more secretive about his work. But his experiments continued. In March, 1926, on a farm near Auburn, Massachusetts, he launched a twelve-foot liquid-propellant rocket to an altitude of 184 feet, an achievement as important to today's technology as the first flights of the Montgolfier balloon or the Wright brothers' airplane.

When he learned of Goddard's achievement, Charles Lindbergh exercised his influence to secure a significant grant from the philanthropist Daniel Guggenheim to further Goddard's rocket studies. From his experiments Goddard developed more than two hundred patents dealing with rocket flight. The father of modern rocketry, Goddard, proved that rockets would operate in a vacuum, and he developed rocket pumps, gyrocontrols, and flight instrumentation.

The experiments of Goddard and the later developments of such rocket geniuses as the German, Wernher von Braun, suddenly came to public attention when on October 4, 1957, the Russians fired Sputnik I, a small, beeping earth satellite, into orbit around the earth.

"Moon over Manhattan" was the banner headline in the *New York Post*, and untold thousands of people along the eastern seaboard rose early to catch a glimpse of *Sputnik* as it raced through the dark, predawn skies.

The space age was born. It would culminate in a series of space spectaculars, many of which were record flights setting F.A.I. official marks as man moved toward fulfillment of his ancient dream, space travel.

On April 12, 1961, the Russians upstaged the much publicized American plan to send Project Mercury astronaut Alan B. Shepard, Jr., on a fifteen-minute suborbital flight, by launching *Vostok 1*, carrying Yuri A. Gagarin into an earth orbit from the Baikonur Cosmodrome in western Siberia. Gagarin was the first man to travel in space.

Georgy Ostroumov, correspondent for the Russian newspaper *Izvestia,* reported the triumphant flight:

> The start was successful. The space ship was not in orbit yet when the cosmonaut replied: "I see the earth in a haze."
>
> Two minutes later, the familiar voice of Levitan broadcasts Tass's report on the beginning of the historic flight.

The space ship needed slightly less than one and one-half hours to carry the first cosmonaut around the globe. In his time, Magellan took three years to circle our planet by sea. Outer space is another, a much shorter route.

Flying over South America, Gagarin radioed: "I am feeling well, the flight proceeds normally."

"The speed is nearly eight kilometers a second. The altitude is almost 200 kilometers. The space around is nearly airless and the frost is so severe that it is difficult to measure the temperature. And yet the flight proceeds normally.

"The route of the space ship lies high above our planet, but the pilot is not isolated from the earth. Soviet cities are transmitting music to outer space. Moscow is transmitting songs about Moscow and Khabarovsk is transmitting the waves of the *Amur Waltz* [a popular Russian song]."

The landing was very successful and Yuri Gagarin without waiting for the helicopter set out himself toward the people who had seen him in the sky.

A helicopter brought Yuri Gagarin to a populated locality where he spoke over the telephone with Nikita Krushchev.

There is no end to the questions asked of a man who has just seen the earth from the outside. Yuri Gagrin says: "The sky is very dark; the earth is bluish. Everything is seen very clearly."

Within eight years the American space team had outdistanced their Russian counterparts by proceeding step-by-step in a planned program to carry men to the moon and back. The goals of Project Mercury, the first step, were to put a man in space, learn about his abilities to function there, and to recover the man and his capsule safely. This program achieved its aims on February 20, 1962, with the earth-orbit flight of astronaut John H. Glenn, Jr. Project Mercury ended its series of successful missions with a 34-hour, 20-minute space flight by astronaut Gordon Cooper in May, 1963. Cooper's flight, however, did not better the record of 94 hours, 10 minutes set in August, 1962, by the Soviet cosmonaut Andrian Nikolayev in *Vostok 3*. And in June, 1963, the Russian cosmonaut Valery F. Bykovsky set an even greater record of 81 revolutions for 118 hours, 7 minutes in the giant spacecraft *Vostok 5*.

Project Mercury was followed by Project Gemini, which established several new records, surpassing Russian milestones with

Astronaut John H. Glenn, Jr. in the *Friendship 7* spacecraft on February 20, 1962.

*(NASA)*

duration flights, space rendezvous, space docking, and astronauts "walking" outside of the craft—extravehicular activity.

Perhaps the most critical of the twelve Gemini missions were the historic flights of *Gemini 6* and 7, flights of endurance and rendezvous. If these functions, the goals of Gemini, could not be performed, man could never reach the moon and return.

On December 4, 1965, astronauts Frank Borman and James A. Lovell, Jr., in *Gemini 7* blasted from Cape Kennedy to begin the world's longest manned orbital flight: 330 hours, 35 minutes —206 times around the globe.

On the eleventh day of the *Gemini 7* flight, December 15, astronauts Walter M. Schirra, Jr., and Thomas P. Stafford in *Gemini 6* were launched from the Cape and began a 100,000-mile six-hour chase of the orbiting *Gemini 7*. No one knew whether the spacecraft could find each other in that great void and thereafter keep station. In 1962, two Russian spacecraft, *Vostok 3* and *4*, had momentarily passed within four miles of each other, but they did so as passenger-carrying projectiles fired from earth, not as manually operated vehicles, flown by pilots. In a true rendezvous the spacecraft stop in space with respect to each other and all relative motion is terminated. The space docking procedure, which would make a trip to the moon possible, could not be accomplished by merely passing in space four miles apart. There had to be a true rendezvous.

With computers on the ground and in the craft providing the precise information necessary to perform the intricate rendezvous maneuver, and with the control centers dotted around the world watching and waiting, Wally Schirra skillfully fired his thrusters to lift *Gemini 6* to the higher orbit of *Gemini 7.*

The two spaceships spun around the earth four times, with *Gemini 6* rising in gradual, stair-step stages to find Borman and Lovell. Five hours into the mission of *Gemini 6,* they had closed to within fifty miles of each other. The two spacecraft had just passed out over the Atlantic beyond Cape Kennedy when announcement of the first visual sighting thrilled the waiting world.

Astronaut Lovell described that moment:

> It was nighttime, just becoming light. We were face down, and coming out of the murky blackness below was this little

Astronauts James A. Lovell, Jr., and Frank Borman as they arrive aboard the U.S. Navy aircraft carrier *Wasp* after their record flight.
**(NASA)**

pinpoint of light. The sun was just coming up and was not illuminating the ground yet, but on the adapter of Gemini 6 we could see sunlight glinting, and as it came closer and closer, just like it was on rails, it became a half-moon. At about half a mile we could see the thrusters firing, like water from a hose. And just in front of us it stopped. Fantastic!

After the successful rendezvous, the two craft flew next to each other 189 miles above the Pacific Ocean.

Wally Schirra, piloting *Gemini 6* with deft precision, greeted his counterparts with "Having fun?"

*Gemini 7* replied, "Hello, there!"

Gently Schirra nudged his vehicle to within a foot of *Gemini 7*. The astronauts could easily see each other through their windows. Schirra complained to the ground controller in Hawaii, "There seems to be a lot of traffic up here!"

Answered Borman in the companion spaceship, "Call a policeman."

Each of the Gemini missions that followed made its own special contribution to the American space effort. It was *Gemini 8* with astronauts Neil Armstrong and David Scott that rendezvoused with an unmanned Atlas Agena rocket and then accomplished the first space docking, an important first that almost ended in disaster.

*Gemini 8* had drawn close to the Agena. The astronauts pushed a switch that extended a guide bar on the capsule's nose, and Armstrong applied short, delicate thruster bursts to guide the *Gemini 8*'s nose into the Agena's docking cone. Three spring-loaded mooring latches gripped the nose and the docking collar stiffened. *Gemini 8* was docked with the Agena.

Following the scheduled program, Armstrong shut down *Gemini 8* in order to utilize the Agena as a power source. Suddenly the docked space vehicle began a pronounced rolling and slewing movement. Thinking the unwanted motion was coming from the Agena, the astronauts quickly switched off the Agena's power and tried to stabilize the combined spacecraft with *Gemini*'s thrusters. The motion got worse. They turned off the *Gemini* thrusters only to have the rolling and twisting become so violent that they feared the spacecraft would break up. They did not learn until after the flight that a circuit failure was activating a *Gemini* thruster located where they could neither see nor hear the firing.

By manually flying his spacecraft, Armstrong gained stability just long enough to separate the two vehicles; but once undocked, the maverick thruster sent the *Gemini* capsule into an end-over-end roll, spinning in a somersault once every second. The tracking ship *Coastal Sentry Quebec,* on station in the Pacific off the coast of China, picked up the first word of the trouble. "We consider this problem serious," radioed Armstrong. "We're tumbling end over end, but we are disengaged from the Agena."

Calmly the two astronauts began running procedures to try to determine the cause of the violent spiraling. The orbital-attitude-and-maneuvering system, the regular control system, was completely inoperative. In the emergency Armstrong turned to *Gemini*'s reentry control system, but it would not work either.

"We're in a violent left roll at the present time. Our RCS [reentry control system] is armed but we can't fire it," reported Armstrong.

His next message was more encouraging: "We are regaining control of the spacecraft slowly in RCS direct."

Now the reentry system was beginning to function and its thrusters were bringing the craft under control.

The two spacemen finally restored stability to their capsule and guided it in an emergency reentry to a Pacific landing. While they waited for the rescue ship *Mason* to pick them up, the astronauts, seeing that frogmen had firmly affixed the flotation gear, opened the capsule's hatch doors and ate a leisurely lunch in the sun.

Project Gemini ended with the spectacular flight of *Gemini 12* and the lengthy space walk of Edwin E. Aldrin, which tested procedures and equipment modified from earlier extravehicular experiences of astronauts Edward H. White, Eugene Cernan, Michael Collins, and Richard Gordon. After Project Gemini came Project Apollo and the lunar landings.

The manned Apollo missions began disastrously. On January 27, 1967, three astronauts, Virgil I. Grissom, Edward H. White, and Roger B. Chaffee were strapped into the Apollo capsule for a runthrough of the final countdown for the first manned Apollo

mission. The hatch was closed and sealed. Pure oxygen under
16.7 pounds per square inch of pressure had been pumped into
the pilot's chamber, when a communication problem developed
that made it necessary to interrupt the simulated countdown.

Before the countdown could be resumed, at 6:31 P.M. tragedy
struck quickly and without warning. A chafed electric wire arced
in the pure oxygen atmosphere.

The first voice from the capsule was calm: "Fire ... I smell
fire."

In two seconds the voice of the first American to walk in space,
Ed White, cried out, "Fire in the cockpit!"

Another voice cried, "There's a bad fire in the spacecraft!"

This was followed by movement and activity as the astronauts,
garbed in cumbersome space suits, struggled with an unyielding
hatch.

The last voice to be heard was that of Chaffee: "We're burning
up!" Then a shriek of a final pain, and three brave men were
dead.

The Apollo program was stopped while the capsule was mod-
ified and other corrections were made. Twenty months later, on
October 11, 1968, *Apollo 7* carried astronauts Walter M. Schirra,
Jr., Donn F. Eisele, and Walter Cunningham into earth orbit.
The successful ten-day mission put the space program back on
the track.

During Christmas week, 1968, a powerful Saturn V rocket lifted
*Apollo 8* and astronauts Frank Borman, James A. Lovell, Jr.,
and William A. Anders from the earth in one of the greatest
events of the century, a voyage around the moon.

"When you see the earth slowly recede from you, there is
a sensation in the stomach that is hard to describe," said Astronaut
Lovell of the record flight for which the past had no equal and
the future no bounds.

The *Apollo 8* crew described the moon during television presen-
tations beamed back to earth from lunar orbit. Frank Borman
said, "It is a vast, lonely, forbidding type of existence, a great
expanse of nothing, that looks rather like clouds and clouds of
pumice stone. It certainly would not appear to be a very inviting
place to live or work." And Lovell added, "The vast loneliness
of the moon up here is awe-inspiring, and makes you realize

just what you have back there on earth. The earth from here is a grand oasis to the big vastness of space.''

The one critical maneuver of the *Apollo 8* flight was the rocket firing for trans-earth injection, in which a single engine boosted the spacecraft out of lunar orbit and sent it roaring back to earth. The firing took place on the far side of the moon, beyond the voice or ears of earth control centers.

Just before the Apollo craft slid behind the moon, a final message was sent: ''*Apollo 8*, Houston. We have three minutes until LOS [loss of signal]. All systems are go.''

''Roger,'' replied the voice from the moon. ''Thank you.''

Then silence. Houston and the world waited and listened. When the signal came, the voice of Frank Borman was calm and happy.

''CapCom,'' radioed the astronaut, ''please be informed there is a Santa Claus!''

While the success of *Apollo 8* was being hailed around the world, an even more spectacular space feat was in the offing.

On July 16, 1969, another 365-foot, three-stage Saturn V rocket rose majestically from its launch pad at the Kennedy Space Center

The launching of Apollo 11, July 16, 1969.

**(NASA)**

and headed for the moon. Thousands of spectators watched the launching of *Apollo 11* from along the roads and beaches near the Space Center, and millions more saw it on television. Seven and one-half million pounds of thrust from five rocket engines lifted the payload from the earth. After two and one-half minutes the first stage fell away. Another million pounds of rocket fuel burned for six and one-half minutes to put *Apollo 11* into earth orbit at better than 17,000 m.p.h.

Within the capsule the crew of *Apollo 11* prepared to leave the earth. After one earth orbit, 225,000 pounds of thrust from the Saturn's third stage pushed the capsule outward, breaking the grip of earth's gravity and projecting the vehicle and three Apollo astronauts on an epochal lunar journey.

By the nineteenth of July, the spacemen had entered a sixty-nine-mile-high moon orbit, and the following day astronauts Neil A. Armstrong and Edwin E. Aldrin, Jr., entered the *Eagle,* the lunar module (LM), for their descent to the moon. Michael Collins, a former test pilot, remained in the Apollo spacecraft *Columbia.* The separation of the *Eagle* and the *Columbia* took place on the far side of the moon beyond radio contact with the earth communicators.

Throughout America and most of the civilized world, eyes and ears were transfixed to television and radio sets as millions waited anxiously.

Behind the moon, descent from lunar orbit had begun. At the Houston Space Center apprehensive eyes glanced often at the sweeping hands of the clock. On schedule, the voice of "Buzz" Aldrin cracked across a quarter of a million miles. "Apogee fifty-seven point two. Perilune nine point one."

A quick smile flashed over the face of flight director Eugene F. Kranz. Now they were on their way down. "Okay," he nodded, "we're off to a good start. Play it cool."

The burn had been precisely on time, and the LM carrying the astronauts upside down and backward was swinging in a wide descending arc out of orbit and down. They were approaching fifty thousand feet, from which point the descent engine would fire them along a three-hundred-mile track to a landing. Inside *Eagle,* Armstrong and Aldrin, in standing positions like motormen in an interplanetary streetcar, carefully monitored the dancing luminescence of the instrument panels. Down through the triangular windows the astronauts observed their approach upon the western edge of the cocoa-brown lunar crater Mt. Marilyn. They were at fifty thousand feet. At Houston, Eugene Kranz polled his six flight controllers, "Okay, all flight controllers, go/no-go for powered descent."

Each flight controller monitered a separate special phase of the total mission. Each gave a "Go."

Kranz's voice was even as he said: "CapCom, we are go for powered descent."

CapCom, the capsule communicator for the mission, astronaut Charles M. Duke, Jr., sent the message. "*Eagle,* Houston. If you read, you are go for powered descent."

The radio connection failed. A secondary circuit via relay by Michael Collins in the orbiting *Columbia* was used, but to no avail. The controllers in Houston, however, had a solution for the communications problem.

"Pitch two twelve, yaw thirty-seven. Why don't you try it.?" suggested Kranz to Duke.

"*Eagle*, Houston," radioed CapCom. "If you'd like to try high again, pitch two twelve, yaw thirty-seven. Over."

A moment passed as the radio beam flashed across the void to the spacemen and then returned. Aldrin's voice snapped into Mission Control with amazing clarity. "Affirmative. I think I've got you on high gain now."

Kranz looked around the room. "Okay, flight controllers, thirty seconds to ignition."

The large hand on the clock swept halfway around.

Then from the *Eagle*: "Dips on. Ullage. Starting burn."

Again, the radio failed.

Steven Bales, the guidance-control officer, was having other problems. As he motioned the guidance system, he noticed that the LM's on-board guidance system had a fourteen-mile-per-hour navigational error. He knew that if the error enlarged to a twenty-four-mile-per-hour difference he would have to signal a cancelation of the moon landing. Each of the controllers was responsible for recommending an abort if there was a failure in his flight-control area. Bales's fists clenched and unclenched as he watched his monitors. The error increased to twenty. His hands were sweating. Now it was holding steady.

Kranz looked across the console at Bales. "No change,"

reported Bales, "that's downtrack. I know it. Down to eighteen now. We're going to make it."

The spidery craft was propelling itself toward the craggy surface, pocked with craters and scarred with rills. It was five minutes into the descent burn, coming up on another critical moment. The module passed through 38,000 feet, dropping like a spent bullet. Up to this point if the mission had been terminated, the LM could have returned to the circling *Columbia* using its descent engine. As its altitude decreased, however, it could return only by an unscheduled firing of its ascent engine.

"Okay, flight controllers," directed Kranz. "I'm going around the horn for your go/no-go reports."

Six men gave six Go's. Duke radioed the module. "*Eagle,* you are go to take it all at five minutes."

The surface of the moon was growing bigger beneath them. They would continue upside down, with the thrust engine propelling them downward until 7,200 feet, when the guidance computer would order rocket firings to tilt the LM upright, then lower them to the surface on a fiery column of rocket flame.

At thirty thousand feet trouble began developing in the electronic nerve system of the *Eagle*. The landing radar was locked onto the lunar surface, but it reported 2,900 feet lower than the electronic calculations of the guidance computer. Aldrin snapped the switch to feed the radar input into the guidance computer for the final stages of the landing. At mission control an alarm light flashed.

"Alarm twelve-oh-two!" The spacecraft computer was overloading.

The plunging module's computer was a sort of Mr. Everybody. Its functions were to guide the spacecraft over a predetermined trajectory, steer the craft and maintain its proper attitude, update itself using current information transmitted to it from the radar impulses pinging from the lunar surface, supervise the other systems of the module, and at the same time continuously report to itself how it was doing. "Alarm 1202" meant that the computer couldn't keep up with all its jobs.

"We're on that, Flight," Steven Bales shouted to Kranz, anticipating the concern. "We're on that alarm."

Mission Control switched to a mode designed to permit the

larger computers at the Center to handle the nonessential functions of the on-board computer. At the same time Aldrin and Armstrong were swiftly dealing with the computer crises, overriding the alarms on advice from Houston coupled with their own on-the-spot determinations.

Duke's voice remained steady and assuring. "At seven minutes you're looking great to us," he said. The calm transmission from the planet earth was heartening to the two astronauts hurling upside down toward the moon while attempting to translate the computerized crises of unprogrammed electronic anguish.

They approached 7,200 feet. Beyond this point, as the craft was turned, they were committed to land on the moon, either correctly or eternally.

Six controllers gave Eugene Kranz the nod.

"*Eagle*," said CapCom, "you're go for landing."

"Roger, understand," replied Aldrin. "Go for landing."

The craft rolled upright, and from their windows the astronauts gazed upon a "stark and strangely different place," as Neil Armstrong later described the moon.

The ten-thousand-pound thrust descent engine of the LM was unlike most rocket engines: it was throttleable. Power could be reduced to 10 percent or increased to 94 percent as the liquid hydrazine aerozine 50 and nitrogen tetroxide provided power without spark in the airless envelope around the moon. Thus by a reduction of power the *Eagle* could be gently lowered down to a landing, while smaller rocket thrusters provided directional control for the unique lunar lander.

Suddenly Aldrin called. "We have an Alarm twelve-oh-one."

In rapid succession two more alarms flashed on the computer console. In its calibrated consternation the electronic brain was giving the astronauts and Houston erroneous warnings.

"Guidance, you happy?" Kranz looked quickly at Bales as the signals came in.

"We're go!" shouted Bales. He knew from the signals that the problem was in the computer overload and not a malfunction of the LM.

Charles Duke remained silent. With the men in *Eagle* preparing to land on the moon, he knew that unneeded communications could be disconcerting.

Armstrong and Aldrin looked out of their windows at the gray-brown terrain rushing toward them. The close horizon of the moon made it difficult to see any distance ahead, especially at their lowering altitude. A crater the size of a football stadium loomed below. Armstrong momentarily considered trying to land in the crater, but when he noticed rocks and boulders strewn over the floor of the crater, he thought better of such an attempt. If the LM in landing should cock over more than 30 degrees, takeoff from the moon would be impossible.

At one thousand feet Armstrong could see that the automatic guidance system was carrying them directly into a field where "boulders big as Volkswagens [were] strewn all around."

Aldrin called altitude and forward movement. "Six hundred feet. Five hundred forty feet. Attitude hold. Okay at hold."

Armstrong punched Program 66 on the guidance computer, putting the module on manual control. He was a pilot again, flying the weird moon vehicle with his hands, confident and sensitive to the controls. With one hand he directly controlled the attitude and horizontal velocity and with the other he gave manual signals to the computer to increase or decrease the power of the adjustable descent rocket.

At Houston the men in Mission Control knew something was happening, but didn't know what.

"Two hundred feet," radioed Aldrin. "Five and a half down. None forward."

As the dive flattened a red warning light flashed on the instrument panel. *Eagle* was running out of fuel. If the engine stopped before touchdown the wingless craft would dash itself and its occupants to their destruction below. Only a swift and dangerous firing of the ascent engine could snatch the astronauts from death if the descent engine failed.

With less than one hundred seconds of fuel remaining, the four gold-paddled legs of the LM groped down toward the powdery surface of the moon and to the most extraordinary landing in the experience of man. Beyond the second crater Armstrong spotted a flat area the size of a house lot ringed by craters on one side and boulders on the other. He dropped the *Eagle* down toward it.

Back on earth millions clutched the edges of their chairs, twisted their hands, bit the ends of pencils, and prayed.

Mission Control had a more knowledgeable worry. A fuel warning light was flashing there, too.

"Sixty seconds." Duke advised Armstrong of the fuel time. A very small margin of safety.

"Down two and a half," said Aldrin, his voice steady, "Forward. Forward. Picking up some dust. Thirty feet, two and a half down. Faint shadow. Four forward."

Neither man in the *Eagle* could now see the surface because of blowing dust, dust which had not been disturbed in four and a half billion years. The rocket blast spewed the dust at high speeds in a trajectory that was low and parallel to the surface.

Armstrong tilted the LM forward, pointing the rocket rearward for a clear look below.

"Four forward," announced Aldrin. "Drifting to the right a little."

"Thirty seconds," replied CapCom.

"Jesus Christ," prayed someone in Mission Control. "Get it down! Get it down!"

It happened quickly. Neil Armstrong did not see the first contact light go on as he eased his power and the lunar module dropped softly to the ground.

"Contact light," said Aldrin. The *Eagle*'s golden pads had settled into the gray, volcanic pumice dust.

"Okay, engine stop."

The roar disappeared, the great rocket power went off. The module rocked slightly to and fro before it became solid, secure, and silent.

"Override off. Engine arm off," announced Aldrin.

Duke's voice cut in, "We copy you down, *Eagle*."

Then across the empty chasm between moon and earth, to the waiting ears at Mission Control and the earthbound millions glued to their TV and radio sets, came the voice of Neil Armstrong. His speech was clear, he used the clipped language of a pilot. At the same time, that slight quiver in his voice when he and Aldrin had just accomplished the feat was captured on the radio waves that carried his message to the waiting world.

"While the whole world watched, Armstrong and Aldrin walked upon the surface of the moon."

*(NASA)*

"Houston," said Armstrong. "Tranquillity Base here. The *Eagle* has landed."

"You got a bunch of guys about to turn blue," replied Charlie Duke with a heavy sigh. "We're breathing again."

Hours later, while the world watched, Armstrong and Aldrin walked upon the surface of the moon. And when they returned home, a proud nation showered them with honors and adulation, giving literal translation to the prophecy of Dr. John Wilkins, who wrote in his treatise *A Discourse Concerning a New World and Another Planet* in 1640: "'Tis likely enough that there may be means invented of journeying to the moon; and how happy they shall be that are first successful in this attempt."

# Acknowledgments, Permissions, and Credits

Our personal thanks to Myron A. Roth, the Assistant Executive Director of the National Aeronautic Association (N.A.A.) for his constant urging over the years to complete this aviation narrative and world flying-records book. To M. J. Randleman for his careful checking of our N.A.A. and F.A.I. (Fédération Aéronautique Internationale) record lists. Photographs were received from the U.S. Air Force, the U.S. Navy, the National Archives and Records Center, the Library of Congress, the National Air and Space Museum, Smithsonian Institution, and NASA.

For the following literary sources—books and periodicals—that we have quoted, we are most appreciative:

Chapter 1: *The New York Times,* "1,132 M.P.H.," by Peter Twiss; *Nicholson's Journal,* "On Aerial Navigation," by George Cayley, 1809; the *Washington Post,* the Washington *Evening Star* and the Boston *Globe* for the Langley Aerodrome quotes; *Flying* magazine, "How We Made the First Flight," by Orville Wright, 1919; Dodd, Mead and Co., "The Story of the Winged-S," by Igor I. Sikorsky; *The New York Times* for the Louis Blériot and Wright brothers quotations; and the London *Daily Mail* for the reference editorial on the future of air power.

Chapter 2: Frederick A. Stokes Co., *The Curtiss Aviation Book* by Glenn H. Curtiss, 1912; *The New York Times* for the Jimmie Doolittle quotations; Don Dwiggins for his kind personal remarks about the manuscript and his permission to quote from his book *They Flew the Bendix Race,* published by J. B. Lippincott Co.; Fairchild Industries, *Pegasus* magazine, "Air Racing Was Like This" by Roscoe Turner; and the Royal Air Force *Flying Review*, "I Tested Messerschmitts," by Flug Kapitan Fritz Wendel.

Chapter 3: William Morrow and Co., for the Charles E. Yeager quotations from *Across the High Frontier*, by William Lundgren; The American Heritage Publishing Co., Inc., for the quotation about Yeager's broken ribs from *The American Heritage History of Flight*, 1962; *The New York Times* for the editorial quotation about the Robert J. Collier Trophy winners; the U. S. Air Force, for the Iven G. Kincheloe and Mel Apt quotations; *Flying* magazine, "I Hold the World's Speed Record," by Marion Carl for the Carl quotations; and *Science* magazine for the quotation from "The Pilot's Seat," by William H. Dana, 1968.

Chapter 4: Scribner, Armstrong and Co., N.Y., for the James Glaisher quotations from *Wonderful Balloon Ascents* (from the French of Fulgence Marion), 1874; the National Geographic Society for their special permission to quote from the *National Geographic Magazine* article, "Man's Farthest Aloft," by Capt. Albert W. Stevens, January, 1936; and Doubleday and Co., for the quotations from *Man High*, by David Simons, 1960.

Chapter 5: T. Werner Laurie, publisher for the Louis Blériot quotations in *The Aeroplane*, by Claude Grahame-White and Harry Harper, 1911; Longmans, Green and Co., for quotations from *Flying*, by Gustav Hamel and Charles C. Turner, 1914; Harcourt, Brace and. Co., *A History of Aeronautics*, by E. Charles Vivian, 1921, for the quotation by the author; *L'Auto Magazine* for quotations of Georges Legagneaux from an interview published in a 1913 article; Doubleday and Co., Inc., for quotations by the author from *Knights of the Air*, by Lester J. Maitland, 1929; *U. S. Air Service* magazine, "Airplane Reaches Altitude of 7.75 Miles," by John A. MacReady; *The New York Times* for the Wiley Post quotations; and the U. S. Air Force for the Carl F. Greene remarks.

Chapter 6: Quotations from "Marquis d'Arlandes' Letter To A Friend," Kurt R. Stehling and William Beller, authors of *Skyhooks*, Doubleday and Co., 1962, and The Smithsonian Institution; and *Les Ballons* by M. Julien Turgan, published by Plon Frères Éditions, 1851, for the quotations of Jean-Pierre Blanchard and Dr. John Jeffries.

Chapter 7: The New York *Sun* for the Edgar Allan Poe story of Monck Mason's "The Atlantic Crossed in Three Days," April 13 issue, 1884; and To-day Printing and Publishing Co., Chicago, for quotations from *Through the Air* by John Wise, 1873.

Chapter 8: The Century Co., New York, for the Alberto Santos-Dumont quotations from his book *My Airships*, 1904; and the Hearst Newspapers for quotations by their correspondents Lady Drummond Hay and Karl H. von Wiegand, who were on the *Graf Zeppelin* flight around the world in 1929.

Chapter 9: For the special permission from the National Geographic Society for the Ross and Keith Smith quotations from their article "A Personal Narrative of the First Aerial Voyage Half Around the World," in the March, 1921, issue of the *National Geographic Magazine.*

Chapter 10: The Houghton Mifflin Co., Boston, for quotations from the "Round the World Flight" as related to Lowell Thomas, 1924, and for Mr. Thomas' personal permission.

Chapter 11: For the special permissions from the National Geographic Society for the Gen. Umberto Nobile quotations from his article "Navigating the *Norge* from Rome to the North Pole and Beyond," in the August, 1927, issue of the *National Geographic Magazine;* and *The New York Times* and the St. Louis *Post-Dispatch* for the Comdr. Richard E. Byrd, Russell D. Owen, Frederick Ramm, and Captain George H. Wilkins quotations.

Chapter 12: Penlington & Somerville Co., publishers, Sydney, 1928, for the Kingsford-Smith quotations from the *Story of the Southern Cross Trans-Pacific Flight, 1928,* by C. E. Kingsford-Smith and C. P. T. Ulm.

Chapter 13: *The New York Times* for Wiley Post and Harold Gatty quotations, 1931 and 1933, James Mattern's remarks, 1933, and those of William Odom, 1947; Funk and Wagnall Co., New York, for the John Heinmuller quotations from his book *Man's Fight To Fly,* 1944; and Gordon Williams for making available his article about the Boeing B-52 Stratofortresses' flight around the world (Operation PowerFlight), which appeared in *Boeing Magazine,* February, 1957.

Chapter 14: *The New York Times* for its editorial of January 13, 1920; to *Izvestia* for the Georgy Ostroumev quotation; and the National Aeronautics and Space Administration for astronaut quotations from the original tapes of the Project Gemini and Project Apollo flights.

Personal thanks to John M. Fritz and Maj. Gen. Leigh Wade for the vital information they gave us in interviews.

The selections in this book are used by permission and special arrangements with the proprietors of the respective copyrights who are listed above. The authors and publisher give their profound thanks to all for making this book possible.

The authors have made every effort to trace the ownership of the material contained herein. It is our belief that the necessary permissions have been obtained from publishers, authors, and authorized agents. In the event of any questions arising as to the use of any material, the authors express regret for any error unconsciously made and will be pleased to set the record straight. We welcome correspondence about the records in the book. We are most pleased with the National Geographic Society's decision to allow us to use a considerable amount of material from their magazine, *National Geographic,* because we are dedicated to the same purpose—"and the fact that the information you have compiled and the F.A.I. records will constitute a valuable reference source and a contribution to scientific knowledge."

MARK P. FRIEDLANDER, JR.
GENE GURNEY

# *Record Flights*

## *Appendix 1*
## *Official F.A.I. Records*

### *How They Are Classified*

To establish uniformity in the recognition of the many possible aircraft performances, a standard record classification has been adopted by the F.A.I. for Absolute World and World "Class" Records. Records which fall in this classification are referred to as F.A.I. records. National records are recognized following these F.A.I. classifications.

### *Absolute World Records*

Absolute World Records are defined as maximum performances regardless of the class or type of aircraft used. The following are recognized:

**A—Aircraft**
Distance in a straight line.
Distance over a closed course.
Altitude: aircraft launched from a carrier airplane.
Altitude in horizontal flight.
Speed over a straight course.
Speed over a closed course.

**B—Manned Spacecraft Records**
Duration (from launch to point of termination of the performance).

Altitude (above the earth's surface).

Greatest mass lifted to altitude.

Distance (along the trajectory measured from the point of launch to the point at which the planned operation is terminated).

Extravehicular duration (time spent outside the spacecraft with an autonomous life support system).

Greatest number of astronauts simultaneously outside of spacecraft.

Accumulated time in space (by one astronaut).

Total time in space (by one astronaut).

### World "Class" Records

All other records which are international in scope are necessarily the best World performances for a particular type of aircraft are termed World "Class" Records to differentiate from the foregoing maximum achievements. World "Class" Records, therefore, are defined as the best international performances for the classes and categories of aircraft recognized by the F.A.I. The aircraft classes which have been adopted by the F.A.I. for the purpose of providing a standard classification are:

Free Balloons . . . . . . . . . . . . . . . . . .Class A
Airships . . . . . . . . . . . . . . . . . . . . . .Class B
Landplanes . . . . . . . . . . . . . . . . . . .Class C-1
Seaplanes . . . . . . . . . . . . . . . . . . . . .Class C-2
Amphibians . . . . . . . . . . . . . . . . . . .Class C-3
Gliders . . . . . . . . . . . . . . . . . . . . . . .Class D
Rotorplanes . . . . . . . . . . . . . . . . . . .Class E
Model Aircraft . . . . . . . . . . . . . . . . .Class F
Parachutes . . . . . . . . . . . . . . . . . . . .Class G
Jetlift Aircraft . . . . . . . . . . . . . . . . . .Class H
Man-powered Aircraft . . . . . . . . . .Class I
Space Vehicles . . . . . . . . . . . . . . . . .Class K
Air Cushion Vehicles . . . . . . . . . .Class L
Recognized Courses
Commercial Air Routes

Group I—Piston engines
Group II—Turboprop engines
Group III—Jet engines
Group IV—Rocket
  engines

In the case of Landplanes, Seaplanes, Amphibians, and Rotorplanes, there is a further subdivision by gross weight, in which there are classified in separate categories as follows:

| *Light Airplanes*<br>(Gross Weight) | *Light Seaplanes, Light Amphibians*<br>(Gross Weight) |
|---|---|
| Class C-1.a (under 1,102 lbs.) | Less than 1,323 lbs. |
| Class C-1.b (1,102 to 2,204 lbs.) | 1,323 to 2,645 lbs. |
| Class C-1.c (2,204 to 3,858 lbs.) | 2,645 to 4,630 lbs. |
| Class C-1.d (3,858 to 6,614 lbs.) | 4,630 to 7,496 lbs. |

| *Business Airplanes* | *Helicopters* |
|---|---|
| Class CJ-1.a (6,614 to 13,227 lbs.) | Class E-1.a (under 1,102 lbs.) |
| Class CJ-1.b (13,227 to 17,636 lbs.) | Class E-1.b (1,102 to 2,204 lbs.) |
| Class CJ-1.c (17,636 to 26,455 lbs.) | Class E-1.c (2,204 to 3,858 lbs.) |
| Class CJ-1.d (26,455 to 35,274 lbs.) | Class E-1.d (3,858 to 6,614 lbs.) |
| Class CJ-1.e (35,274 to 44,092 lbs.) | Class E-1.e (6,614 to 9,920 lbs.) |
| Class CJ-1.f (44,092 to 57,320 lbs.) | |

The contest aircraft must be weighed in the full takeoff configuration in the presence of an official observer to determine the proper weight class.

For Landplanes, Seaplanes, Amphibians, and Rotorplanes, the World "Class" Records recognized are:

## Without Load

1. Greatest distance in a straight line without landing or refueling.
2. Greatest distance in a closed circuit without landing or refueling.
3. Greatest altitude or height above the sea level.
4. Greatest altitude in a horizontal sustained flight.
5. Greatest speed over a straight course (3 Kms. and 15/25 Kms.).
6. Greatest speed in a closed circuit over an established course for each of the following distances: 100 kms. (62.137 miles); 500 kms. (310.685 miles); 1,000 kms. (621.369 miles); 2,000 kms. (1,242.739 miles); 5,000 kms. (3,106.849 miles) and 10,000 kms. (6,213.698 miles).
7. Speed around-the-world; speed around the world over the poles; speed from equator to equator over a pole.
8. Time to climb to 3,000; 6,000; 9,000; 12,000; and 15,000 meters and

additional 5,000 meters consecutively (Light Aircraft excluded):

*With Payload of 1,000 kgs. (2,204.6 lbs.); 2,000 kgs. (4,409.2 lbs.); 5,000 kgs. (11,023 lbs.); 10,000 kgs. (22,046 lbs.); or additional 5,000 kgs. consecutively (Light Aircraft excluded).*

1. Greatest altitude or height.
2. Greatest speed in a closed circuit over an established course for each of the following distances: 1,000 kms. (621.369 miles); 2,000 kms. (1,242.739 miles); 5,000 kms. (3,106.849 miles); and 10,000 kms. (6,213.698 miles).
3. Greatest payload lifted to a height of 2,000 meters (6,561 feet).

For Gliders, the World "Class" Records recognized are:

Greatest distance to a fixed point and return.
Greatest distance in a straight line.
Greatest distance to a fixed point.
Greatest height or altitude above sea level.
Greatest gain in height.
Speed for 100 kilometers over a triangular course.
Speed for 300 kilometers over a triangular course.
Speed for 500 kilometers over a triangular course.

World "Class" Records for Airships, Gas Balloons, and Hot Air Balloons: In each of these classes, records for altitude, distance, and duration are recognized. Records for gas balloons and hot-air balloons are further divided into ten subclasses according to the capacity of the balloon. Altitude With Payload records may also be established in the unlimited classification for gas and hot-air balloons.

## Speed Over a Recognized Course

The F.A.I. recognizes maximum speed performances between selected national capitals and internationally important cities. These performances must be made between previously designated cities.

## Speed On a Commercial Air Route

In additional to speed records over a recognized course, the F.A.I. recognizes the best performances in speed accomplished by aircraft with normal certificate of airworthiness belonging to regular airlines flying over regular air routes.

### Feminine Records

Feminine Records are recognized in all classes except those with payloads and light aircraft classified according to weight.

## *Appendix 2*

# *Official F.A.I. Absolute World Records (Maximum Performance in Any Class)*

*A. Aircraft*
1962—Jan 11
DISTANCE IN A STRAIGHT LINE      U.S.A.    *12,532.28 miles.*
Major Clyde P. Evely, U.S.A.F.
Boeing B52-H
(8) Pratt & Witney TF-33-P-3 engines
Kadena, Okinawa, to Madrid, Spain

1962—June 6-7
DISTANCE OVER A CLOSED CIRCUIT    U.S.A.    *11,336.92 miles.*
Capt. William Stevenson, U.S.A.F.
Boeing B52-H
(8) Pratt & Whitney TF-33-P-3 engines
Seymour-Johnson, North Carolina; Kindley, Bermuda;
Sondrestrom, Greenland; Anchorage, Alaska
March AFB, California; Key West, Florida
Seymour-Johnson, North Carolina

1961—Apr 28
ALTITUDE          U.S.S.R.    *113,890.8 ft.*
Gueorgui Mossolov

E66A Airplane
(1) TDR engine and (1) GDR engine
Podmoskovnoe, U.S.S.R.

| | | |
|---|---|---|
| 1962—Jul 17 | | |
| ALTITUDE: AIRCRAFT LAUNCHED | | |
| FROM A CARRIER AIRPLANE | U.S.A. | *314,750 ft.* |
| Major Robert M. White, U.S.A.F. | | |
| North American X-15-1 (NASA Aircraft) | | |
| (1) Reaction Motors XLR-99 Rocket Engine | | |
| Edwards Air Force Base, California | | |

1962—Jul 17
ALTITUDE: AIRCRAFT LAUNCHED
 FROM A CARRIER AIRPLANE          U.S.A.          *314,750 ft.*
Major Robert M. White, U.S.A.F.
North American X-15-1 (NASA Aircraft)
(1) Reaction Motors XLR-99 Rocket Engine
Edwards Air Force Base, California

1965—May 1
ALTITUDE IN HORIZONTAL FLIGHT          U.S.A.          *80,257.86 ft.*
Col. R. L. Stephens, U.S.A.F.
Lockheed YF-12A
(2) Pratt & Whitney J58 engines
Edwards Air Force Base, California

1965—May 1
SPEED OVER A STRAIGHT COURSE          U.S.A.          *2,070.101 m.p.h.*
Col R. L. Stephens, U.S.A.F.
Lockheed YF-12A
(2) Pratt & Whitney J58 engines
Edwards Air Force Base, California

1967—Oct 5
SPEED OVER A CLOSED CIRCUIT          U.S.S.R.          *1,852.61 m.p.h.*
Mikhail Komarov
E-266 Jet
(2) RD 11,000 kgs. engines

*B. Manned Spacecraft*

1970—Jun 1-19
DURATION          U.S.S.R.          *424 hrs., 58 min., 55 sec.*
A. G. Nikolayev
V. I. Sevastyanov
Spacecraft Soyuz 9

1968—Dec 21-27
ALTITUDE          U.S.A.          *234,672.5 miles*
Frank Borman, James A.
Lovell, Jr., William Anders
Spacecraft Apollo 8

1968—Dec 21-27
GREATEST MASS LIFTED                U.S.A.                  *282,197 lbs.*
Frank Borman, James A.
Lovell, Jr., William Anders
Spacecraft Apollo 8


1970—Jun 1-19
DISTANCE                            U.S.S.R.              *7,387,499 miles*
A. G. Nikolayev
V. I. Sevastyanov
Spacecraft Soyuz 9


1972—Dec 12-14
DURATION OF STAY OUTSIDE OF
    SPACECRAFT                      U.S.A.        *21 hrs., 32 min., 35 sec.*
Eugene A. Cernan
Spacecraft Apollo 17 & LM Challenger

1969—Mar 15
GREATEST NUMBER OF ASTRO-
    NAUTS SIMULTANEOUSLY OUT-
    SIDE OF SPACECRAFT             U.S.S.R.                      *2*
A. Elisseiev and E. Khrounov
Spacecraft Soyuz 5

1970—May 17
TOTAL TIME IN SPACE                U.S.A.
James A. Lovell, Jr.                  *29 days, 19 hrs., 4 min., 57 sec.*
Gemini 7 12/4-18/65                 *13 days, 18 hrs., 35 min., 00 sec.*
Gemini 12 11/11-15/66                *3 days, 22 hrs., 34 min., 34 sec.*
Apollo 8 12/21-27/68                  *6 days, 3 hrs., 00 min., 42 sec.*
Apollo 13 4/11-17/70                 *5 days, 22 hrs., 54 min., 41 sec.*

## Appendix 3

# Official F.A.I. World Class Balloon Records

### Class A

**Subclass A-1**
**Less than 250 Cubic Meters Capacity**

Duration
  None
Distance
  1972—Aug 12
            Wilma Piccard in a Piccard S-10 Holiday
            Balloon at Indianola, Ind.
            *– 17.6 miles*

  None
Altitude
  1960—Jul 24
            Donald L. Piccard in a Piccard S-10 Holiday
            Balloon at Minneapolis, Minn.
            *– 3,740 feet.*

**Subclass A-2**
**Between 250 and 400 Cubic Meters Capacity**

Duration
  1953—May 3
            Audouin Dollfus of France from Senlis to
            Cheverny, France
            *– 4 hours.*
Distance
  1953—May 3
            Audouin Dollfus of France from Senlis to
            Cheverny, France
            *– 129 miles.*
Altitude
  1955—May 1
            Audouin Dollfus of France at Senlis, France
            *– 11,171 feet.*

1962—Aug 24   Donald L. Piccard in a Sioux City Sue Raven Industries Balloon at Sioux City, Iowa – *17,747 feet.*

## Subclass A-3
## Between 400 and 600 Cubic Meters Capacity

Duration
 1922—Jul 1   Georges Cormier, France
        – *17 hours, 32 min.*

 1923—Aug 15-16 Gaston Fleury and George Fleury, France
        – *19 hours, 43 min.*

 1924—Aug 10-11 Georges Cormier, France
        – *22 hours, 34 min.*

 1941—Mar 30  Serge Sinoveev, Dolgoproudnaia, U.S.S.R.
        – *46 hours, 10 min.*

Distance
 1922—Jul 1   Georges Cormier, France
        – *499 miles.*

Altitude
 1940—Aug 31  Boris Nevernov at Dolgoproudnaia, U.S.S.R.
        – *23,286 feet.*

 1964—May 10  Tracy Barnes in a Barnes 14-A Balloon at Rosemount, Minn.
        – *38,650 feet.*

## Subclass A-4
## Between 600 and 900 Cubic Meters Capacity

Duration
 1922—May 14-15 Jules Duboise, France
        – *23 hours, 28 min.*

 1939—Apr 3-6  F. Bourlouzki and A. Aliochine, U.S.S.R. from Moscow to Charaboulski
        – *61 hours, 30 min.*

Distance
  1922—Jul 1          Georges Cormier, France
                      – *499 miles.*

  1935—Mar 25-26      Eug. Stuber and Werner Schafer of Germany
                      from Bitterfeld, Germany, to Pazariche,
                      U.S.S.R.
                      – *747 miles.*

  1939—Apr 3-6        F. Bourlouzki and A. Aliochine of U.S.S.R.
                      from Moscow to Charaboulski, U.S.S.R.
                      – *1,056 miles.*

Altitude
  1940—Oct 4          Alexei Rostine at Dolgoproudnaia, U.S.S.R.
                      – *27,718 feet.*

  1961—July 19        Donald L. Piccard in a "Golden Bear" 600-
                      cubic-meter balloon at Faribault, Minn.
                      – *34,462 feet.*

  1964—May 10         Tracy Barnes in a Barnes 14-A Balloon at
                      Rosemount, Minn.
                      – *38,650 feet.*

## Subclass A-5
## Between 900 and 1200 Cubic Meters Capacity

Duration
  1922—May 14-15      Jules Dubois, France
                      – *23 hours, 28 min.*

  1927—Jul 4-5        D. J. Hill and A. G. Schlosser, Ford Airport
                      to Montvale, Va.
                      – *26 hours, 46 min.*

  1939—Apr 3-6        F. Bourlouzki and A. Aliochine, U.S.S.R.
                      from Moscow to Charaboulski
                      – *61 hours, 30 min.*

Distance
　　1922—Jul 1
　　　　　　　　　　Georges Cormier, France
　　　　　　　　　　*– 499 miles.*

　　1927—Jul 4-5
　　　　　　　　　　S. A. U. Rasmussen, Ford Airport to
　　　　　　　　　　Hookerton, N.C.
　　　　　　　　　　*– 571 miles.*

　　1932—Sep 10
　　　　　　　　　　Jean Herbe of France, St. Cloud-Neuewise,
　　　　　　　　　　Silesia, course
　　　　　　　　　　*– 620 miles.*

　　1932—Sep 25-26
　　　　　　　　　　Georges Ravaine of France from Basle,
　　　　　　　　　　Switzerland, to Tokary, Poland
　　　　　　　　　　*– 769 miles.*

　　1939—Apr 3-6
　　　　　　　　　　F. Bourlouzki and A. Aliochine of U.S.S.R.
　　　　　　　　　　from Moscow to Charaboulski, U.S.S.R.
　　　　　　　　　　*– 1,056 miles.*

Altitude
　　1940—Oct 4
　　　　　　　　　　Alexei Rostine at Dolgoproudnaia, U.S.S.R.
　　　　　　　　　　*– 27,718 feet.*

　　1961—July 19
　　　　　　　　　　Donald L. Piccard in a "Golden Bear" 600-
　　　　　　　　　　cubic-meter balloon at Faribault, Minn.
　　　　　　　　　　*– 34,462 feet.*

　　1964—May 10
　　　　　　　　　　Tracy Barnes in a Barnes 14-A Balloon at
　　　　　　　　　　Rosemount, Minn.
　　　　　　　　　　*– 38,650 feet.*

---

**Subclass A-6**
**Between 1200 and 1600 Cubic Meters Capacity**

Duration
　　1927—Jul 4-5
　　　　　　　　　　D. J. Hill and A. G. Schlosser,
　　　　　　　　　　Ford Airport to Montvale, Va.
　　　　　　　　　　*– 26 hours, 46 min.*

1929—May 4-6     Lt. T. G. W. Settle and Ensign W. Bushnell, Pittsburgh, Pa., to Prince Edward Island, Canada
*– 43 hours, 20 min.*

1941—Mar 13-16     Boris Nevernov and Semion Gaiguerov, from Dolgoproudnaia to Novosibirsk, U.S.S.R.
*– 69 hours, 20 min.*

## Distance

1927—Jul 4-5     S. A. U. Rasmussen, Ford Airport to Hookerton, N.C.
*– 571 miles.*

1932—Sep 10     Jean Herbe of France, St. Cloud-Neuewise, Silesia, course
*– 620 miles.*

1932—Sep 25-26     Georges Ravaine of France, from Basle, Switzerland, to Tokary, Poland
*– 769 miles.*

1941—Mar 13-16     Boris Nevernov and Semiou Gaiguerov of U.S.S.R., from Dolgoproudnaia to Novosibirsk, U.S.S.R.
*– 1,719 miles.*

## Altitude

1901—June 30     Professors Reinhard Süring and Artur Berson, Germany
*– 35,424 feet.* *

1940—Oct 4     Alexei Rostine at Dolgoproudnaia, U.S.S.R.
*– 27,718 feet.*

1961—July 19     Donald L. Piccard in a "Golden Bear" 600-cubic-meter balloon at Faribault, Minn.
*– 34,462 feet.*

*Accepted by F.A.I. but not certified.

| 1964—May 10 | Tracy Barnes in a Barnes 14-A Balloon at Rosemount, Minn.<br>*– 38,650 feet.* |

## Subclass A-7
## Between 1600 and 2200 Cubic Meters Capacity

### Duration

| 1927—Sep 10-12 | Georges Blanchet and Dr. George LeGallee, Gordon Bennett Balloon Race, Detroit, Mich. to Waverley Hall, Ga.<br>*– 49 hours.* |
| 1933—Sep 2-4 | Lt. Comdr. T. G. W. Settle and Lt. Charles H. Kendall, Gordon Bennett Balloon Race, Chicago, Ill.<br>*– 51 hours.* |
| 1935—Sep 15-18 | Z. J. Burzynski and W. Wisocki, Poland, Gordon Bennett Balloon Race<br>*– 57 hours, 54 min.* |
| 1941—Mar 13-16 | Boris Nevernov and Semion Gaiguerov, from Dolgoproudnaia to Novosibirsk, U.S.S.R.<br>*– 69 hours, 20 min.* |

### Distance

| 1927—Sep 10-12 | E. J. Hill and A. G. Schlosser, Gordon Bennett Balloon Race, Detroit, Mich., to Baxley, Ga.<br>*– 745 miles.* |
| 1929—May 4-6 | Lt. T. G. Settle, U.S.N., and Ensign Wilfred Bushnell, U.S.N., from Pittsburgh, Pa., to Prince Edward Island, Canada<br>*– 952 miles.* |

1932—Sep 25-27    Lt. Comdr. T. G. Settle, U.S.N., and Lt. Wilfred Bushnell, U.S.N., the Internation Balloon Race from Basle, Switzerland, to Daugieliski, Poland
*– 963 miles.*

1935—Sep 15-18    Z. J. Burzynski and W. Wisocki of Poland from Warsaw to Tiszkino, Poland
*– 1,025 miles.*

1936—Sep 1    Ernest Demuyter and Pierre Hoffmans of Belgium from Warsaw, Poland, to Miedlesza, U.S.S.R.
*– 1,065 miles.*

1941—Mar 13-16    Boris Nevernov and Semion Gaiguerov of U.S.S.R. from Dolgoproudnaia to Novosibirsk, U.S.S.R.
*– 1,719 miles.*

Altitude
1901—Jun 30    Professors Reinhard Süring and Artur Berson, Germany
*– 35,424 feet.*

1937—Sep 25-27    Josef Emmer at Vienna-Lac de Nuesiedl, Austria
*– 30,755 feet.*

1961—July 19    Donald L. Piccard in a "Golden Bear" 600-cubic-meter balloon at Faribault, Minn.
*– 34,462 feet.*

1964—May 10    Tracy Barnes in a Barnes 14-A Balloon at Rosemount, Minn.
*– 38,650 feet.*

## Subclass A-8
## Between 2200 and 3000 Cubic Meters Capacity

Duration
1927— Sep 10-12      Georges Blanchet and Dr. George LeGallee,
                     Gordon Bennett Balloon Race, Detroit,
                     Mich., to Waverley Hall, Ga.
                     – *49 hours.*

1933—Sep 2-4         Lt. Comdr. T. G. W. Settle and Lt. Charles
                     H. Kendall, Gordon Bennett Balloon Race,
                     Chicago, Ill.
                     – *51 hours.*

1935—Sep 15-18       Z. J. Burzynski and W. Wisocki, Poland,
                     Gordon Bennett Balloon Race
                     – *57 hours, 54 min.*

1941—Mar 13-16       Boris Nevernov and Semion Gaiguerov
                     from Dolgoproudnaia to Novosibirsk,
                     U.S.S.R.
                     – *69 hours, 20 min.*

Distance
1929—May 4-6         Lt. T. G. Settle and Ensign Wilfred Bushnell
                     from Pittsburgh, Pa., to Prince Edward Island,
                     Canada
                     – *952 miles.*

1932—Sep 25-27       Lt. Comdr. T. G. Settle, U.S.N., and Lt.
                     Wilfred Bushnell, U.S.N., the Internation
                     Balloon Race
                     from Basle, Switzerland, to Daugieliski,
                     Poland
                     – *963 miles.*

1935—Sep 15-18       Z. J. Burzynski and W. Wisocki of Poland
                     from Warsaw to Tiszkino, Poland
                     – *1,025 miles.*

| | |
|---|---|
| 1936—Sep 1 | Ernest Demuyter and Pierre Hoffmans of Belgium from Warsaw, Poland to Miedlesza, U.S.S.R.<br>– *1,065 miles.* |
| 1941—Mar 13-16 | Boris Nevernov and Semion Gaiguerov of U.S.S.R. from Dolgoproudnaia to Novosibirsk, U.S.S.R.<br>– *1,719 miles.* |

Altitude

| | |
|---|---|
| 1927—Mar 9 | Capt. Hawthorne C. Gray, Scott Field, Belleville, Ill., U.S.A.<br>– *28,508 feet.* |
| 1937—Sep 25-27 | Josef Emmer at Vienna-Lac de Nuesiedl, Austria<br>– *30,755 feet.* |
| 1961—July 19 | Donald L. Piccard in a "Golden Bear" 600-cubic-meter balloon at Faribault, Minn.<br>– *34,462 feet.* |
| 1964—May 10 | Tracy Barnes in a Barnes 14-A Balloon at Rosemount, Minn.<br>– *38,650 feet.* |

## Subclass A-9
### Between 3000 and 4000 Cubic Meters Capacity

Duration

| | |
|---|---|
| 1927—Sep 10-12 | Georges Blanchet and Dr. George LaGallee, Gordon Bennett Balloon Race, Detroit, Mich., to Waverley Hall, Ga.<br>– *49 hours.* |
| 1933—Sep 2-4 | Lt. Comdr. T. G. W. Settle and Lt. Charles H. Kendall, Gordon Bennett Balloon Race, Chicago, Ill.<br>– *51 hours.* |

1935—Sep 15-18      Z. J. Burzynski and W. Wisocki, Poland, Gordon Bennett Balloon Race, *– 57 hours, 54 min.*

1941—Mar 13-16      Boris Nevernov and Semion Gaiguerov from Dolgoproudnaia to Novosibirsk, U.S.S.R. *– 69 hours, 20 min.*

Distance

1929—May 4-5-6      Lt. T. G. Settle and Ensign Wilfred Bushnell from Pittsburgh, Pa., to Prince Edward Island, Canada *– 952 miles.*

1932—Sep 25-27      Lt. Comdr. T. G. Settle, U.S.N., and Lt. Wilfred Bushnell, U.S.N., the Internation Balloon Race from Basle, Switzerland, to Daugieliski, Poland *– 963 miles.*

1935—Sep 15-18      Z. J. Burzynski and W. Wisocki of Poland from Warsaw to Tiszkino, Poland *– 1,025 miles.*

1936—Sep 1      Ernest Demuyter and Pierre Hoffmans of Belgium from Warsaw, Poland, to Miedlesza, U.S.S.R. *– 1,065 miles.*

1941—Mar 13-16      Boris Nevernov and Semion Gaiguerov of U.S.S.R. from Dolgoproudnaia to Novosibirsk, U.S.S.R. *– 1,719 miles.*

Altitude

1927—Mar 9      Capt. Hawthorne C. Gray, Scott Field, Belleville, Ill., U.S.A. *– 28,508 feet.*

1936—Mar 29      Z. J. Burzynski at Legjonowo, Poland *– 35,607 feet.*

1964—May 10       Tracy Barnes in a Barnes 14-A Balloon at Rosemount, Minn.
*– 38,650 feet.*

## Subclass A-10
## Over 4000 Cubic Meters Capacity

Duration
  1913—Dec 13-17       Hans Kaulen, Germany
*– 87 hours.*

Distance
  1914—Feb 8-10       Emile Berliner, Germany (in same balloon Kaulen used in 1913 record)
*– 1,896 miles.*

Altitude
  1931—May 27       Auguste Piccard and Paul Kipfer of Switzerland at Augsburg, Glacier d'Obergurgl
*– 51,775 feet.*

  1932—Aug 18       Auguste Piccard and Max Cosyns of Switzerland, takeoff from Dubendorf, landing near Volta Montavana, Italy
*– 53,152 feet.*

  1933—Sep 30       G. Profkoviet, E. N. Birnbaum, K. D. Godunow, Moscow, U.S.S.R. The U.S.S.R. claimed an altitude record; it was not verified by FAI but was *accepted as a courtesy.* U.S.S.R. refused to submit scientific data
*– 60,680 feet.*

  1933—Nov 20       Lt. Comdr. T. G. Settle, U.S.N., and Major C. L. Fordney, U.S.M.C., takeoff from Akron, Ohio, landing at Bayside, N.J.
*– 61,236 feet.*

  1935—June 26       (Warigo, Christofil, and Priluchi, U.S.S.R., ascended to 52,800 feet when balloon went into an uncontrolled descent and crew parachuted to safety)

| 1935—Nov 11 | Capt. Orvil Anderson and Capt. Albert Stevens, U.S.A.S., takeoff Rapid City to White Lake, S.D. |
| | *– 72,395 feet.* |

| 1957—Aug 19 | Major David G. Simons, U.S.A.F., takeoff Crosby, Minn., to Frederick, S.D. |
| | *– 101,516 feet.* |

| 1961—May 4 | Comdr. Malcolm D. Ross, U.S.N.R., and V. Prather in a Lee Lewis Memorial Winzen Research Balloon over Gulf of Mexico (Prather killed in the recovery operations) |
| | *– 113,739 feet.* |

In 1965, the F.A.I. also established the same 10 categories for hot-air balloons, calling them Subclass AX-1 through 10.

### Subclass AX-1
### Less than 250 Cubic Meters Capacity

Duration
  None
Distance
  None
Altitude
  None

### Subclass AX-2
### Between 250 and 400 Cubic Meters Capacity

Duration
  None
Distance
  None
Altitude
  None

## Subclass AX-3
### Between 400 and 600 Cubic Meters Capacity

Duration
    1969—Sep 18         George A. Stokes of U.S.A. in a Semco
                              Balloon at Richmond, Va.
                              *– 51 minutes.*

    1970—Oct 5          Raymond Munro of Canada in a Raven S40A
                              Vulcoon Balloon
                              *– 2 hours, 4 min.*

    1971—May 2          Mrs. Lois Elmstrom of U.S.A. in a Piccard
                              Balloon at Lancaster, Calif.
                              *– 2 hours, 6 min., 10 sec.*

Distance
    1969—Sept 18        George A. Stokes of U.S.A. in a Semco
                              Balloon at Richmond, Va.
                              *– 9.6 miles.*

    1970—May 19        Raymond A. Munro of Canada in a Raven
                              S40A Vulcoon Balloon
                              *– 35.57 miles.*

Altitude
    1965—Sep 3          Brenda Bogan of U.S.A. at Anoka, Minn.
                              *– 9,770 feet.*

    1966—Oct 11        Deke Sonnichsen of U.S.A. in a Quick Silver
                              Libra II AX-4 Piccard Balloon at Tracy, Calif.
                              *– 21,250 feet.*

## Subclass AX-4
### Between 600 and 900 Cubic Meters Capacity

Duration
    1966—Oct 5          Deke Sonnichsen of U.S.A. in a Quick Silver
                              Libra II AX-4 Piccard Balloon from Mountain
                              View to Los Altos, Calif.
                              *– 1 hour, 55 min., 10 sec.*

1971—May 2                         Mrs. Lois Elmstrom of U.S.A. in a Piccard
                                   Balloon at Lancaster, Calif.
                                   – *2 hours, 6 min., 10 sec.*

Distance
1966—Oct 11                        Deke Sonnichsen of U.S.A. in a Quick Silver
                                   Libra II AX-4 Piccard Balloon from Tracy
                                   to Salida, Calif.
                                   – *20.24 miles.*

    1970—May 19                    Raymond A. Munro of Canada in a Raven
                                   S40A Vulcoon Balloon
                                   – *35.57 miles.*

Altitude
1966—Oct 11                        Deke Sonnichsen of U.S.A. in a Quick Silver
                                   Libra II AX-4 Piccard Balloon at Tracy, Calif.
                                   – *21,250 feet.*

### Subclass AX-5
### Between 900 and 1200 Cubic Meters Capacity

Duration
1970—Oct 5                         Raymond A. Munro of Canada in a Raven
                                   S40A Vulcoon Balloon
                                   – *2 hours, 4 min.*

1970—Oct 5                         Mrs. Lois Elmstrom of U.S.A. in a Piccard
                                   Balloon at Lancaster, Calif.
                                   – *2 hours, 6 min.*

1972—Mar 31                        Thomas Donnelly of the United Kingdom in a
                                   G. Azer Balloon at (location not listed).
                                   – *2 hours, 28 min.*

Distance
1970—May 19                        Raymond A. Munro of Canada in a Raven
                                   S40A Vulcoon Balloon
                                   – *35.57 miles*

| 1972—Mar 31 | Thomas Donnelly of the United Kingdom in a G. Azer Balloon at (location not listed). |
|---|---|
| | *– 64 miles.* |

Altitude
None

## Subclass AX-6
## Between 1200 and 1600 Cubic Meters Capacity

Duration
   1969—Dec 17     Raymond A. Munro of Canada in a Raven
                   S50A Vulcoon Balloon
                   *– 1 hour, 25 min.*

   1970—Feb 1      Raymond A. Munro of Canada in a Raven
                   S50A Vulcoon Balloon
                   *– 4 hours, 52 min.*

   1972—Feb 1      Matt A. Wiederkehr in a Raven S50A Balloon
                   at St. Paul, Minn.
                   *– 8 hours, 48 min.*

Distance
   1969—Dec 24     Raymond A. Munro of Canada in a Raven
                   S50A Vulcoon Balloon
                   *– 26.433 miles.*

   1972—Mar 29     Matt A. Wiederkehr in a Raven S50A Balloon
                   at St. Paul, Minn.
                   *– 196.71 miles.*

Altitude
   1965—Oct 5      Donald L. Piccard of U.S.A. in a Piccard
                   Balloon at El Mirage, Calif.
                   *– 15,691 feet.*

   1969—Dec 17     Raymond A. Munro of Canada in a Raven
                   S50A Vulcoon Balloon beat his record of Nov.
                   24, 1969 of 17,920 feet
                   *– 25,405.8 feet.*

## Subclass AX-7
### Between 1600 and 2200 Cubic Meters Capacity

Duration
  1970—Feb 1                Raymond A. Munro of Canada in a Raven
                            S50A Vulcoon Balloon
                            – *4 hours, 52 min.*

  1972—Dec 14               Robert Sparks in a Semco Challenger Balloon
                            at Lafayette, Ind.
                            – *11 hours, 14 min.*

Distance
  1970—Feb 1                Raymond A. Munro of Canada in a Raven
                            S50A Vulcoon Balloon
                            – *158.34 miles*

  1972—Mar 29               Matt A. Wiederkehr in a Raven S50A Balloon
                            at St. Paul, Minn.
                            – *196.71 miles.*

Altitude
  1966—Jul 10               William R. Berry of U.S.A. in a Raven S50R
                            Balloon at Livermore, Calif.
                            – *18,980 feet.*

  1969—Dec 17               Raymond A. Munro of Canada in a Raven
                            S50A Vulcoon Balloon beat his record of Nov.
                            24, 1969 of 17,920 feet
                            – *25,405.8 feet.*

## Subclass AX-8
### Between 2200 and 3000 Cubic Meters Capacity

Duration
  1970—Oct 31               Kurt Runzi of Switzerland in a Semco TC-4
                            Balloon at Zumikon, Switzerland
                            – *6 hours, 30 min.*

1972—Dec 14        Robert Sparks in a Semco Challenger Balloon at Lafayette, Ind.
*– 11 hours, 14 min.*

Distance
1970—Oct 31        Kurt Runzi of Switzerland in a Semco TC-4 Balloon at Zumikon, Switzerland
*– 160.82 miles.*

1972—Mar 29        Matt A. Wiederkehr in a Raven S50A Balloon at St. Paul, Minn.
*– 196.71 miles.*

Altitude
1966—Aug 25        Tracy L. Barnes of U.S.A. in a Barnes Balloon at Pittsburgh, Pa.
*– 28,585 feet.*

1971—Jun 9        Karl Stefan of U.S.A. in a Raven S-60 Balloon at Boulder, Colo.
*– 31,000 feet.*

1971—June 12        Chauncy Dunn of U.S.A. in a Raven S-60 Balloon at Boulder/Longmont, Colo.
*– 32,949 feet.*

1972—Jul 14        Julian Nott in an Omega 84 Balloon "GAXVU" at Hereford, Eng.
*– 35,971 feet.*

## Subclass AX-9
## Between 3000 and 4000 Cubic Meters Capacity

Duration
1970—Feb 1        Raymond A. Munro of Canada in a Raven S50A Vulcoon Balloon
*– 4 hours, 52 min.*

| 1972—Dec 14 | Robert Sparks in a Semco Challenger Balloon at Lafayette, Ind. |
| | *– 11 hours, 14 min.* |

Distance
| 1970—Feb 1 | Raymond A. Munro of Canada in a Raven S50A Vulcoon Balloon |
| | *– 158.34 miles.* |

| 1972—Mar 29 | Matt A. Wiederkehr in a Raven S50A Balloon at St. Paul, Minn. |
| | *– 196.71 miles.* |

Altitude
| 1966—Aug 25 | Tracy L. Barnes of U.S.A. in a Barnes Balloon at Pittsburgh, Pa. |
| | *– 28,585 feet.* |

| 1971—June 12 | Chauncy Dunn of U.S.A. in a Raven 6-60 Balloon at Boulder/Longmont, Colo. |
| | *– 32,949 feet.* |

| 1972—July 14 | Julian Nott in an Omega 84 Balloon "GAXVU" at Hereford, Eng. |
| | *– 35,971 feet.* |

## Subclass AX-10
## Over 4000 Cubic Meters Capacity

Duration
| 1970—Feb 1 | Raymond A. Munro of Canada in a Raven S50A Vulcoon Balloon |
| | *– 4 hours, 52 min.* |

| 1970—Oct 1 | Kurt Runzi of Switzerland in a TC-4 Balloon at (location not listed). |
| | *– 6 hours, 30 min.* |

| 1972—Mar 29 | Matt A. Wiederkehr in a Raven S50A Balloon at St. Paul, Minn. |
| | *– 8 hours, 48 min.* |

| 1972—Dec 12 | Robert Sparks in a Semco Challenger Balloon at Lafayette, Ind. |
| | *– 11 hours, 14 min.* |

Distance
| 1970—Feb 1 | Raymond A. Munro of Canada in a Raven S50A Vulcoon Balloon |
| | *– 158.34 miles.* |

| 1970—Oct 31 | Kurt Runzi of Switzerland in a Semco TC-4 Balloon at (location not listed). |
| | *– 160.82 miles.* |

| 1971—Mar 29 | Matt A. Wiederkehr in a Raven S50A Balloon at St. Paul, Minn. |
| | *– 196.71 miles.* |

Altitude
| 1966—Aug 25 | Tracy L. Barnes of U.S.A. in a Barnes Balloon at Pittsburgh, Pa. |
| | *– 28,585 feet.* |

| 1971—Jun 12 | Chauncy Dunn of U.S.A. in a Raven S-60 Balloon at Boulder/Longmont, Colo. |
| | *– 32,949 feet.* |

| 1972—Jul 14 | Julian Nott in an Omega 84 Balloon "GAXVU" at Hereford, Eng. |
| | *– 35,971 feet.* |

## Miscellaneous Balloon Records

| 1957—Jun 2 | Altitude-endurance record for manned, lighter-than-air craft established by Capt. Joseph W. Kittinger, Jr., U.S.A.F., remained aloft in a balloon over Minnesota for 6 hours, 34 minutes, above 96,000 feet for 2 hours. |

| 1959—Nov 16 | Capt. Joseph W. Kittinger, Jr., U.S.A.F., set 3 unofficial world aerial records, ascending in |

an open balloon gondola to an altitude of 76,400 feet, made a *parachute jump* of 76,400 feet, experiencing longest free fall in history, 64,000 feet—2 minutes, 58 seconds—White Sands, N.M.

1960—Aug 16     Capt. John Kittinger, Jr., reached highest altitude in nonpowered balloon flight carrying him 102,800 feet over New Mexico, falling freely for 4¼ minutes before opening parachute at 17,500 feet. Leap to landing—13 minutes, 8 seconds.

1962—Dec 13-14     U.S.A.F.'s Project Stargazer balloon, manned by Capt. Joseph A. Kittinger, Jr., U.S.A.F., and William C. White, U.S.N. civilian astronomer, reached altitude of 82,000 feet in 18½-hour flight over southwestern New Mexico. A telescope mounted atop the gondola gave White the clearest celestial view ever experienced by an astronomer.

## Appendix 4

# Official F.A.I. World Class Dirigible Records Class B

Altitude
  1912—Jun 18     Cohen at Coute, France—*10,102 feet.*

Maximum Speed
  1913—Jul 30     Italians Castracane and Castruccio in a P-5 airship—*40 m.p.h.*

Distance
1913—Jul 30               Italians Castracane and Castruccio in a P-5 airship– *503 miles*.

1928—Nov 29-31      Dr. Hugo Eckener, in the *Graf Zeppelin* airship from Lakehurst, N.J., to Friedrichshafen, Germany – *3,967 miles*.

Duration
1913—Jun 25              Italians Castracane and Castruccio in a P-5 airship– *15 hours*.

1928—Nov 29-31      Dr. Hugo Eckener in the *Graf Zeppelin* airship from Lakehurst, N.J., to Friedrichshafen, Germany– *71 hours, 7 min*.

## Appendix 5

# Official F.A.I. World Records for Altitude Class C

1908—Nov 13              Wilbur Wright
in a Wright airplane at Auvours, France
– *82 feet*.

1908—Nov 13              Henri Farman
in a Voisin airplane at Issy, France
– *82 feet*.

1908—Dec 18              Wilbur Wright won the French Aero Club de la Sarthe 100-meter height prize by an official flight to a height of 110 meters. He also established a world's duration-distance record of 99.8 kilo-

meters in 1 hour, 54 minutes, 53.4 seconds
(Auvours, France)
*– 361 feet.*

1909—Jul 18      Louis Paulhan of U.S.A.
in a Voisin airplane at Dounais, France
*– 492 feet.*

1909—Aug 29      Hubert Latham
in an Antoinette airplane at Rheims, France
*– 508 feet.*

1909—Sep 17      Orville Wright
in a Wright airplane at Berlin, Germany
*– 564 feet.*

1909—Sep 20      Rougier of France
in a Voisin airplane at Brescia, Italy
*– 633 feet.*

1909—Oct 18      Charles de Lambert
in a Wright biplane at Paris, France
*– 984 feet.*

1909—Dec 1      Hubert Latham
in an Antoinette airplane at Chalon, France
*– 1,486 feet.*
*– 3,445 feet* (Jan 7, 1910).

1910—Jan 12      Louis Paulhan
in a H. Farman airplane at Los Angeles, Calif.
(Los Angeles Flying Meet)
*– 4,164 feet.*

1910—Jun 14      Walter Brookins
in a Wright airplane at Indianapolis, Ind.
*– 4,380 feet.*

1910—Jul 7           Hubert Latham
in an Antoinette airplane at Rheims, France
– *4,541 feet.*

1910—Jul 7           Jan Olieslaegers
in a Blériot airplane at Brussels, Belgium
– *5,643 feet.*

1910—Jul 10         Walter Brookins
in a Wright biplane at Atlantic City, N.J.
(won $5,000 Atlantic City Aero Club prize)
– *6,259 feet.*

1910—Aug 11        Armstrong Drexel of U.S.A.
in a Blériot airplane at Lanark, Scotland
– *6,605 feet.*

1910—Aug 29        Leon Morane
in a Blériot airplane at Le Havre, France
– *7,054 feet.*
at Deauville, France
– *8,471 feet* (Sep 3, 1910).

1910—Sep 8          Georges Chavez
in a Blériot airplane at Issy, France
– *8,487 feet.*

1910—Oct 1          Henry Wijnmalen
in an H. Farman airplane at Mourmelon,
France
– *9,121 feet.*

1910—Oct 10        Armstrong Drexel
in a Blériot airplane at Philadelphia, Pa.
– *9,449 feet.*

1910—Oct 31        Ralph Johnstone
in a Wright biplane at Belmont Park, N.J.
(Belmont Park International Meet)
– *9,712 feet.*

1910—Dec 8             Georges Legagneaux
in a Blériot airplane at Pau, France
– *10,204 feet.*

1910—Dec 26          Archibald Hoxsey
in a Wright airplane at Los Angeles, Calif.
– *10,474 feet.*

1911—Jul 9             Marcel Loridan
in an H. Farman airplane at Buc, France
– *10,499 feet.*

1911—Aug 5           Capt. Julien Félix
in a Blériot airplane at Étampes, France
– *10,991 feet.*

1911—Aug 17          Lincoln Beachy
in a Curtiss airplane at Chicago, Ill.
– *17,573 feet.*

                      (1915—Mar 14—Lincoln Beachy, world-famous
stunt flyer, was killed at the San Francisco
Exposition when, as he pulled out of a dive, the
wings broke off from the fuselage of his airplane.)

1911—Sep 4             Roland Garros
in a Blériot airplane at St. Malo, France
– *12,960 feet.*
at Dinard, France
– *16,274 feet* (Sep 6, 1912).

1912—Sep 17          Georges Legagneaux
in a Morane airplane at Issy, France
– *17,891 feet.*

1912—Dec 11          Roland Garros of France
in a Morane airplane at Tunis, Tunisia
– *18,406 feet.*

1913—Mar 11

Édouard Perreyon
in a Blériot airplane at Buc, France
– *19,325 feet.*

1913—Dec 29

Georges Legagneaux
in a Nieuport airplane at St. Raphael, France
– *20,080 feet.*

1914—Jul 9

Gino Linnekogel
in a Rumpler airplane at Johannisthal, Germany
– *21,654 feet.*

1914—Jul 14

Harry Oelerich
in a D.F.W. airplane at Leipzig, Germany
– *25,755 feet.*

1918—Sep 18

R. W. Schroeder
in a Bristol airplane at Dayton, Ohio
– *28,897 feet.*

1919—May 26

Jean Casale
in a Nieuport airplane at Issy, France
– *29,937 feet.*
– *30,511 feet* (June 7, 1919).
– *31,233 feet* (June 14, 1919).

1919—Sep 18

Roland Rohlf
in a Curtiss triplane K-12 at Garden City, N.J.
– *31,420 feet.*

1919—Oct 4

Major R. W. Schroeder
in a Le Père "Liberty 400" at Dayton, Ohio
– *31,821 feet.*
– *33,114 feet* (Feb 27, 1920)

1921—Sep 28

Lt. John A. Macready
in a Le Père biplane at Dayton, Ohio
– *34,508 feet.*

1923—Sep 5
Sadi Lecointe
in a Nieuport Delage airplane at Villacoublay,
France
– *35,239 feet.*
at Issy, France
– *36,565 feet* (Oct 30, 1923).

1927—Jul 25
Lt. C. C. Champion
in a Wright P & W 425 at Anacostia, D.C.
– *38,474 feet.*

1929—May 25
Willi Neuenhofen
in a Junkers airplane at Dessau, Germany
– *41,794 feet.*

1930—Jun 4
Lt. Apollo Soucek
in a Wright "Apache" at Anacostia, D.C.
– *43,166 feet.*

1932—Sep 16
Capt. Cyril F. Uwins of Great Britain
in a Vickers airplane at Filton, Bristol, Eng.
– *43,976 feet.*

1933—Sep 28
G. Lemoine
in a Potez airplane at Villacoublay, France
– *44,819 feet.*

1934—Apr 11
Comdr. Ronato Donati
in a Caproni airplane at Montecello, Italy
– *47,352 feet.*

1936—Aug 14
George Detre
at Villacoublay, France
– *48,697 feet.*

1936—Sep 28

Squadron Leader S. R. D. Swain
in a Briston "Special" at S. Farnborough, Great
Britain
– *49,944 feet.*

1937—May 8

Col. Mario Pezzi
in a Caproni airplane at Montecello, Italy
– *51,361 feet.*

1937—Jun 30

Flt. Lt. M. J. Adam
in a Bristol airplane at S. Farnborough, Great
Britain
– *53,936 feet.*

1938—Oct 22

Mario Pezzi
in a Caproni airplane at Montecello, Italy
– *56,046 feet.*

### Jet Aircraft

1948—Mar 23

John Cunningham
in a De Havilland airplane at Hatfield, Great
Britain
– *59,445 feet.*

1953—May 4

Walter F. Gibb
in an Electra airplane at Bristol, Great Britain
– *63,668 feet.*
– *65,889 feet* (Aug 29, 1955).

1957—Aug 28

Michael Randrup
in a Canberra airplane at Luton, Great Britain
– *70,310 feet.*

1958—Apr 18

Lt. Comdr. George C. Watkins, U.S.N.,
in a Grumman F11-1F at Edwards Air Force
Base, California
– *76,932 feet.*

1958—May 7          Major Howard Johnson, U.S.A.F.,
                    in a Lockheed F-104A at Palmdale, Calif.
                    – *91,243 feet.*

1959—Jul 14         Vladimir Iljiuchin
                    in a T-437 airplane at Podmoskovnoe, U.S.S.R.
                    – *94,635 feet.*

1959—Dec 6          Comdr. Lawrence E. Flint, U.S.N.,
                    in a McDonnell F4H Phanton II at Edwards Air
                    Force Base, California
                    – *98,557 feet.*

1959—Dec 14         Capt. Joe B. Jordan, U.S.A.F.,
                    in a Lockheed F-104C at Edwards Air Force
                    Base, California
                    – *103,389 feet.*

1961—Apr 28         Gueorgui Mossolov
                    in a E-66-A at Podmoskovnoe, U.S.S.R.
                    – *113,890 feet.*

## Appendix 6

# Official F.A.I. World Records for Maximum Speed Class C Airplanes – Piston Engine, Land*

1906—Nov 12         Santos-Dumont
                    in a Dumont airplane at Bagatelle, France
                    – *25.6 m.p.h.*

*In 1930s this record was established over a 1.8 mile course (3 kilometers).

1907—Oct 26

Henri Farman
in an H. Farman airplane at Issy, France
– *32.7 m.p.h.*

1909—May 20

Paul Tissandier
in an Antoinette airplane at Pont. Long, France
– *34 m.p.h.*

1909—Aug 23

Glenn H. Curtiss
in a Curtiss airplane at Rheims, France
– *43.38 m.p.h.*

1909—Aug 28

Louis Blériot
in a Blériot airplane at Rheims, France
– *47.8 m.p.h.*

1910—Apr 23

Hubert Latham
in an Antoinette airplane at Nice, France
– *48.2 m.p.h.*

1910—Jul 10

Léon Morane
in a Blériot airplane at Rheims, France
– *66.18 m.p.h.*

1910—Oct 29

Alfred Leblanc
in a Blériot airplane at Belmont Park, France
– *67.9 m.p.h.*

1911—May 9

Edouard Nieuport
in a Nieuport biplane at Chalon, France
– *68.3 m.p.h.*

1911—Apr 12

Alfred Leblanc
in a Blériot airplane at Pau, France
– *69.5 m.p.h.*

1911—May 11          Édouard Nieuport
                     in a Nieuport airplane at Chalon, France
                     – *74 m.p.h.*

1911—Jun 12          Alfred Leblanc
                     in a Blériot airplane at Étampes, France
                     – *77.67 m.p.h.*

1911—Jun 21          Édouard Nieuport
                     in a Nieuport biplane at Chalon, France
                     – *82.7 m.p.h.*

1912—Jan 13          Jules Védrines
                     in a Deperdussin airplane at Pau, France
                     – *90 m.p.h.*
                     at Chicago, Ill.
                     – *108 m.p.h.* (Sep. 9, 1912).

1913—Sep 29          Maurice Provost
                     in a Deperdussin airplane at Rheims, France
                     – *127 m.p.h.*

1919—Oct 15          Sadi Lecointe
                     in a Spad airplane at Paris, France
                     – *153.9 m.p.h.*

1919—Oct 22          Bernard de Romanet
                     in a Nieuport airplane at Villacoublay, France
                     – *166.9 m.p.h.*

1920—Feb 7           Sadi Lecointe
                     in a Nieuport biplane at Villacoublay, France
                     (under a new F.A.I. regulation covering a
                     kilometer course in both directions)
                     – *171 m.p.h.*

1920—May 3           Francesed Brack-Papa
                     in a Fiat 700 airplane at Turin, Italy
                     – *172 m.p.h.*

1920—Feb 28     Jean Casale
in a Spad airplane at Villacoublay, France
– *176 m.p.h.*

1920—Oct 9     Bernard de Romanet
in a Spad airplane at Buc, France
– *181.8 m.p.h.*

1920—Oct 20     Sadi Lecointe
in a Nieuport biplane at Villacoublay, France
– *188 m.p.h.*

1920—Nov 4     Bernard de Romanet
in a Spad airplane at Buc, France
– *192 m.p.h.*

1921—Sep 26     Sadi Lecointe
in a Nieuport biplane at Villacoublay, France
– *205 m.p.h.*

1922—Aug 26     Francesed Brack-Papa
in a Fiat 700 airplane at Turin, Italy
– *208.6 m.p.h.*

1922—Dec 31     Sadi Lecointe
in a Nieuport-Delage airplane
– *216 m.p.h.*

1922—Oct 18     Brig. Gen. William Mitchell
in a Curtiss 375 airplane at Detroit, Mich. (one-kilometer course)
– *223 m.p.h.*

1923—Jan 15     Sadi Lecointe
in a Nieuport biplane at Istres, France
– *233 m.p.h.*

1923—Mar 29          Lt. R. L. Maughan, U. S. Air Service,
                     in a Curtiss 465 airplane at Dayton, Ohio
                     – *236.6 m.p.h.*

1923—Nov 2           Lt. H. J. Brow, U.S.N.,
                     in a Curtiss 500 airplane at Mineola, New York
                     – *259 m.p.h.*

1923—Nov 4           Lt. Al J. Williams, U.S.N.,
                     in a Curtiss 500 airplane at Mineola, New York
                     – *267 m.p.h.*

1924—Dec 11          Warrant Officer Bonnett
                     in a Ferbois airplane at Istres, France
                     – *278 m.p.h.*

1932—Sep 3           James H. Doolittle
                     in a Granville Gee-Bee at Cleveland, Ohio
                     – *294 m.p.h.*

1933—Sep 4           James R. Wedell
                     in a Wedell-Williams airplane at Glenville, Ill.
                     – *305 m.p.h.*

1934—Dec 25          Ralph Delmotte
                     in a Caudron C-460 at Istres, France
                     – *314 m.p.h.*

1935—Sep 13          Howard Hughes
                     in a Hughes "Special" airplane at Santa Ana,
                     Calif.
                     – *352 m.p.h.*

1937—Nov 11          Dr. Ing Herman Wurster
                     in a BF-113R airplane at Augsburg, Germany
                     – *379.6 m.p.h.*

1939—Apr 26          Fritz Wendel
                     in a Messerschmitt B.F. 109R at Augsburg,

Germany
– *469 m.p.h.*

1969—Aug 16    Darryl Greenamyer
in a F8F Grumman Bearcat at Edwards Air
Force Base, Calif.
– *482.462 m.p.h.*

## JETS — 1.8-Mile Course (3 Kilometers)

1948—Sep 15    Major Richard L. Johnson
in a North American F-86 at Muroc (Edwards)
Air Force Base, Calif.
– *679 m.p.h.*

1952—Nov 19    Capt. James J. S. Nash
in a North American F-86D at Salton Sea, Calif.
– *699 m.p.h.*

1953—Oct 3    Lt. Comdr. James B. Verdin
in a Douglas XF-4D at Salton Sea, Calif.
– *753 m.p.h.*

1961—Aug 28    Lts. Huntington Hardesty and Earl H. DeEsch
in a McDonnell F-4H-1 at White Sands, N.M.
– *902 m.p.h.*

## JETS—9.3-Mile Course (15 Kilometers)

1953—Oct 29    Lt. Col. Frank K. Everest
in a North American YF-100A at Salton
Sea, Calif.
– *755 m.p.h.*

1955—Aug 20    Col. H. A. Hanes
in a North American F-100C at Palmdale, Calif.
– *822 m.p.h.*

1956—Mar 10       L. Peter Twiss of Great Britain
                  in a Fairey Delta-2 at Ford-Chichester, England
                  – *1.132 m.p.h.*

1958—May 16       Capt. Walter W. Irwin, U.S.A.F.,
                  in a Lockheed F-104 at Edwards Air Force Base,
                  Calif.
                  – *1,404 m.p.h.*

1959—Oct 31       Gueorgui Mossolov of U.S.S.R.
                  in a E-66 jet monoplane-triangular wing at
                  Joukovski, U.S.S.R.
                  – *1.482 m.p.h.*

1959—Dec 15       Major Joseph W. Rogers, U.S.A.F.,
                  in a Convair F-106A at Edwards Air Force
                  Base, Calif.
                  – *1,524 m.p.h.*

1961—Nov 22       Lt. Col. Robert W. Robinson, U.S.M.C.,
                  in a McDonnell F-4H-1 at Edwards Air Force
                  Base, Calif.
                  – *1,605 m.p.h.*

1962—Jul 7        Gueorgui Mossolov of U.S.S.R.
                  in a E-166 jet airplane at Podmoskovnoe,
                  U.S.S.R.
                  – *1,664 m.p.h.*

1965—May 1        Col. R. L. Stephens, U.S.A.F., in a Lockheed
                  YF-12A at Edwards Air Force Base, Calif.
                  – *2,070 m.p.h.*

## *Appendix 7*

# *Official F.A.I. World Records for Distance Class C*

### In a Closed Circuit

1906—Sep 14
Santos-Dumont
in a Santos-Dumont airplane at Bagatelle, France
– *25.8 feet.*

1906—Nov 12
Santos-Dumont
in a Santos-Dumont airplane at Bagatelle, France
– *733 feet.*

1908—Mar 21
Henri C. Farman
in a Voisin airplane at Issy, France
– *1.24 miles.*

1908—Sep 16
Léon Delagrange
in a Voisin airplane at Issy, France
– *14.9 miles.*

1908—Dec 31
Wilbur Wright flew 124.7 kilometers in 2 hours,
20 min., 23.2 sec., to establish a world duration-
distance record at Le Mans, France, winning the
Michelin Trophy and $4,000.
– *77 miles.*

1909—Aug 25
Louis Paulhan of U.S.A.
in a Voisin airplane at Betheny, France
– *83 miles.*

1909—Aug 26
Hubert Latham

in an Antoinette airplane at Betheny, France
– *96 miles.*

1909—Nov 4         Henri Farman
in an H. Farman airplane at Mourmelon, France
– *145 miles.*

1910—Jul 9         René Labouchère
in an Antoinette airplane at Rheims, France
– *211 miles.*

1910—Jul 20       Jan Olieslaegers
in a Blériot airplane at Rheims, France
– *244 miles.*

1910—Oct 20       Maurice Tabuteau
in an M. Farman airplane at Étampes, France
– *289 miles.*

1910—Dec 11       Georges Legagneux
in a Blériot airplane at Pau, France
– *320 miles.*

1910—Dec 30       Maurice Tabuteau
in an M. Farman airplane at Étampes, France
– *363 miles.*

1911—Jul 16       Jan Olieslagers
in a Blériot airplane at Kiewit, Belgium
– *388 miles.*

1911—Sep 1        Georges Fourny
in an M. Farman airplane at Buc, France
– *449 miles.*

1911—Dec 24       André Gobe
in a Nieuport biplane at Pau, France
– *459 miles.*

1912—Sep 11            Georges Fourny
                       in an M. Farman airplane at Étampes, France
                       – *628 miles.*

1913—Oct 13            Augustin Seguin
                       at Buc-le-Bard, France
                       – *634 miles.*

1920—May 3-4           Lucien Boussoutrut and Jean Bernard
                       in a Farman Goliath at Villesauvage, France
                       – *1,189 miles.*

1923—Apr 16-17         Lts. Oakley C. Kelly and John A. Macready
                       in a Fokker T-2 transport at Dayton, Ohio
                       – *2,516 miles.*

1925—Aug 7-9           Maurice Drouhin and Jules Landry
                       in a Farman biplane at Étampes-Chartres, France
                       – *2,734 miles.*

1927—Aug 3-5           Cornelius Edzard and Johann Risztics
                       in a Junkers W-33 at Dessau, Germany
                       – *2,895 miles.*

1928—May 31-           Arturo Ferrarin and Carlo P. Del Prete
Jun 1-2                in a Savoia-Marchetti S-64 at Casale del Prati,
                       Anzio, Italy
                       – *4,763 miles.*

1929—Dec 15-17         Dieudonne Costes and Paul Codos
                       in a Breguet airplane at Istres, France
                       – *4,988 miles.*

1930—May 31-           Maj. Umberto Maddalena and Lt. Fausto
Jun 1-2                Cecconi in a Savoia-Marchetti S-64, at
                       Monteclio-Stazion Ladispoli, Italy
                       – *5,088 miles.*

1931—Mar 30-           Anthoine Paillard and Jean Mermoz

Apr 2                        at Oran, France
                             – *5,567 miles.*

1931—June 7-10               Joseph Le Brix and Marcel Doret
                             in a Dewoitine *The Hyphen* at Istres, France
                             – *6,444 miles.*

1932—Mar 23-26               Lucien Boussoutrut and Maurice Rossi
                             in a Blériot 110 monoplane at Oran, France
                             – *6,587 miles.*

1938—May 13-15               Comdt. Yuzo Fujita, Fukujiro Takahashi, and
                             Chikakichi Sekine, mechanic, in a Koken mono-
                             plane at Kisarasu, Japan
                             – *7,239 miles.*

1939—Jul 30-Aug 1            Angelo Tondi, Roberto Dagasso, Ferrucio
                             Vignoli, and Aldo Stagliano
                             at Rome, Italy
                             – *8,037 miles.*

1947—Aug 1-2                 Lt. Col. O. F. Lassiter, Capt. W. J.
                             Valentine, and crew, U.S.A.F., in a Boeing B-29
                             at Tampa, Fla.
                             – *8,854 miles.*

1960—Dec 14                  Lt. Col. J. R. Grissom and Lt. Col. J. P. Bosley
                             in a Boeing B-52 G at Edwards Air Force Base,
                             Calif.
                             – *10,078 miles.*

### In a Straight Line

1919—June 14-15              First nonstop Atlantic crossing from St. Johns,
                             Newfoundland, to Clifden, Ireland, was accom-
                             plished by Capt. John Alcock and Lt. A. W.
                             Brown of England in a Vickers aircraft in 15

hours, 57 min. They divided the $50,000 London
*Daily Mail* prize.
– *1,936 miles.*

1925—Feb 3-4    Capts. Ludovic Arrachart and Henri Le
Maître in a Breguet 19 (B-2) from Étampes,
France, to Cisneros, Greece
– *1,987 miles.*

1926—Jun 26-27    Capts. Ludovic Arrachart and Paul Arrachart
in a Breguet 19 from Le Bourget, France, to
Shaibah, Mesopotamia
– *2,674 miles.*

1926—Jul 14-15    Capt. André Girier and Lt. Francis Dordilly
in a Breguet 19 from Le Bourget, France, to
Omsk, Siberia
– *2,930 miles.*

1926—Aug 31-
Sep 1    Lt. Leone Challe and Capt. René Weiser
in a Breguet 19 from Le Bourget, France to
Bender-Abbas, Iran
– *3,214 miles.*

1926—Oct 28-29    Lt. Dieudonne Costes and Capt. Georges Riguot
in a Breguet 19 from Le Bourget, France to
Jask, Iran
– *3,352 miles.*

1927—May 20-21    Charles A. Lindbergh
in a Ryan monoplane from New York to Paris,
France
– *3,609 miles.*

1927—June 4-6    Clarence Chamberlin and Charles A. Levine in a
Bellanca-Wright powered monoplane from New
York to Isleben, Germany
– *3,910 miles.*

1928—Jul 3-5   Major Arthur Ferrarin and Major Carlo P. Del
Prete in a Savoia-Marchetti S-64 from Rome,
Italy, to Touros, Brazil
*– 4,466 miles.*

1929—Sep 27-29  Dieudonne Costes and Maurice Bellonte
in a Breguet 19 airplane from Le Bourget,
France, to Coulant, China
*– 4,911 miles.*

1931—Jul 28-30  Russell N. Boardman and J. Polando
in a Bellanca monoplane from Brooklyn,
New York, to Istanbul, Turkey
*– 5,011 miles.*

1933—Feb 6-8   O. R. Grayford and C. E. Nicholetts of Great
Britain in a Fairey airplane from Cranwell,
England, to Walvis Bay, South Africa
*– 5,308 miles.*

1933—Aug 5-7   Maurice Rossi and Paul Codos of France in a
Blériot-Zapata monoplane *Joseph Le Brix* from
Floyd Bennet Field, New York, to Rayack,
Syria (also "broken line" distance record—
5,658.4 miles)
*– 5,657 miles.*

1937—Jul 12-14  Col. Mikhail Gromov, Comdt. Andre
Youmachev, and Eng. Serge Danilin of U.S.S.R.
in an ANT-25 monoplane from Moscow,
U.S.S.R., to San Jacinto, Calif.
*– 6,305 miles.*

1938—Nov 5-7   R. Kellett, R. T. Gething, and M. L. Gaine
(1st airplane); A. N. Combe, B. K. Burnett,
and H. B. Gray (2nd airplane) of Great Britain
from Ismalia, Egypt, to Darwin, Australia
*– 7,158 miles.*

1945—Nov 19-20    Col C. S. Irvine, Lt. Col. G. R. Stanley,
                  U.S.A.A.F., and crew in a Boeing B-29 from
                  Guam to Washington, D.C.
                  – *7,916 miles.*

1946—Sep 29-Oct 1 Comdr. T. D. Davies, Comdr. E. P. Rankin,
                  Comdr. W. S. Reid, Lt. Comdr. R. A. Tabeling,
                  U.S.N., in a Lockheed P2V-1 *Truculent Turtle*
                  from Perth, Australia, to Columbus, Ohio
                  – *11,235 miles.*

## JET CLASS — IN A STRAIGHT LINE

1955-Mar 1        Elisabeth Boselli of France
                  in a Mistral aircraft, Creil to Agadir
                  – *1,448 miles.*

1957—Nov. 11-13   Gen. Curtis E. Le May and crew flew Boeing
                  KC-135, establishing world distance record from
                  Westover Air Force Base, Mass., to Buenos
                  Aires, Argentina. (Return trip on Nov. 13—he set
                  another F.A.I. record flying from Buenos Aires
                  to Washington, D.C.: speed of 471.451 m.p.h.
                  —11 hours, 3 min., 57.38 sec., 5,204 miles.)
                  – *6,322 miles.*

1958—Apr 7-8      Brig. Gen W. E. Eubank and crew flew Boeing
                  KC-135, establishing world distance record from
                  Tokyo to Lajes, Azores. (He set a world speed
                  record on same flight of 492.262 m.p.h. from
                  Tokyo to Washington, D.C., in 13 hours, 45 min.,
                  46.5 sec.)
                  – *10,229 miles.*

1962—Jan 10-11    U.S.A.F. Boeing B-52H, piloted by Maj. Clyde P.
                  Evely, set eight F.A.I. course records in flight
                  from Tokyo to Madrid at speed of 328.78 m.p.h.
                  in 20 hours, 22 min., 12 sec. Other F.A.I. course

records varied in speeds from 456.97 m.p.h. (Seattle—Madrid in 11 hours, 34 min., 9.22 sec.) to 604.44 m.p.h. (Ft. Worth—Washington, D.C., in 2 hours, 26.66 sec.). Maj. Evely also established world distance record in straight line of 12,532.28 miles from Kadena, Okinawa, to Madrid.
– *12,532 miles.*

## JET CLASS—CLOSED CIRCUIT

1955—Feb 21
Elisabeth Boselli
in a Mistral single-engine jet at Oran-Monte de Marsan Course, France
– *1,143 miles.*

1957—Sep 11
Joury Alacheev, Valentine Kovalev, and crew
in a TU-104A at Moscow, U.S.S.R.
– *1,244 miles.*

1958—Sep 26
U.S.A.F. Boeing B-52D, piloted by Lt. Col. Victor L. Sandacz, set world distance and speed records. Distance record 6,233.98 miles, and speed record over 10,000 kilometers 560.75 m.p.h. (Flight involved two laps over Ellsworth Air Force Base, S. Dak-Douglas, Ariz.-Newberg, Ore.-Ellsworth Air Force Base, S. Dak. course.)
– *6,233 miles.*

1960—Dec 14
U.S.A.F. Boeing B-52G, piloted by Lt. Col. T. R. Grissom and Capt. J. P. Bosley, established world distance record. (Edwards Air Force Base, Calif.-Texas-Washington, D.C.-Newfoundland-Alaska-Montana-Edwards Air Force Base, Calif.)
– *10,078 miles.*

1962—June 6-7      Capt. William Stevenson, Piloting a U.S.A.F.
                   Boeing B-52H, established a world distance
                   record. (Seymour-Johnson, N.C.-Kindley,
                   Bermuda-Sondrestrom, Greenland-Anchorage,
                   Alaska-March Air Force Base, Calif.-Key West,
                   Fla.-Seymour-Johnson, N.C.)
                   – *11,336 miles.*


## Appendix 8

# *Selected Chronology of Round-the-World Flights*

1924—Apr 6         (Apr. 6 to Sep. 28) U.S. Air Service officers made
                   the first round-the-world air trip, the first trans-
                   Pacific flight, and the first westbound Atlantic
                   crossing. Leaving from and returning to Seattle,
                   they flew 26,345 miles in 363 hours' flying time—
                   elapsed time of 175 days. The aircraft used were
                   the Douglas World Cruisers.

1928—Jun 29-       John H. Mears and Capt. C. B. D. Collyer in 23
Jul 22             days, 15 hours, 21 minutes from New York,
                   N.Y., and return.

1929—Aug 14-       *Graf Zeppelin* made trip in 20 days, 4 hours; from
Sep 4              Friedrichshafen, Germany, via Tokyo, Los
                   Angeles, and Lakehurst, N.J.

1931-June 23       Wiley Post and Harold Gatty left New York on
                   round-the-world flight in *Winnie Mae* (Lockheed
                   P & W 550). They completed the trip Jul. 1—
                   15,474 miles—8 days, 15 hours, 51 minutes.

1933—Jul 15          Wiley Post began first solo round-the-world flight, 15,596 miles—7 days, 18 hours, 49 minutes, 30 seconds. Completed Jul. 22.

1934—Oct 9           The Gold Medal of the F.A.I. presented to Wiley Post for his world flight.

1935—Aug 15          Will Rogers and Wiley Post were killed in a take-off crash near Point Barrow, Alaska.

1937—May 21          A. Earhart and Fred Noonan left from San Francisco on west-east round-the-world flight, ending on Jul. 2 when fliers disappeared in the Pacific.

1938—Jul 10          Howard Hughes, pilot, and three-man crew began flight around the world: New York, Paris, Moscow, Omsk, Yakutsk, Fairbanks, Minneapolis, and New York—14,791 miles—3 days, 19 hours, 8 minutes.

1941—Oct 30          Maj. Alva L. Harvey completed record-making flight around the world in B-24, a 3,150-mile nonstop flight from Great Britain to Moscow. Personnel of Harriman Mission were carried. Distance 24,700 miles, 17 days' elapsed time.

1945—Oct 4           First Skymaster round-the-world flight completed by Air Transport Command when a Douglas C-54 landed in Washington. The flight covered 23,279 miles in 149 hours, 44 minutes, including 33 hours, 21 minutes' ground time.

1945—Nov 30          B-26 Martin "Marauder," piloted by Col. Joseph Holzapple, completed flight totaling 96 hours, 50 minutes' flying time on Nov. 30.

1947—Apr 15          *Reynolds Bombshell,* a converted A-26 piloted by Capt. William P. Odom, landed at La Guardia

Field, N.Y., setting a new record of 78 hours, 56 minutes for 20,000-mile round-the-world flight. To Carroll Sallee, flight engineer, and Milton J. Reynolds, navigator.

1947—Aug 7      William P. Odom, solo, flew same 20,000 mile course as earlier, setting new record, 73 hours and 5 minutes, New York City and return.

1948—Jul 22-
Aug 6      Three B-29s departed from Davis-Monthan Air Force Base, Ariz., and encircled the globe. The entire flight covered approximately 20,000 miles in 103 hours, 50 minutes. Only two aircraft completed the flight; one B-29 crashed into the Arabian Sea (17 dead, one survivor). The two aircraft completing the flight were *Gas Gobbler,* commanded by Lt. Col. R. W. Kline, and *Lucky Lady,* commanded by Lt. A. M. Neal.

1948—Dec 13      Col. Edward P. F. Eagan, New York, N.Y., and return, 20,559 miles in 147 hours, 15 minutes.

1949—Mar 2      Carswell Air Force Base, Texas, U.S.A.F. Boeing B-50 *Lucky Lady II,* Capt. James Gallagher as pilot, completed first nonstop, round-the-world flight in history, covered 23,452 miles, 94 hours, 1 minute; being refueled in air over Azores, Arabia, the Philippines, and Hawaii.

1949—Dec 2-7      Thomas G. Lanphier, Jr., New York, N.Y., and return, 22,180 miles in 119 hours, 47 minutes.

1957-Jan 18      Commanded by Maj. Gen. Archie J. Old, Jr., U.S.A.F., 3 B-52 Stratofortresses completed 24,325-mile round-the-world nonstop flight in 45 hours, 19 minutes, average speed 534 m.p.h. First globe-circling nonstop flight by jet aircraft.

1959—Aug 22-
Sep 20
Peter Gluckmann in a solo world flight of 22,800 miles in 29 days from San Francisco, Calif., and return (Meyers 200 airplane).

1961—Mar 8
Max Conrad, pilot and Dick Jennings, observer, established record for light airplanes by completing flight around the world, 8 days, 18 hours, 35 minutes, 57 seconds.

1963—Aug 3-4
Sam Miller and Louis Fodor from New York, N.Y., and return, 46 hours, 28 minutes.

1964—Apr 17
Mrs. Jerrie Mock became first woman pilot to fly solo around the world when she landed her Cessna 180 *Spirit of Columbus* at Columbus, Ohio, at end of 29-day flight —22,858.8 miles and 21 stops.

1964—May 12
Miss Joan Merriam became second woman pilot to circumnavigate the earth alone when she landed her Piper Apache at Oakland, Calif. Following Amelia Earhart's route, she flew 27,750 miles in 56 days.

1965—Feb 17
Mrs. Joan Merriam Smith, who in 1964 flew her small plane around the world, and Trixie Anne Schubert, pilot and aviation writer, were killed in an aircraft crash on a California mountain.

# F.A.I. Recent Official-Round-the-World Flight Records

## Speed Around the World Category

### Class C-1 Group I (Piston Engine)
### Without Payload

1966—Jun 1-7      Robert and Joan Wallick from Manila, Philippines, and return, in a Beechcraft Baron, 23,129 miles in 5 days, 6 hours, and 17 minutes.
*– 186.53 m.p.h.*

### Class C-1c Group I (Piston Engine) Light Airplanes
### Payload of 2,204 to 3,858 lbs.

1967—May 18-
Jun 20      Miss Sheila Scott of United Kingdom in a Piper Comanche, London, England, and return, 28,633 miles in 33 days, 03 minutes elapsed time.
*– 36.15 m.p.h.*

1969—April 3-16      Alvin Marks of the U.S.A. in a Cessna 210, 23,356 miles in 13 days, 8 hours, and 41 minutes from Sacramento, Calif., to Sacramento, Calif.
*– 73.45 m.p.h.*

### Class C-1d Group I (Piston Engines) Light Airplanes
### Payload of 3,858 to 6,614 lbs.

1966—Jun 1-7      Robert and Joan Wallick from Manila, Philippines, and return, in a Beechcraft Baron, 23,129 miles in 5 days, 6 hours, and 17 minutes.
*– 186.53 m.p.h.*

1971—Aug 5-10        T. K. Brougham of Australia in a Beechcraft
Baron.
*– 197.77 m.p.h.*

### Class C-1 Group III (Jet)
### Without Payload

1965—Nov 15-17      Jack L. Martin, Fred L. Austin, Harrison Finch,
Robert N. Buck, and James R. Gannett in a
Boeing 707/320C from Honolulu, Hawaii, and
return, in 62 hours, 27 minutes.
*– 420.75 m.p.h.*

### Class C-1f Group III (Jet Business) Aircraft
### Payload of 13,227 to 17,636 lbs.

1966—May 23-26    Henry G. Beaird and John O. Lear in Lear Jet
Model 24 from Wichita, Kansas, and return,
22,992 miles in 65 hours, 39 minutes.
*– 350.11 m.p.h.*

### Class C-1g Group III (Jet) Business Aircraft
### Payload of 17,636 to 26,455 lbs.

1966—Jun 4-7         Arthur Godfrey, Richard Merrill, Fred Austin,
and Karl Keller from New York, N.Y., and
return, in a Jet Commander, 23,333 miles in 86
hours, 9 minutes.
*– 271.31 m.p.h.*

## *Appendix 9*

# *Selected Chronology of Transcontinental Flights*

| | |
|---|---|
| 1911—Sep 17 | Calbraith P. Rodgers in a Burgess-Wright biplane began the first transcontinental flight, New York to Pasadena, Calif. The trip—*3,390 miles*—required 49 days. |
| 1912—Feb 17 | Second transcontinental flight. Robert G. Fowler flew his Wright biplane from Los Angeles to Pasadena, Yuma, Tucson, Douglas, El Paso, Sweetwater, Ft. Worth, Houston, Orange, New Iberia, New Orleans, Biloxi, Flomston, Evergreen, Troy, Bainbridge, Quitman, Pablo Beach *– 2,520 miles.* |
| 1918—Dec 4 | First Army transcontinental flight by four Curtiss JN-4s under Maj. Albert D. Smith, from San Diego to Jacksonville—reached on Dec. 22. |
| 1919—October | Start of Army transcontinental reliability and endurance test, New York to San Francisco and return. Forty-four planes completed westbound; 15 eastbound; 10 made the round trip. On basis of elapsed time Lt. B. W. Maynard in a DH-4 won east-west and round trip and Maj. Carl Spaatz in a DH-4B won west-east. |
| 1921—Feb 21-24 | Lt. William D. Coney, Air Service, made a solo transcontinental flight from Rockwell Field, Calif., to Jacksonville, Fla., in 22 hours, 27 minutes. |

1921—Feb 22-23    Jack Knight and E. M. Allison flew the first transcontinental airmail flight, San Francisco to New York, in 33 hours, 20 minutes. Knight flew at night from North Platte, Nebr., to Chicago.

1922—Sep 4    First transcontinental crossing within a single day made by Lt. J. H. Doolittle in a rebuilt DH-4B Liberty 400, from Pablo Beach, Fla., to Rockwell Field, San Diego—2,163 miles in 21 hours, 20 minutes' flying time.

1923—May 2-3    First nonstop transcontinental flight, 2,516 miles, New York to San Diego, flown by Lts. O. G. Kelly and J. A. Macready in a Fokker T-2 Liberty 400; flying time 26 hours, 50 minutes, 3 seconds. DFC's and Mackay Trophy were awarded for the flight.

1923—Sep 13    (Sept. 13 to Dec. 14) Round-trip transcontinental tour, anticipating national airways, made by Lts. J. F. Whitely, H. D. Smith, and crew in a Martin-2 Liberty 400, from Langley Field, Va., to San Diego and return—8,000 miles.

1924—June 23    Daylight transcontinental flight, New York to San Francisco, in PW-8 D12 Curtiss 375, by Lt. R. L. Maughan—2,670 miles in 21 hours, 48 minutes, 30 seconds, including five brief refueling stops.

1928—Aug 19-20    Arthur Goebel and Harry Tucker in Lockheed-Vega monoplane flew cross-country from Los Angeles to Curtiss Field, Long Island, new record of 18 hours, 58 minutes.

1928—Oct 24-25    Capt. C. B. D. Collyer and Harry Tucker, New York, N.Y., to Los Angeles—24 hours, 51 minutes.

1929—Jun 27

Capt. Frank Hawks established a record round-trip, transcontinental flight from New York to Los Angeles, Calif., and return. To Los Angeles —19 hours, 10 min., 32 sec. Return to New York —17 hours, 38 min., 10 sec. (Aug. 12-15, 1930, round-trip New York to Los Angeles and return. To New York—14 hours, 50 min. To Los Angeles—12 hours, 25 min., 3 sec.) He was killed in a plane crash at East Aurora, N.Y., Aug. 23, 1938.

1929—Aug 15

Lt. Nicholas B. Mamer and Arthur Walker, in Buhl Spokane *Sun God* with Wright Whirlwind engine, flew from Spokane, Wash., to East Coast and back, record nonstop distance flight of 7,200 miles—refueled in air 11 times.

1932—Nov 14

Roscoe Turner, in a Wedell-Williams, set new transcontinental east-west record. Flight from Floyd Bennett Field, N.Y., to Burbank, Calif., 12 hours, 33 minutes, stopped twice en route.

1934—Nov 8

Capt. E. V. Rickenbacker, Silas Morehouse, and Capt. Charles W. France flew from Los Angeles to Newark, N.J., in 12 hours, 3 minutes, 50 seconds, setting new record for passenger transport.

1935—Jan 15

Maj. J. H. Doolittle, with two passengers, flew nonstop from Los Angeles to New York—11 hours, 59 minutes—transcontinental record for passenger transport airplanes and nonstop west-east transcontinental record.

1937—Jan 19

Howard Hughes flew from Burbank, Calif., to Newark, N.J., in 7 hours, 28 minutes, 25 seconds, setting new transcontinental speed record.

1938—Aug 29

Maj. Alexander De Seversky set east-west transcontinental speed record—10 hours, 2 minutes, 55.7 seconds—2,457-mile flight.

1945—Dec 8    Lt. Col. H. F. Warden and Capt. G. W. Edwards in a Douglas XB-42 monoplane, Los Angeles, Calif., to Washington, D.C. F.A.I. course record. Elapsed time: 5 hours, 17 minutes, 34 seconds; distance—2,295 miles; average speed—433.6 m.p.h.

1945—Dec 11

Col. C. S. Irvine and Lt. Col. G. R. Stanley set an F.A.I. course record between Los Angeles, Calif., and New York (2,457 miles)—speed 450.385 m.p.h. in 5 hours, 27 minutes, 19.2 seconds in B-29. (F.A.I. Record for multi-engined military aircraft)

1946—Jan 26    In Lockheed P-80, Col. W. H. Councill set an F.A.I. course record between Los Angeles and New York (2,453.807 miles)—speed 580.935 m.p.h. in 4 hours, 13 minutes, 26 seconds. (F.A.I. record for Jet aircraft)

1946—Aug 1    An F.A.I. course record for multi-engined military aircraft between New York and Los Angeles (2,453.805 miles)—speed 328.598 m.p.h. in 7 hours, 28 minutes, 3 seconds set by Captains B. L. Grubaugh and J. L. England in B-29.

1947—Sep 3    A. Paul Mantz in a North American P-51 from New York City to Burbank, Calif., F.A.I. course record. Distance—2,453.8 miles; elapsed time—7 hours, 4 seconds; average speed—350.49 m.p.h.

1949—Mar 29    North American P-51 flown by Joe de Bona set new cross-country F.A.I. record for piston-type aircraft by flying from Burbank, Calif., to La Guardia, N.Y., 5 hours.

1950—Jan 22

Paul Mantz sets new F.A.I. transcontinental record, for "Single Reciprocating Engine—Solo" flight in a North American P-51 "Mustang" (Allison) from Burbank, Calif., to La Guardia Field, N.Y., in 4 hours, 52 minutes, 58 seconds.

1954—Jan 2

Col. Willard W. Millikan, ANGUS, established new coast-to-coast record (F.A.I. course) by flying an F-86F from Los Angeles to New York with speed of 559.91 m.p.h.—4 hours, 6 minutes, 16 seconds.

1954—Feb 13

Joe de Bona set transcontinental speed record for piston-engine aircraft when he piloted an P-51 Mustang 2,467 miles from Los Angeles to New York—4 hours, 24 minutes, 17 seconds.

1954—Apr 1

Aided by strong tail winds, Lt. Comdr. Francis X. Brady, U.S.N., established transcontinental jet aircraft speed record flying an F9F "Cougar" 2,438 miles from San Diego to Brooklyn—3 hours, 45 minutes, 30 seconds. In same type aircraft two Navy pilots came within minutes of setting the same record.

1955—Mar 9

Piloting a Republic F-84F, Lt. Col. Robert R. Scott, U.S.A.F., established F.A.I. course record 652.522 m.p.h., 2,445.9-mile flight, Los Angeles to New York—3 hours, 44 minutes, 53.88 seconds.

1955—May 21

Piloting an F-86A, Lt. John M. Conroy, ANGUS, established speed record of 432.616 m.p.h. in F.A.I. course flight—Los Angeles to New York and return—4,891.8 miles, in 11 hours, 18 minutes, 27 seconds.

1957—Mar 21-22

Comdr. Dale V. Cox, U.S.N., and crew, United States, Douglas A3D "Skywarrior." Elapsed

time: 5 hours, 12 minutes, 39.24 seconds. New York to Los Angeles
– *469 m.p.h.*
Los Angeles to New York to Los Angeles. Elapsed time: 9 hours, 31 minutes, 35 seconds
– *513 m.p.h.*

1957—Jul 16    F8U-1P Crusader, piloted by Maj. J. H. Glenn, Jr., U.S.M.C., broke transcontinental speed record by flying from Los Alamitos, Calif., to Long Island—3 hours, 22 minutes, 50 seconds— average speed 723.51 m.p.h. The first upper atmosphere, supersonic, west-coast-to-east-coast flight.

1957—Nov 27    Capt. Ray W. Schrecengost, Jr., U.S.A.F., United States, McDonnell RF-101C "Voodoo," Los Angeles to New York
– *749.95 m.p.h.*
New York to Los Angeles
– *607.8 m.p.h.*
Los Angeles-New York-Los Angeles
– *721.85 m.p.h.*

1957—Nov 27    Capt. Robert J. Kilpatrick, U.S.A.F., United States, McDonnell RF-101C "Voodoo," Los Angeles to New York
– *765.69 m.p.h.*

1957—Nov 27    Flying an RF-101 Voodoo jet aircraft, Lt. Gustave B. Klatt, U.S.A.F., set a transcontinental F.A.I. record in 3 hours, 7 minutes, 43.64 seconds (west to east)
– *781.7 m.p.h.*

1957—Nov 27    Flying an RF-101, Capt. Robert M. Sweet, U.S.A.F., established a round-trip transcontinental F.A.I. course record of 721.853 m.p.h. in 6 hours, 46 minutes, 36.23 seconds. Return trip set

F.A.I. course record of 677.726 m.p.h. in 3 hours, 36 minutes, 32.36 seconds (west to east).

1958—Jun 12    Flying a Boeing KC-135 jet tanker. Pilots: Capts. William H. Howell, Richard F. Haley, and Gene Gurney, Lt. Charles P. Krantz; 3 hours, 42 minutes, 45 seconds, from Los Angeles to New York City.
*– 670 m.p.h.*

1959—Jan 20    Richard J. Scoles, pilot; Loren W. Davis, copilot; Barney Parker, flight engineer; Douglas RB-66A, International Airport, Ontario, *Calif., to* Andrews Air Force Base, Md. Elapsed time: 3 hours, 35 minutes, 59.1 seconds. Distance: 2,269.33 statute miles
*– 630.413 m.p.h.*

1959—Jan 22    Richard J. Scoles, pilot; Loren W. Davis, copilot; Barney Parker, flight engineer; Douglas RB-66A, Andrews Air Force Base, Md. to Ontario International Airport, Ontario, Calif. Elapsed time: 4 hours, 58 minutes, 15.9 seconds. Distance: 2,269.33 statute miles
*– 456.506 m.p.h.*

1961—May 24    Lt. Richard F. Gordon, Jr., and Lt. Bobbie R. Young, U.S.N., flew an F4H-1 from Los Angeles to New York City in 2 hours, 47 minutes, 19.75 seconds with speed of 869.73 m.p.h., winning the Bendix Trophy race.

1962—Mar 5    Capt. Robert G. Sowers, U.S.A.F., piloting B-58, established three F.A.I. course records in round-trip flight from Los Angeles to New York at speed of 1,044.46 m.p.h. in 4 hours, 41 minutes, 14.98 seconds. Other two records were: Los Angeles to New York, speed 1,214.65 m.p.h. in 2 hours, 58.71 seconds; and New York to Los Angeles, speed 1,081.8 m.p.h. in 2 hours, 15 minutes, 50.08 seconds.

## Appendix 10

# Selected Chronology of Transatlantic Flights

| | |
|---|---|
| 1919—May 16 | Lt. Comdr. Albert C. Reed and crew of five left Trepassy Bay, Newfoundland, in an NC-4, arrived at the Azores on May 17 and at Lisbon, Portugal, on May 27 (4,116 miles), thus completing the first crossing of the Atlantic by air. Two other planes which started the trip did not complete the flight. |
| 1919—May 18 | Harry G. Hawker, an English pilot, with Comdr. K. MacKenzie Grieve as the navigator made the first attempt to pilot an airplane across the Atlantic Ocean. They were among the first entries for the London *Daily Mail* prize of $50,000 for the first transatlantic flight. Hawker and Grieve started May 18, 1919, from the Pearl Aerodrome near St. Johns, Newfoundland. Their destination was nonstop to Ireland—over 1,925 sea miles— but engine trouble developed. They descended on the ocean after sighting the tramp steamer *Mary* and were rescued. |
| 1919—June 14-15 | First nonstop Atlantic crossing from St. Johns, Newfoundland, to Clifden, Ireland, 1,936 miles, was accomplished by Capt. John Alcock and Lt. A.W. Brown of England in a Vickers 2 Rolls-Royce 400 in 15 hours, 57 minutes. They divided the $50,000 London *Daily Mail* prize. |
| 1919—Jul 2-13 | First lighter-than-air transatlantic flight. The British dirigible *R-34,* commanded by Maj. |

George H. Scott, left Firth of Forth, Scot. (July 2) and touched down at Mineola, L.I., 108 hours later. The eastbound trip was made in 75 hours.

1926—Sep 15    Capt. René Fonck, leading French WWI ace (75 kills), and Lt. Lawrence M. Curtin survived crash of Sikorsky airplane on takeoff to set record for New York to Paris flight. Two other members were killed—Jacob Isliamoff and Charles Clavier.

1927—May 8     Capt. Charles Nungesser and Capt. François Coli, French WWI aces, attempted a North Atlantic flight from Paris to New York and were lost at sea.

1927—May 20-21  First solo nonstop transatlantic flight. Charles Augustus Lindbergh in a Wright-powered Ryan monoplane, *Spirit of St. Louis,* from Roosevelt Field, L.I., in 33 hours, 39 minutes and covering 3,600 miles to Le Bourget Field, Paris.

1927—June 4    Clarence D. Chamberlin and Charles A. Levine made the first nonstop flight from Roosevelt Field, L.I., N.Y., to Eisleben, Germany, 3,911 miles, in 43 hours, 49 minutes, 33 seconds, in a Bellanca-15 Wright 200.

1927—June 29-  Lt. Comdr. Richard E. Byrd, Lt. G. O. Noville,
Jul 1          Bert Acosta, and Bernt Balchen, in airplane *America* established record four-passenger flight. Flew from Roosevelt Field, N.Y., to Ver-Sur-Mer, France, an airplane distance of 3,477 miles, in 46 hours, 6 minutes.

1927—Oct 11    George Haldeman and Ruth Elder are forced to land in ocean alongside a freighter in attempted flight across the Atlantic.

| | |
|---|---|
| 1927—Oct 14-15 | First South Atlantic crossing, a French team, Lt. Dieudonne Costes and Lt. Joseph Le Brix in a Breguet biplane from St. Louis, Senegal, to Rio de Janeiro, Brazil. |
| 1927—Dec 23 | Oskar Omdal, pilot; Brice Goldsborough, navigator; Mrs. Frances Grayson; and Fred Koehler take off from Roosevelt Field in an attempted flight to Harbour Grace, Newfoundland, from which point Mrs. Grayson had planned to fly to Denmark. Plane is lost at sea. |
| 1928—Mar 13 | Capt. W. R. Hinchcliffe is lost at sea with Elsie Mackay in attempted east-west flight across the Atlantic. |
| 1928—Apr 12 | First east-west transatlantic crossing. Baron Guenther von Huenefeld, piloted by German Capt. Hermann Koehl and Irish Capt. James Fitzmaurice, left Dublin for New York City (Apr. 12) in a single-engine Junkers monoplane, *Bremen*. Some 37 hours later they crashed on Greely Island, Labrador. They were uninjured. |
| 1928—June 17-18 | Amelia Earhart, first woman to cross the Atlantic, flies in the *Friendship* from Newfoundland to Wales, with Wilmer Stultz, and Lou Gordon as navigator, in 20 hours, 40 minutes. |
| 1928—Jul 3-5 | Two Italian pilots, Major C. P. Del Prete and Capt. Arturo Ferrarin, flew nonstop from Italy to Brazil. |
| 1930—June 24-25 | Charles Kingsford-Smith and a crew of three made the first crossing of the North Atlantic from west to east. |
| 1930—Sep 1 | First nonstop Paris to New York flight. Dieu- |

donne Costes and Maurice Bellonte in a Breguet biplane, *Question Mark.*

1931—Jan 7-10    Lt. William S. McLaren and Mrs. Beryl Markham forced down between Bermuda and the Azores on attempted transatlantic flight in a Bellanca seaplane.

1931—June 23    Ruth Nichols crashes at St. Johns, Newfoundland, in first attempt by a woman to fly the Atlantic.

1932—May 20    Amelia Earhart in Wasp-powered Lockheed Vega flew first solo flight across the North Atlantic by a woman. From Harbour Grace to Londonderry, Ireland—15 hours, 20 minutes.

1932—Aug 20    The first solo east-to-west North Atlantic crossing—James Mollison, Port Marnock, Ireland to Pennfield Ridge, New Brunswick.

1933—Jul 23    Capt. and Mrs. James A. Mollison (Amy Johnson) complete nonstop east-west crossing of Atlantic from Wales to Stratford, Conn.

1935—Nov 15    Jean Batten flies solo from England to Brazil, setting record of 61 hours. The South Atlantic crossing, the first by a woman, made in 13 hours, 15 minutes.

1936—Sep 4-5    First east-to-west crossing of the North Atlantic, solo, by a woman pilot. Mrs. Beryl Markham flew from Abingdon Airfield, Berkshire, England, in 24 hours, 40 minutes to Baleine, Nova Scotia, where she crashed, uninjured.

1936—Sep 14    Harry Richman and Henry T. (Dick) Merrill,

transatlantic round trip, New York to London and return.

1936—Oct 29-30    Capt. James A. Mollison flew from Newfoundland to London—distance of 2,300 miles—13 hours, 17 minutes. Fastest west-to-east crossing to date.

1937—May 9-10    Henry T. Merrill and John S. Lambe, pilots, United States, Lockheed Electra monoplane; elapsed time—20 hours, 29 minutes, 45 seconds New York to London (F.A.I. course record).

1938—Jul 18    Douglas "Wrong Way" Corrigan arrived in Dublin, Ireland, 28 hours, 13 minutes after leaving New York in 9-year-old Curtiss Robin.

1938—Aug 11-14    Alfred Henke and Rudolf Freiherr von Moreau, pilots; Paul Dierberg, *radiomécanicien* and Walter Kober, *radiotélégraphiste;* Germany, Focke-Wulf Fw. 200 Condor airplane; elapsed time—24 hours, 56 minutes for Berlin to New York; elapsed time—19 hours, 55 minutes for New York to Berlin leg: Berlin to New York—158.759 m.p.h. New York to Berlin—199.409 m.p.h.

1951—Jan 31    Charles F. Blair, Jr., flew a North American P-51 from New York to London, 7 hours, 48 minutes, set a new record for the route.

1951—Aug 31    Wing Comdr. R. P. Beamont and crew, Great Britain; Canberra bomber; elapsed time—4 hours, 18 minutes, 24.4 seconds. Belfast to Gander, Newfoundland—481.099 m.p.h. (F.A.I. course record)

1952—Jul 31    Two U.S.A.F. MATS Sikorsky H-19 helicopters completed first transatlantic helicopter flight, having flown in five stages from Westover Field, Mass., to Prestwick, Scotland.

1952—Aug 25     Wing Comdr. R. P. Beamont, pilot; P. Hillwood, copilot; D. A. Watson, navigator; Great Britain, English Electric Canberra VX 185. Gander, Newfoundland, to Belfast, Ireland—605.527 m.p.h. (F.A.I. course record) Belfast-Gander-Belfast—411.992 m.p.h.

1953—Jul 28     U.S.A.F. B-47 Stratojet bomber set transatlantic speed record in completing a 2,925-mile flight, Limestone Air Force Base, Maine, to Fairford, England—4 hours, 43 minutes, average of 618 m.p.h.

1955—Aug 23     Captain John Hackett, with Mr. Peter Moneypenny as his navigator, flew an English Electric Canberra Mark 7 photographic reconnaissance jet aircraft from London Airport to Floyd Bennett Field, New York, and back. They completed the 6,920-mile flight in 14 hours, 21 minutes, 45 seconds, including a 35-minute stop at Floyd Bennett for refueling. The average speed for the round trip was 481.5 m.p.h.

1958—Jun 27-29  KC-135 piloted by Maj. Burl B. Davenport and Lt. James J. Jones set west-east transatlantic F.A.I. course speed record in flight from New York to London, June 27, 630.223 m.p.h. in 5 hours, 29 minutes, 14.64 seconds. Return trip, June 29, they set another F.A.I. course record flying from London to New York at 587.458 m.p.h. in 5 hours, 53 minutes, 12.77 seconds.

1959—June 28    Russian TU-114, largest passenger aircraft in world, completed first nonstop flight from Moscow to New York—5,092 miles in 11 hours, 6 minutes.

1961—May 26     A B-58, Lt. Col. William R. Payne, pilot, set two F.A.I. course records. From New York to Paris at speed of 1,089.36 m.p.h. in 3 hours, 19 minutes, 44.53 seconds. Other from Washington, D.C., to Paris at 1,048.68 m.p.h. in 3 hours, 39 minutes, 49 seconds.

1963—May 19-21     Thirty world records (F.A.I. course) established in the U. S. Presidential aircraft, a VC-137C, by Col. James B. Swindal in flights from Washington, D. C., to Moscow and return. Washington—Moscow flight (May 19) made at speed of 561.6 m.p.h. in 8 hours, 39 minutes, 2.2 seconds. Return flight, Moscow-Washington, D.C., (May 20-21) made at speed of 490.6 m.p.h. in 9 hours, 54 minutes, 48.5 seconds. Fifteen records established on each one-way flight.

1967—June 1     Two HH-3H helicopters flew nonstop from New York to Paris in 30 hours, 46 minutes, 10 seconds with 9 air refuelings.

## Appendix 11

# Selected Chronology of Transpacific Flights

1925—Aug 31     (Aug. 31 to Sept. 8) In Navy's attempted San Francisco-Honolulu flight, Comdr. John Rodgers and crew alighted short of their mark, but set a nonstop seaplane record of 1,841 miles. (Comdr. Rodgers was killed in an air crash on Aug. 27, 1926.)

1927—June 28-29     First nonstop Hawaiian flight, from Oakland, Calif., to Wheeler Field, Honolulu, made by Lts. L. J. Maitland and A. F. Hegenberger in a Fokker C2-3 Wright 220—flew 2,407 miles in 25 hours, 50 minutes, navigation accomplished by directional beacons of San Francisco and Maui. The Mackay Trophy for 1927 and DFC were awarded for the flight.

1927—Aug 16     Arthur C. Goebel and Lt. W. V. Davis, U.S.N., won the Dole Oakland-Honolulu race in 26 hours, 17 minutes, 33 seconds. No other plane completed the flight.

1927—Oct 15     Capt. W. N. Lancaster and Mrs. Keith Miller started their flight to Australia. Complete flight from London to Port Darwin, Australia, 12,500 miles on March 19, 1928.

1928—May-June 10     Capt. Charles E. Kingsford-Smith, Capt. C. T. P. Ulm, pilots, Lt. Comdr. Harry W. Lyon, navigator, and James Warner, radio operator, in Fokker trimotored Wright Whirlwind monoplane, Southern Cross, fly from Oakland, Falif., to Brisbane, Australia, first transpacific flight, stopping at Honolulu, Fiji Islands, and Brisbane, 7,400 miles in 83 hours, 15 minutes, flying time. Kingsford-Smith was lost on an England-Australia flight during Nov. 1935. Ulm was lost with two companions in an attempt to fly from California to Australia in 1934.

1931—Jul 29-     Col. and Mrs. Charles Lindbergh fly from Glenn
Aug 26     Curtiss Airport, North Beach, N.Y., to Tokyo, Japan, via Canada, Alaska, and Siberia, in a Lockheed Sirius seaplane.

1931—Oct 3     Clyde Pangborn and Hugh Herndon, Jr., began the first nonstop flight between Japan and U.S.

Flying a Bellanca P & W 420, they landed at
Wenatchee, Wash., Oct. 5.

1935—Jan 11-12    Amelia Earhart, in Lockheed Vega with P & W
Wasp engine, made the first solo flight from
Hawaii to Calif.—18 hours, 16 minutes.

1945—Sep 3    Air Transport Command C-54 Skymaster, commanded by Maj. G. E. Cain, and carrying films
of formal Japanese surrender, set new flight
record of 31 hours, 25 minutes between Tokyo
and Washington.

1945—Oct 20    Three B-29s commanded by Lt. Gen. N. F
Twining landed in Washington after blazing new
trail from Guam via India and Germany. Time
was 59 hours, 30 minutes for 13,167 miles.

1947—Feb 28    Lt. Col. Robert E. Thacker, pilot; 1st Lt. John M.
Ard, copilot; North American P-82 monoplane,
from Hickam Field, Honolulu, to La Guardia
Airport, New York. Elapsed time: 14 hours, 31
minutes, 50 seconds. Distance: 4,968.852 miles.
Average speed: 341.959 m.p.h.

1948—Aug 28    Navy transport *Caroline Mars* landed at Chicago
after nonstop flight from Honolulu in record time
—24 hours, 9 minutes. It carried 42 persons and
14,000-pound payload.

1948—Dec 8    A 6-engine B-36 completed 9,400-mile nonstop
flight from Ft. Worth-Hawaii-Ft. Worth without
refueling.

1949—Jan 13    William P. Odom, in Beechcraft Bonanza, set a
world distance record for light planes—*2,400-mile*
nonstop flight from Honolulu to Oakland.

1949—Mar 8    W. P. Odom in Beechcraft Bonanza set new world distance record for light planes, 4,957-mile flight, in 36 hours, from Honolulu to Teterboro, N.J.

1957—Aug 21   With Lt. Comdr. James M. Pruitt, U.S.N., pilot, a twin-jet Douglas A3D Skywarrior flew from Hawaii to Calif., in 4 hours, 12 minutes, record for eastward flight.

1957—Oct 11   Navy Douglas A3D Skywarrior speed record from San Francisco to Honolulu in 4 hours, 29 minutes, 55 seconds.

1958—Mar 27   U.S.A.F. Boeing KC-135 Stratotanker completed first nonstop flight from Calif. to New Zealand, distance of approximately 6,000 miles in 15 hours.

1958—Jul 11   U.S.A.F. Boeing KC-135 Stratotanker made first nonstop flight from Washington, D.C., to Honolulu, covering 5,000 miles in 11 hours, 8 minutes.

1963—Oct 16   Air Force Convair B-58 piloted by Maj. Sidney J. Kubesch established three world records (F.A.I. course) in flight from Tokyo, Japan, to London, England, in 8 hours, 35 minutes, 20.4 seconds at average speed of 692.7 m.p.h. The other two records were from Tokyo to Anchorage, Alaska, and from Anchorage to London at speeds of 1,093.44 m.p.h. and 826.91 m.p.h., respectively.

## Appendix 12

# Selected Chronology
# of Polar Flights

| | |
|---|---|
| 1926—May 8-9 | First flight to the North Pole area made by Richard Byrd, navigator, and Floyd Bennett, pilot, in a Fokker monoplane, from Kings Bay, Spitsbergen. |
| 1926—May 12 | Lincoln Ellsworth, Roald Amundsen, and Umberto Nobile flew from Spitsbergen over North Pole to Teller, Alaska, in dirigible *Norge*. |
| 1928—Apr 15-21 | First eastbound Arctic crossing made in a Lockheed Vega monoplane with skis by Capt. G. H. Wilkins and Lt. C. B. Eielson, Point Barrow to Green Harbor, Spitsbergen, 2,200 miles in 20 hours, 20 minutes flying time. En route plane was grounded five days by storm. |
| 1928—May 24-25 | Umberto Nobile crossed North Pole in airplane *Italia,* May 24, crashed May 25. Roald Amundsen was lost trying to effect a rescue by airplane. |
| 1928—Dec 20 | First airplane flight over Antarctic, 10 hours' duration, made by Sir Hubert Wilkins and Lt. Carl Ben Eielson. |
| 1929—Nov 29 | Comdr. R. E. Byrd, in a Ford trimotor *Floyd Bennett* piloted by Bernt Balchen, made first flight over South Pole. |
| 1935—Nov 23 | (Nov. 23 to Dec. 5) Lincoln Ellsworth and pilot |

Herbert Hollick-Kenyon flew 2,100 miles from Dundee Island, Antarctica, to the Bay of Whales.

1937—May 21       Otto Schmidt of U.S.S.R. landed at North Pole by plane and established a camp on the ice. After drifting for 9 months they were rescued at Jan Mayen.

1951—May 29       Charles F. Blair, Jr., flew across the North Pole in a converted P-51, first man to make the trip alone in a single-engine plane.

## Appendix 13

# Selected Chronology of X-Model Rocket Aircraft Flights

1946—Dec 9       The Army Air Forces revealed first powered test flight of XS-1. Flown by Chalmers Goodlin, a Bell test pilot, it reached 550 m.p.h.

1947—Aug 25       World speed record of 650.92 m.p.h. set by Maj. Marion E. Carl, U.S.M.C. in Douglas D-588-1 which had been flown by Comdr. Turner F. Caldwell in setting previous record of 640.74 m.p.h. five days earlier.

1947—Oct 14       The first faster-than-sound flight was made by Capt. Charles E. Yeager at Muroc, Calif., in a rocket-powered Air Force research plane, Bell XS-1.

1948—Jun 10       Air Force confirmed repeated attainment of supersonic speeds by X-1 (formerly XS-1) flown by Capt. C. E. Yeager.

| | |
|---|---|
| 1949—Jan 7 | U.S.A.F. announced X-1, flown by Capt. C. E. Yeager, climbed 23,000 feet from takeoff, at record rate 13,000 feet per minute. |
| 1949—Apr 6 | Curtiss-Wright announced that the X-1 rocket plane (made by Bell, engine by Curtiss-Wright) flew an unofficial world-record speed, 1,100 m.p.h., for piloted planes. |
| 1949—Nov 22 | U. S. Navy announced that its D-558-2 Douglas Skyrocket had repeatedly exceeded the speed of sound at Muroc, Calif. |
| 1951—Aug 7 | U. S. Navy D-558-2 Skyrocket, piloted by Bill Bridgeman, reached speed of 1,238 m.p.h., a new world's record. |
| 1951—Aug 15 | At Muroc, Calif., Bill Bridgeman flew U. S. Navy D-558-2 Skyrocket to highest altitude ever reached by a human being—79,494 feet. |
| 1953—Aug 31 | Flying the D-558-2 Skyrocket research aircraft, which had been launched from B-29 Superfortress at 34,000 feet, Lt. Col. Marion E. Carl, U.S.M.C., attained altitude of 83,235 feet, Edwards Air Force Base, Calif. |
| 1953—Nov 20 | In a D-558-2 which was launched from a B-29, test pilot Scott Crossfield established speed record of 1,327 m.p.h. at Edwards Air Force Base, Calif. |
| 1953—Dec 12 | In Bell X-1A launched from a B-36 bomber, Maj. C. E. Yeager, U.S.A.F., attained speed of 1,650 m.p.h., about twice that of sound, Edwards Air Force Base, Calif. |
| 1954—Jun 4 | Maj. Arthur Murray, U.S.A.F., attained an unofficial altitude of 91,000 feet in the Bell X-1A. |

1954—Aug 25

A Bell X-1A rocket-propelled aircraft launched from a B-29 Superfortress over Edwards Air Force Base, Calif. Maj. A. Murray, U.S.A.F., reached altitude of 90,443 feet, greatest official height.

1956—June 23

At Edwards Air Force Base, Calif., Lt. Col. Frank K. Everest, U.S.A.F., flew Bell X-2 rocket-powered plane at record speed just over 1,900 m.p.h.

1956—Sep 7

Capt. Iven C. Kincheloe, U.S.A.F., set altitude record for manned flight at Edwards Air Force Base, Calif., piloting a Bell X-2 rocket-powered aircraft to height of 126,200 feet.

1956—Sep 27

An X-2 rocket-powered plane launched from a B-50 bomber set speed record of 2,094 m.p.h. over Mojave Desert, Calif., flown by Capt. Melburn G. Apt. Flight killed pilot in aircraft crash.

1958—Jul 26

Capt. I. C. Kincheloe, U.S.A.F., Korean War ace, who set an altitude record of 126,200 feet in 1956 for manned flight, killed in crash of jet-powered aircraft at Edwards Air Force Base, Calif.

1959—Jun 8

Piloted by Scott Crossfield, the 7½-ton North American X-15 rocket plane, designed for speeds up to 4,000 m.p.h. and altitudes to 100 miles, dropped from a B-52 more than 7 miles above the Mojave Desert for a nonpowered glide test—its first free flight.

1959—Sep 17

A B-52 dropped the X-15 rocket plane, S. Crossfield as pilot, which attained a speed over 1,400 m.p.h. and reached altitude over 50,000 feet—its first powered flight.

| | |
|---|---|
| 1960—Aug 12 | Maj. Robert White, U.S.A.F., flew the X-15 to altitude of 136,500 feet. |
| 1960—Nov 15 | X-15 flown for the first time with new XLR-99 engine. NASA pilot S. Crossfield attained speed of about 2,000 m.p.h. and altitude approaching 80,000 feet. |
| 1961—Mar 30 | NASA pilot Joseph A. Walker reached highest altitude in manned flight flying the X-15, equipped with XLR-99 rocket engine to altitude of 169,600 feet. |
| 1961—Apr 21 | Maj. Robert White, U.S.A.F., established an unofficial speed record in first full-throttle flight of the X-15. Altitude of 79,000 feet, attained speed of 3,074 m.p.h. before coasting upward to altitude of 105,100 feet. |
| 1961—Jun 22 | Maj. Robert White, U.S.A.F., set new unofficial world speed record for manned airplanes, flying the X-15 at speed of 3,603 m.p.h., attaining this speed with full-throttle operation of XLR-99 engine for 75 seconds. |
| 1961—Nov 9 | Major Robert White, U.S.A.F., attained a top speed of 4,093 m.p.h. in X-15 while flying at full throttle at an altitude of 101,600 feet. |
| 1962—Apr 30 | X-15, piloted by Joseph A. Walker, climbed to a record altitude of 246,700 feet for piloted aircraft. |
| 1962—June 27 | NASA pilot Joseph A. Walker piloted X-15 No. 1 at record speed of 4,159 m.p.h. in climb from 96,000 to 120,000 feet. |
| 1962—Jul 17 | Maj. Robert White, U.S.A.F., piloted X-15-1 to a world record altitude of 58.7 miles (314,750 feet) |

in first flight on which X-15 achieved its original design altitude. Maximum speed was 3,784 m.p.h.

1962—Jul 19 Maj. Robert M. White, the first man to fly a winged aircraft into outer space, received his astronaut's wings. NASA and the military established the altitude of 50 miles as the qualifying height for astronaut's wings.

1963—Jun 27 Maj. Robert A. Rushworth, U.S.A.F., piloted X-15 to an altitude of 285,000 feet to become second military pilot to earn astronaut's wings for space flight in a winged aircraft.

1963—Jul 19 NASA pilot Joseph A. Walker flew X-15 No. 3 to unofficial record height of 347,800 feet at speed of 3,710 m.p.h.

1963—Aug 23 NASA pilot Joseph A. Walker flew X-15 No. 3 to unofficial record height of 354,200 feet.

1967—Oct 3 Maj. William J. Knight, U.S.A.F., flew the X-15 to a record 4,534 m.p.h.

1967—Nov 15 Maj. Michael J. Adams was killed in an X-15 crash, the first fatality since the program began in 1959.

1968—Oct 24 The 199th and final X-15 flight.

### Appendix 14

# Selected F.A.I. Manned Spacecraft Record Flights

## Class K
### ALTITUDE WITHOUT EARTH ORBIT

1961—May 5      Comdr. Alan B. Shepard, Jr., U.S.N., became first Project Mercury astronaut to cross the space frontier, on a 14.8-minute flight that reached an altitude of *116 miles,* carrying him 302 miles to a landing in the Atlantic after a launching from Cape Canaveral. His maximum speed, in the *Friendship 7* capsule, 5,100 m.p.h.

1961—Jul 21      America's second Project Mercury astronaut, Capt. Virgil I. Grissom, U.S.A.F., attained altitude of *118 miles* and speed of 5,310 m.p.h. in a 303-mile suborbital space flight from Cape Canaveral in the *Liberty Bell 7* capsule launched by a Mercury-Redstone 4 booster. Not certified by F.A.I.—capsule sank after landing and was not recovered.

### GREATEST ALTITUDE WITH EARTH ORBIT (1 Astronaut)

1961—Apr 12      *Vostok 1* (U.S.S.R.) carried cosmonaut Yuri A. Gagarin. Landed after one revolution *– 203.19 statute miles.*

### GREATEST ALTITUDE WITH EARTH ORBIT (2-4 Astronauts)

1964—Oct 12-14      *Voskhod 1* (U.S.S.R.) carried cosmonaut

Vladimir Komarov; Konstantin Feoktistov, a scientist and spacecraft designer; and Boris Yegorov, a physician. Landed after 16 revolutions
– *253.51 miles.*

1965—Mar 18-19     *Voskhod 2* (U.S.S.R.) carried cosmonauts Pavel Belyayev and Alexei A. Leonov. Leonov left spacecraft for 10 minutes. Landed after 17 revolutions
– *307.5 miles.*

1966—Jul 18-21     *Gemini 10* (U.S.A.) carried astronauts John W. Young and Michael Collins. Performed rendezvous and docking and 87 minutes of extravehicular activity. Used Agena target vehicle engine to reach record 476-mile altitude. Landed after 43 revolutions
– *476 miles.*

1966—Sep 12-15     *Gemini 11* (U.S.A.) carried astronauts Charles Conrad, Jr., and Richard F. Gordon, Jr. Performed first-orbit rendezvous and docking and two hours and 47 minutes of extravehicular activity. Used Agena engine to climb to new record altitude. Landed after 44 revolutions
– *850.65 miles.*

## DISTANCE WITH EARTH ORBIT (1 Astronaut)

1961—Aug 6-7     *Vostok 2* (U.S.S.R.) carried cosmonaut Gherman S. Titov. Landed after 17.5 revolutions
– *436,912 miles.*

1962—Aug 11-15     *Vostok 3* (U.S.S.R.) carried cosmonaut Andrian G. Nikolayev. Landed after 64 revolutions
– *1,640,168 miles.*

1963—Jun 14-19     *Vostok 5* (U.S.S.R.) carried cosmonaut Valery F.

Bykovsky. Landed after 81 revolutions
*– 2,066,654 miles.*

## DISTANCE WITH EARTH ORBIT (2-4 Astronauts)

1965—Aug 21-29    *Gemini 5* (U.S.A.) carried astronauts L. Gordon
Cooper, Jr., and Charles Conrad, Jr. Set manned
duration record—190.9 hours in space. Landed
after 120 revolutions. It established five world
records, including four previously established by
the U.S.S.R.
*– 3,309,506 miles.*

1965—Dec 4-18    *Gemini 7* (U.S.A.) carried astronauts Frank
Borman and James A. Lovell, Jr. Set new manned
duration record—330.5 hours in space. Landed
after 206 revolutions. The 14-day flight by astronauts Borman and Lovell aboard the *Gemini 7*
spacecraft and the rendezvous with astronauts
Stafford and Schirra in *Gemini 6* completed the
U.S.'s most successful space mission. *Gemini 7*
established 11 world records for manned space
flights, including the first rendezvous of two
manned maneuverable spacecraft
*– 5,719,457 miles.*

1970—June 1-19    *Soyuz 9* (U.S.S.R.) carried cosmonauts A. G.
Nikolayev and V. I. Sevastyanov. Set new
manned duration record—424 hours, 58 minutes,
55 seconds in space
*– 7,387,499 miles.*

## DURATION WITH EARTH ORBIT (1 Astronaut)

1961—Apr 12    *Vostok 1* (U.S.S.R.) carried cosmonaut Yuri A.
Gagarin. Landed after one revolution
*– 108 minutes.*

1961—Aug 6-7    *Vostok 2* (U.S.S.R.) carried cosmonaut Gherman

S. Titov. Landed after 17.5 revolutions
– *25 hours, 11 minutes.*

1962—Aug 11-15  *Vostok 3* (U.S.S.R.) carried cosmonaut Andrian
G. Nikolayev. Landed after 64 revolutions
– *94 hours, 10 minutes.*

1963—June 14-19  *Vostok 5* (U.S.S.R.) carried cosmonaut Valery F.
Bykovsky. Landed after 81 revolutions
– *118 hours, 57 minutes.*

## DURATION WITH EARTH ORBIT (2-4 Astronauts)

1965—Aug 21-29  *Gemini 5* (U.S.A.) carried astronauts L. Gordon
Cooper, Jr., and Charles Conrad, Jr. Set manned
duration record—190.9 hours in space. Landed
after 120 revolutions
– *190 hours, 56 minutes.*

1965—Dec 4-18  *Gemini 7* (U.S.A.) carried astronauts Frank
Borman and James A. Lovell, Jr. Set new manned
duration record—330.5 hours in space. Landed
after 206 revolutions
– *330 hours, 35 minutes.*

1970—June 1-19  *Soyuz 9* (U.S.S.R.) carried cosmonauts A. G.
Nikolayev and V. I. Sevastyanov. Set new
manned duration record
– *424 hours, 58 seconds.*

## GREATEST MASS LIFTED WITH EARTH ORBIT

1961—Apr 12  *Vostok 1* (U.S.S.R.) carried cosmonaut Yuri A.
Gagarin. Landed after one revolution
– *10,417 lbs.*

1964—Oct 12-13  *Voskhod 1* (U.S.S.R.) carried cosmonaut
Vladimir Komarov; Konstantin Feoktistov, a
scientist and spacecraft designer; and Boris

Yegorov, a physician. Landed after 16
revolutions
*– 11,729 lbs.*

1968—Oct 26-30  *Soyuz 3* (U.S.S.R.) carried cosmonaut Georgiy
Beregovoi. Landed after 64 revolutions
*– 14,495 lbs.*

1968—Dec 21-27  *Apollo 8* (U.S.A.) carried Frank Borman, James
A. Lovell, Jr., and William Anders.
*– 282,197 lbs.*

## GREATEST MASS LIFTED TO LUNAR ORBIT
## FROM THE EARTH

1971—Jul 26-29  *Apollo 15* (U.S.A.) carried astronauts David R.
Scott, James B. Irwin, and Alfred M. Worden, Jr.
*– 76,278 lbs.*

## LUNAR AND PLANETARY MISSIONS (1 Astronaut)
### Duration in Lunar Orbit

1972—Apr 19-24  *Apollo 16* (U.S.A.) Thomas K. Mattingly
*– 125 hours, 46 minutes*

1972—Dec 10-16  *Apollo 17* (U.S.A.) Ronald I. Evans
*– 147 hours, 41 minutes*

## GREATEST MASS LANDED ON THE MOON (2-4 Astronauts)

1969—Jul 20  Lunar Module *Eagle* (U.S.A.) carried astronauts
Neil A. Armstrong and Edwin Aldrin, Jr., from
Spacecraft *Apollo 11*
*– 16,153 lbs.*

1972—Apr 20  Lunar Module *Orion* (U.S.A.) carried astronauts
John W. Young and Charles M. Duke from
Spacecraft *Apollo 16*
*– 18,208 lbs.*

## GREATEST MASS LIFTED TO LUNAR ORBIT FROM THE SURFACE OF THE MOON

1969—Jul 21  Lunar Module *Eagle* (U.S.A.) carried astronauts Neil A. Armstrong and Edwin Aldrin, Jr., to Spacecraft *Apollo 11*
– *5,928.6 lbs.*

1972—Apr 23  Lunar Module *Orion* (U.S.A.) carried astronauts John W. Young and Charles M. Duke to Spacecraft *Apollo 16*
– *10,949 lbs.*

## DISTANCE TRAVELED ON THE LUNAR SURFACE

1971—Aug 1  Astronauts David R. Scott and James B. Irwin (U.S.A.) from Spacecraft *Apollo 15* and Lunar Module *Falcon*. Used Lunar Rover
– *16,470 ft.*

1972—Dec 13  Astronauts Eugene A. Cernan and Harrison A. Schmitt (U.S.A.) from Spacecraft *Apollo 17* and Lunar Module *Challenger*. Used Lunar Rover
– *25,029 ft.*

## DURATION OF STAY OUTSIDE THE SPACECRAFT ON THE SURFACE OF THE MOON

1971—Feb 5-6  Astronaut Alan B. Shepard (U.S.A.) from Spacecraft *Apollo 14* and Lunar Module *Antares*
– *9 hours, 12 minutes.*

1971—Jul 31-
Aug 2  Astronaut David R. Scott (U.S.A.) from Spacecraft *Apollo 15* and Lunar Module *Falcon*
– *18 hours, 18 minutes.*

1972—Dec 12-14  Astronaut Eugene A. Cernan (U.S.A.) from Spacecraft *Apollo 17* and Lunar Module *Challenger*
– *21 hours, 32 minutes.*

## DURATION OF MISSION TO THE MOON AND RETURN
### (2-4 Astronauts)

1969—Dec 14-24     Astronauts Charles Conrad, Jr., Richard F. Gordon, Jr., and Alan L. Bean (U.S.A.) in Spacecraft *Apollo 12*
*– 244 hours, 36 minutes.*

1972—Dec 7-19     Astronauts Eugene A. Cernan, (U.S.A.) Harrison A. Schmitt, and Ronald E. Evans in Spacecraft *Apollo 17*
*– 301 hours, 51 minutes.*

## MISCELLANEOUS SPACE FLIGHT CHRONOLOGY

1962—Feb 20     Lt. Col. John H. Glenn, Jr., U.S.M.C., completed a three-orbit flight around the earth in *Friendship 7,* a Mercury spacecraft, and became America's first orbital flyer. After 4 hours, 56 minutes of flight he parachuted into the Atlantic east of Grand Turk Island. (Not listed as F.A.I. record)

1965—Mar 23     *Gemini 3,* first U.S. two-man space flight, is blasted off at Cape Kennedy after an almost flawless 420-minute countdown. Crew of the GT-3 on its three-orbit mission is Virgil Grissom and John Young. Another first was accomplished when GT-3 changed orbit during the mission. (Not listed as F.A.I. record)

1965—Jun 4     Air Force space pilots Maj. James A. McDivitt and Edward H. White set a United States space endurance record lasting 97 hours, 30 seconds in a 63-orbit trip. During the *Gemini 4* mission, White took a 23-minute walk in space to become the first U. S. astronaut to accomplish this feat.

1967—Jan 27     A tragedy occurred at Cape Kennedy when fire erupted inside the Apollo spacecraft during ground testing. The fire resulted in the deaths of U. S. astronauts Lt. Col. Virgil I. Grissom, Lt. Colonel Edward H. White, II, and Lt. Comdr. Roger B. Chaffee.

1967—Apr 24      Vladimir Komarov, U.S.S.R. cosmonaut, was killed when parachute straps of his spacecraft became entangled in a space recovery landing.

1968—Mar 27      Yuri Gagarin, U.S.S.R. cosmonaut, who flew the world's first manned space flight on April 12, 1961, was killed in a military jet training-flight accident.

1971—Jun 30      U.S.S.R. cosmonauts Georgi T. Dobrovolsky, Vladislav N. Volkov, and Viktor I. Patsayev were found dead in their seats when *Soyuz 11* landed after a record 24 days in orbit. The deaths have been attributed to a loss of pressurization that followed the failure of a hatch to seal properly.